D1556647

THE
WOLF PACKS
GATHER

THE
WOLF PACKS
GATHER

Mayhem in the Western Approaches
1940

BERNARD EDWARDS

Pen & Sword
MARITIME

First published in Great Britain in 2011 by
PEN & SWORD MARITIME
an imprint of
Pen & Sword Books Ltd
47 Church Street
Barnsley
South Yorkshire
S70 2AS

ISBN 978 1 84884 624 1

A CIP catalogue record for this book is
available from the British Library

Typeset in Ehrhardt
by Chic Media Ltd

Printed and bound in England
by CPI

Pen & Sword Books Ltd incorporates the imprints of
Pen & Sword Aviation, Pen & Sword Family History, Pen & Sword Maritime,
Pen & Sword Military, Pen & Sword Discovery, Wharncliffe Local History,
Wharncliffe True Crime, Wharncliffe Transport, Pen & Sword Select,
Pen & Sword Military Classics, Leo Cooper, Remember When,
The Praetorian Press, Seaforth Publishing and Frontline Publishing

For a complete list of Pen & Sword titles please contact
PEN & SWORD BOOKS LIMITED
47 Church Street, Barnsley, South Yorkshire, S70 2AS England
E-mail: enquiries@pen-and-sword.co.uk
Website: www.pen-and-sword.co.uk

Contents

The book is dedicated to the memory of
Captain 'Fearless Freddie' Parker, OBE,
who in his ageing 7½-knotter, bristling with guns,
took great delight in putting the fear of God into the enemy.

'If you are going through hell, keep going.'
Winston S. Churchill

Author's Note

Almost three-quarters of a century ago, but still within the memory span of many who now watch distant conflicts unfold through the medium of wide-screen television, the Second World War was waged in comparative isolation. Great armies clashed, cities burned, empires fell, and all without the benefit of today's high-tech media coverage. And in this long-drawn-out conflict no action was conducted in greater isolation than the Battle of the Atlantic. This was a battle fought out of sight, over the far horizon, mainly in darkness, and frequently in foul weather. It began within a few short hours of the declaration of war on 3 September 1939, and ranged over millions of square miles of deep ocean, from Bishop Rock to Barbados, and from Greenland to the Cape of Good Hope, ending only with the surrender of Germany on 7 May 1945; five years and eight months of sea warfare of incredible intensity and brutality.

Dunkirk, the Battle of Britain, Alamein and Normandy are forever enshrined in the annals of this country's history, and remembered annually with due reverence. The Battle of the Atlantic, on the other hand, in which so many Allied civilian seamen refused to bend the knee to a ruthless and heavily-armed enemy, slipped unrecognized into the mists of time almost as soon as the last torpedo was fired and the last stricken merchant ship went spiralling to the bottom.

This book attempts to paint a true picture of the early days of the Battle of the Atlantic, when Hitler's U-boats were in the ascendancy, and reaping a rich harvest virtually unopposed by a depleted Royal Navy. Their killing ground was in the Western Approaches, where ships and convoys from all points of the compass converged as they left or entered the confines of the North Channel, the only clear access to Fortress Britain.

Chapter 1

The Betrayal

The slow convoy SC 7, thirty-five superannuated merchant ships huddled together for mutual protection, inched its way across the broad reaches of the North Atlantic in the worst winter ever recorded in that great ocean. Scouting bravely ahead, and rolling her weather rails under in the mountainous seas, was SC 7's sole escort, a 14-knot ex-Admiralty survey vessel.

'The U-boats won't even know you're coming,' they had been assured, 'and in any case they can't operate beyond 17 degrees West, by which time the destroyers of Western Approaches Command will be there to look after you.' Ever the optimist, the Admiralty was wrong on all counts.

The story begins on the other side of the world in the early summer of 1940.

Sitting squat and sluggish in the water, the heavily laden British steamer *City of Baghdad* was 'smelling the mud' as she made her way out of Lourenço Marques on the morning of 28 June, 1940. Even with a continuous stream of helm and engine orders, it was taking all the combined navigational skills of Captain J. Armstrong-White and his Portuguese pilot to hold the wayward ship in the buoyed channel. Both were aware that if she strayed just a few yards to either side, she would be aground, and all those thousands of miles she had covered since sailing from her British loading ports would have been in vain.

The 7506-ton *City of Baghdad* started life in 1919 as the *Geierfels* of the German Hansa Line, was handed over to the British Government as part of war reparations, and taken under the wing of the London-based Ellerman Lines. On her current voyage, she was carrying 9,324 tons of steel, chemicals and machinery, all consigned to Penang.

When the *City of Baghdad* sailed from Liverpool at the end of May, she had left behind her a country seemingly on the brink of humiliating defeat. Hitler's Panzers were rampaging across the plains of Europe unchecked, France was contemplating surrender, and the shattered remnants of the British Expeditionary Force were retreating in disarray to the Channel coast. It was with great reluctance that Captain Armstrong-White and his officers had left their families behind to face a very uncertain future, but in the end their inherent loyalty to the ship had decided the issue. Not one man was missing when the time came for sailing.

On the long passage south to the Cape, the news from home became even more depressing. Benito Mussolini, Italy's preening dictator, eager to climb aboard Hitler's rolling bandwagon, declared war on the Allies on 10 June. Twelve days later, France, her much overrated Maginot Line outflanked, abandoned all resistance, and signed an armistice with Germany. Britain, the bulk of her guns and equipment lost in the fiasco of Dunkirk, was left to face alone the might of the greatest war machine ever known to man.

At sea, in the North Atlantic, a similarly desperate situation was developing.. When France threw in the towel, the German Navy found itself in control of the whole of the coastline of western Europe from the North Cape to the Spanish frontier, which for the U-boats was a dream come true. Hitherto, based in Kiel and Wilhelmshaven, they had been forced to make the long and hazardous voyage around the north of Scotland to reach their hunting grounds in the Western Approaches. Now they had the choice of the key ports in the Bay of Biscay, Brest, Lorient, La Pallice, St. Nazaire and Bordeaux, any one of which brought them nearly 1,000 miles closer to their main hunting ground. The astute Admiral Dönitz had already made preparations for this. While Von Rundtstedt's Panzers were steam-rolling their way through Northern France, Dönitz had ordered a train to stand by loaded with all the essentials required to keep U-boats operational, ready to be despatched to the Biscay ports as soon as the French surrendered.

Operation 'Dynamo', the evacuation of the last-ditch rearguard of British and French forces from the beaches of Dunkirk, had cost Britain's navy dear. Six of its finest destroyers were sunk, and another nineteen so badly damaged that it would be months before they were able to go to sea again. Those destroyers still fit for action, along with most of the other small escort ships, were being held in the Channel to face the growing threat of invasion. As a direct result of this chronic shortage of escorts, the Admiralty was forced to send convoys across the North Atlantic completely unescorted, or, if one was available, under the so-called protection of a single armed merchant cruiser.

In desperation, Churchill made frantic representations to America for the loan of fifty US Navy destroyers mothballed since the end of the First World War. It was little to ask of Britain's traditional ally, but such was the opposition from the powerful isolationists in Washington that it would be well into autumn of 1940 before the first of these old four-stackers arrived. Meanwhile, with Italy in the war, Dönitz had at his disposal 100 Italian submarines, although he doubted the ability and commitment of their crews. At the same time, the fall of France had presented the Luftwaffe with dozens of serviceable airfields on the coast of Biscay and Northern France, all within easy flying distance of the convoy routes. The situation was succinctly described by an anonymous U-boat man:

> We had reason to believe that our hunger blockade against England would soon result in her downfall. On land, moreover, our armies had driven deep into enemy territory. Following our seizure of Poland, Norway had been defeated almost overnight, Holland, Belgium and France were overrun within a few weeks and Denmark occupied. Our capital ships controlled European waters far into the Arctic region. It seemed to me that one thing remained to be done: intensify the U-boat offensive against England, starve the British and force them to surrender. Once we held the British Isles, the war would be won.

With all other approaches blocked by minefields, the Admiralty was routing all convoys around the north of Ireland and into the North Channel. The plan was for these convoys to come under the protection of ships of Western Approaches Command before the U-boats reached them, but the reality proved to be very different. Sufficient escorts were available only to supply cover for convoys as far as 17 degrees West, while the U-boats, now based in the Biscay ports, were able to operate as far as 25 degrees West. That left a gap of up to thirty-six hours steaming during which the convoys were without protection, apart from the odd long-range Sunderland making a brief appearance overhead. This, the U-boats' killing ground, lay some 300 miles to the west of the appropriately named Bloody Foreland.

Bloody Foreland, dark and forbidding, juts out into the Atlantic from

Ireland's Donegal coast like an accusing finger pointing back to times long past. Contrary to expectations, *Cnoc Fola* (the hill of blood), as it is known in the Gaelic language, takes its name not from battles fought or blood spilt on its rocky shores, but from a completely benign quirk of nature. Given a clear sunset, the rays of the dying sun appear to bathe the headland in a blood red glow, which in autumn is enhanced when the ferns growing on the cliff faces turn a russet brown. It then requires little stretch of the imagination to associate this lonely outcrop of the British Isles with the forces of evil. But it was not until the autumn of 1940, when the North Atlantic became a battlefield and the blood of hundreds of slaughtered seamen began to lap at its silver sand beaches that, for the first time, Bloody Foreland lived up to its sinister name.

Dönitz choose Lorient as the main U-boat base in Biscay. Situated at the mouth of the River Blavet, with a sheltered deep water approach, Lorient had been a French naval base, and still had excellent dockyard and repair facilities. Using French labour under German supervision, the port was ready to accept its first U-boat at the beginning of July, 1940. Ironically, the first boat in was Fritz-Julius Lemp's U-30, which had opened the war at sea on 3 September 1939 by sinking the British liner *Athenia*.

Far to the east of the Atlantic's troubled waters, much to Captain Armstrong-White's disgust, the *City of Baghdad* had been ordered into the Portuguese East African port of Lourenço Marques to top up her bunkers before setting off on the long haul across the Indian Ocean to Malaya. Lourenço Marques was a pleasant enough place for a brief call; the climate was agreeable, the beer passable, but Armstrong-White was well aware that the supposedly neutral port was crawling with German agents, all observing closely the movements of Allied ships. He was not surprised, then, when as the *City of Baghdad* passed close to Reuben Point on her way out of the harbour he caught the glint of the sun on glass as someone focused their binoculars on the ship. It was almost certain that they were being watched by enemy eyes.

Armstrong-White's assumption was correct. As the *City of Baghdad* cleared the harbour and lifted to the first of the long Indian Ocean swells, a telegram was on its way to Berlin with details of the British ship, her cargo, time of sailing, and destination. From then on, the *City of Baghdad* was a marked ship, and unknown to those on board she had an appointment with a close relative.

The German armed merchant cruiser *Atlantis,* was also an ex-Hansa Line vessel, but younger by eighteen years than the *City of Baghdad*. She matched the British ship in tonnage and size, but there the resemblance ended. The *Atlantis*, ex-*Goldenfels*, powered by two six-cylinder MAN diesels, had a cruising speed of 17½ knots, and was armed with six 5.9-inch guns, four 21-inch torpedo tubes, and various smaller guns. She also carried two Heinkel spotter aircraft, and was manned by a hand-picked crew of 347 officers and ratings, all Navy men. They sailed under the command of *Fregattenkapitän* Bernhard Rogge, a popular and highly experienced officer.

After breaking out into the Atlantic, via the north of Scotland, at the beginning of April, the *Atlantis* had steamed some 11,000 miles, lingering only off the Cape of Good Hope to lay her deadly cargo of ninety-two mines in the shipping lane. In mid-June she was to be found cruising in the Indian Ocean near the Equator. Since leaving German waters she had adopted a variety of disguises, and was now masquerading as the Norwegian motor vessel *Tarifa*. Flying the Norwegian flag and authentically painted with black hull, white upperworks and two pale blue bands adorning her funnel, she looked every inch the smart Wilhelmsen Far East trader she purported to be. However, behind this innocent facade there was a very formidable surface raider.

Meanwhile, the *City of Baghdad* was making her leisurely way north-east across the Indian Ocean, passing outside the island of Madagascar and west of Mauritius, before setting course for the north-western tip of Sumatra, after which she would enter the Malacca Straits. Before sailing from Lourenço Marques, Captain Armstrong-White had been warned of the presence of a German raider in the Indian Ocean, a niggling worry he had lived with each time the sun came up. But the *City of Baghdad* was steering a lonely course, and day after day no threat appeared on the horizon. After more than a week at sea with no sign of the enemy, Armstrong-White had begun to feel more confident of reaching port unmolested.

Fregattenkapitän Rogge, on the other hand, was experiencing the frustration of an empty horizon. After laying the minefield off the Cape, the *Atlantis* changed her disguise, a coat of paint and adjustments to the superstructure turning her into a credible replica of the Dutch Royal Interocean Line's cargo *Abbekerk*. Then, for four weeks she had scoured the Indian Ocean trade routes for a likely prize, but had sighted nothing but the occasional Arab dhow running north on the first winds of the monsoon. By the middle of June, when Rogge was on the point of concluding that all Allied merchantmen had been confined to port, he chanced upon the 7,230-ton Norwegian-flag *Tirranna*. The *Tirranna,* ironically a sister ship of the real *Tarifa*, was on passage from Australia to Mombasa, carrying a British Admiralty cargo, which included 5,500 cases of beer, 300 cases of tobacco, 3,000 cases of canned peaches and 17,000 cases of jam. The Norwegian ship offered no resistance, and was soon on her way to Germany with a prize crew on board, but not before the crew of the raider had appropriated their share of the abundant luxuries she carried in her holds.

Before her capture, the *Tirranna's* radio operator had sent out a QQQ signal, indicating that she was being attacked by an enemy merchant raider, and Rogge fully expected the Royal Navy to come hunting for the *Atlantis*. Fortunately for her, few British warships could be spared to patrol these waters, and for another month the *Atlantis* had cruised in the vicinity of the Cape-Far East route without interference. Neither did she catch sight of as much as a single promising masthead in that time.

Morning star sights taken on 11 July put the *City of Baghdad* in a position just south of the Equator, and in longitude 90 degrees East. She was less than 500 miles from the north-western end of Sumatra, and only three days steaming from Penang, her first port of call. At 0700, Captain Armstrong-White, freshly bathed and shaved, was on the bridge of the Ellerman ship enjoying his first pot of tea of the day, served, as always, on a silver tray by his Indian steward. As the rising sun chased away the last cold airs of the night, White also looked out on yet another empty horizon. As he sipped his tea, he contemplated with satisfaction the prospect of a long voyage soon to be safely completed.

For some reason – possibly atmospheric interference – the *City of Baghdad's* radio room had not picked up the stricken *Tirranna's* call for help, and Captain Armstrong-White had no inkling of any danger that might be threatening. Then, as he poured his second cup of the strong brew – Broken Orange Pekoe from Ceylon, of course – the officer of the watch informed him that another ship was in sight on the starboard beam, and on a converging course.

Not over-concerned, the British captain ran his binoculars over the approaching ship, and by her colours identified her as belonging to the

Royal Interocean Line,and probably on a similar voyage to that of his own ship. He continued to enjoy his morning tea.

On the bridge of the *Abbekerk*, alias *Atlantis*, now within 4 miles of the *City of Baghdad*, Bernhard Rogge was in turn examining the unsuspecting ship through his powerful *Zeiss* binoculars. She was not flying an ensign, but she was plainly British. Moreover, she was fully loaded, and although she mounted a 4-inch on her poop, there was no indication that the gun was manned. Satisfied that he had another prize within his grasp, Rogge increased speed and closed the gap to about 2 miles. The *Atlantis's* forward guns were manned, but still hidden behind their screens.

Rogge checked his watch and continued to stalk his prey, waiting for the right moment to strike, which was as soon as the radio silence period ended. Even in wartime, international regulations required all radio stations, on ship and on shore, to cease all transmissions for three minutes at fifteen minutes to and fifteen minutes past the hour. During these 'silent periods' all stations listened on 500 kHz for distress signals. It was a simple, but very effective arrangement that had saved many lives at sea over the years, and Rogge knew that if he challenged the British ship in the silence period her calls for help would be heard all over the world.

The three-minute silence period over, Rogge quickly crossed astern of the *City of Baghdad* and came up on her port quarter. At 1½ miles, he raised the shutters hiding his guns, and hoisted a flag signal ordering the other ship to stop at once and not to use her radio.

The German's signal was observed from the bridge of the *City of Baghdad*, but as there was little wind and the flags hung limp, the message could not be read. However, not surprisingly, by now the strange behaviour of the other ship had thoroughly aroused Captain Armstrong-White's suspicions. Hesitating no longer, he ordered the radio room to send out the QQQ signal.

The distress signal was monitored by radio operators aboard the *Atlantis*, who at once alerted the bridge of the raider. Rogge now had no alternative but to open fire on the British ship. The raider's 5.9s thundered, and salvo after salvo was hurled at the *City of Baghdad*, which was now stern-on and desperately attempting to take herself out of range of the enemy's guns.

Armstrong-White's gallant action was doomed from the start. The

German gunners were firing from almost point blank range, and within minutes their shells were bracketing the *City of Baghdad*, then striking home. Rogge's first aim was to silence the ship, and this his gunners quickly achieved, one shell demolishing her radio room, another bringing down her fore topmast, and the main aerial with it. The First Radio Officer, who had stuck bravely to his post transmitting the distress, was seriously injured.

When Captain Armstrong-White still refused to heave to, the raider's guns were turned on the *City of Baghdad's* bridge, creating carnage. Soon, three Lascar seamen lay dead, and the quartermaster of the watch was lying in a pool of blood by his wheel. Only then did Armstrong-White concede defeat. By this time, the *City of Baghdad* had been hit by forty-two enemy shells.

As the crippled ship slowly came to a halt, an armed boarding party, led by her first lieutenant, Ulrich Mohr, put out from the *Atlantis*. When they reached the *City of Baghdad,* they found Captain Armstrong-White and his small band of British officers attempting to control their panicking Lascar crew, who greatly outnumbered them. Torn from their villages in the Sundarbans of India by the need to earn a living, these men were traditionally fine seamen. However, now that they found themselves involved in a fighting war that was really none of their business, they were frightened and bewildered. Complete chaos reigned on board the *City of Baghdad*. Lifeboats were being lowered without orders, men were hurling themselves into the water.

The guns of *Leutnant* Mohr eventually restored order, but by this time all but one of the ship's boats had been taken away by the crew. Mohr ordered Captain Armstrong-White and his officers into the remaining boat, which then pulled clear of the ship, leaving the German boarding party in complete control. Mohr then carried out a thorough search of the prize and, to his great surprise and delight, he discovered that all the *City of Baghdad's* secret code books had been left in her chartroom. The books were in their weighted canvas bags ready for dumping over the side, but had obviously been overlooked in the confusion created by the shelling and the mutiny of the Lascar crew.

Scuttling charges were planted in the *City of Baghdad's* engine-room, and shortly after Mohr and his boarding party left, she blew up and sank in less than eight minutes.

When *Fregattenkapitän* Rogge realized the significance of the captured code books, he immediately set a course for the nearest Japanese held port, where the books were landed and sent to Germany. Within weeks of the *City of Baghdad* being shelled and sunk, and Captain Armstrong-White and his hapless crew being carried off into captivity, Berlin was able to decode most signals sent to and from Allied merchant ships. Some months were to pass before the Admiralty realized that its radio communications with the convoys were no longer secret. Meanwhile, ships were being sunk, and men were dying in ever increasing numbers.

Chapter 2

The First Pack Runs

Due in no small measure to the acquisition of the *City of Baghdad's* code books, by the time August 1940 drew to a close, Britain and her maritime allies were losing more than a quarter of a million tons of merchant shipping a month. Much of this was in the North Atlantic, and down to the U-boats. At the same time, Britain's shipyards were working at full capacity, but these calamitous losses were completely beyond their ability to replace. Thanks largely to the bravery and determination of the men of RAF Fighter Command, Hitler had been forced to abandon his plan to invade the British Isles, and now it was on the sea that the war would be won or lost.

There had been little change in this situation when, on the morning of 24 August 1940, Convoy SC 2 was making ready for sea. Anchored in the sheltered waters of Sydney, Cape Breton, one of the principal convoy assembly points on Canada's eastern seaboard, were fifty-three British and Allied merchantmen. Between them they carried more than 250,000 tons of cargo, steel, grain, timber, iron ore, all desperately needed on the other side of the Atlantic.

In the early afternoon of the 24th, led by the 6,216-ton *Empire Tarpon*, with the convoy commodore Rear Admiral Edye Boddam-Whetham aboard, the long line of deep-loaded, rust-stained ships slowly made their way out of Sydney harbour. With their tall 'Woodbine' funnels belching black smoke, this collection of ageing tramps made a brave sight. On reflection, however, their prospects for survival did not look good. Few of them were armed, and most were barely capable of making 8 knots with a fair wind. A man could run faster. It was just as well that none of the 2,500 men manning these ships had the slightest inkling that they would soon reap the whirlwind sown by the *City of Baghdad* and her abandoned code books.

After a great deal of agonized manoeuvring, urged on by the *Empire Tarpon's* flag hoists and clacking signal lamps, SC 2 was finally formed up into nine columns abreast, and ready to challenge the Atlantic crossing. The convoy's local escort, two Canadian destroyers, flags flying and bow-waves foaming, made a great show of chasing imaginary enemies, but their presence was no more than a temporary morale booster. Three days later, when the convoy was to the south of Newfoundland, the Canadian warships signalled their goodbyes, and peeled away, heading for the comfort of their base at St John's. Only then did the reality of the parlous state of Britain's Navy dawn on those committed to sail with SC 2. They discovered that they were to face the perils of the Atlantic battleground alone.

In an ideal world, a convoy of the size and importance of SC 2 would warrant a substantial naval escort to see it safely across the North Atlantic. In the real world of 1940, this was out of the question. Twelve months into total war, Britain had simply run out of suitable long-range escorts.

The Royal Navy had begun the war with 150 destroyers, but at least half of these dated back to the First World War, and in peacetime would have been ready for the knacker's yard. Bearing in mind that convoy escort work involved almost continuous zig-zagging with frequent high speed dashes, few of the available destroyers had the fuel capacity to complete the Atlantic crossing. British shipyards were beginning to turn out the new all-weather, long-range corvettes, but it would be many months before they were available in any significant numbers. Meanwhile, Prime Minister Churchill was negotiating hard with America for fifty old destroyers in exchange for air and naval bases in the West Indies, but that might well prove to be a pipe dream. In the summer of 1940, the only escorts able to cover a convoy for the whole of the Atlantic crossing were a handful of armed merchant cruisers. These were large, ex-passenger liners pressed into service and armed with a few obsolete guns. In the case of Convoy SC 2, not even one of these make-believe warships could be found to give protection.

Saying goodbye to her Canadian escort off Cape Race, SC 2 faced up to the prospect of crossing 2,000 miles of hostile ocean alone; fifty-three slow, ungainly merchantmen huddled together for mutual protection. It would not be until they reached longitude 17 degrees West, within 300 miles of the Irish coast, that they would be met by ships of the Royal

Navy's Western Approaches Command. The rendezvous was chosen on the basis that this was at the extreme limit of the U-boats, but no one at he Admiralty seems to have appreciated that since the fall of France the war at sea had moved westwards. When SC 2 sailed from Sydney, the Biscay ports of Brest, La Pallice and Lorient were fully functional as U-boat bases, and Dönitz's 'grey wolves' had gained another 350 miles out into the Atlantic.

Although SC 2, with its attendant cloud of black smoke generated by the predominance of old coal burners hovering overhead, was visible from well over the horizon, its chances of crossing the Atlantic unmolested were still good. The ocean was wide, the U-boats were not yet radar-equipped, and due to the reluctance of Reich Marshal Herman Goering to share his resources, they had no air reconnaisance. That being so, the horizon of the U-boats was restricted to what they could see from the conning tower. And as this was the wild Atlantic, so often lashed by blinding rain, or blanketed by fog, poor visibility was ever the U-boat commander's curse. Furthermore, at this stage of the war, the number of U-boats operational at any one time was severely restricted. The following entry in Admiral Dönitz's war diary for 1 September 1940 serves to illustrate the constraints of his command:

1.9.1940 Distribution of U-boats.

In the Atlantic Operations Area: U-28, 32, 38, 46, 56, 60, 65, 101, 124 (One of these, in this case U-124 was acting as 'weather boat', sending in 4-hourly weather reports for the Luftwaffe, and was therefore not available for operations).

On outward passage from home: U-61 in the North Sea, U-47 west of the Orkneys.

On return passage home: U-57.

On return passage to Lorient: U-59, 100.

In Lorient: U-48, 58, 99, 100.

Konteradmiral Karl Dönitz, *Befehlshaber* (C-in-C) *der U-Boote* (BdU), was by this time ensconced in his new Paris headquarters overlooking the Bois de Boulogne. It was here that, on 30 August, he received news from *xB-Dienst* (the cryptanalysis section of German Naval Intelligence) that Convoy SC 2 had sailed from Canada. The *City of Baghdad's* code books, having reached Berlin, enabled xB–Dienst to supply Dönitz not only with news of the sailing of SC 2, but also the composition of the convoy, its route, and exact details of where it would rendezvous with its local escort off Ireland. Confident that his code breakers at last had the upper hand, Admiral Dönitz decided that the time was now right to put the much argued over *Rudeltaktik* to the test again.

The *Rudeltaktik*, or 'pack tactic', was the brainchild of First World War U-boat ace Hermann Bauer, who as early as 1917 advocated a prearranged ambush of a convoy by a pack of U-boats controlled and directed from the shore by wireless. The war ended in defeat for Germany before Bauer was able to try out his new method of attack, and it was left to Karl Dönitz to resurrect the idea in 1935, when he was appointed to command the 1st U-boat Flotilla.

Dönitz's *Rudeltaktik* called for a pack of six to ten U-boats to deploy in the expected path of a convoy in line abreast, much like a fisherman's drift net. The boats would so spaced as to be able to keep watch on 50 to 100 miles of the ocean, depending on the visibility. The first boat to sight the enemy ships would not attack independently, but follow in the wake of the convoy, keeping out of sight, and sending hourly position reports by radio. It should then be a simple matter for the controlling station ashore to call in the other boats to mount a concerted attack. In the years leading up to the outbreak of war Dönitz had spent a great deal of time and effort rehearsing his U-boats in the pack attack. In October 1939 he was given the first opportunity to put *Rudeltaktik* into practice.

Convoy HG 3 sailed from Gibraltar on 12 October, one of the earliest convoys of the war. It consisted of twenty-five ships sailing unescorted, but covered by air patrols from Gibraltar. All the merchantmen were classified as 'fast', i.e. being capable of speeds in excess of 9 knots, and with the total passage to UK waters being only 1,200 miles, the convoy was not considered to be at great risk.

Not surprisingly, given that all movements of Allied ships were closely monitored by German agents in Algeciras, Dönitz was informed of the sailing of HG 3, and had acted without delay.

With HG 3 at sea, Dönitz ordered six U-boats to set up an ambush off Cape Trafalgar. In operational command in U-37, was the experienced 38-year-old *Korvettenkapitan* Werner Hartmann, a veteran of the Spanish Civil War. Hartmann had orders to mount a massed attack under the cover of darkness, when the convoy would be without air cover, sinking as many ships as possible. The first U-boat wolf pack was about to bare its fangs.

The plan misfired badly when three of the pack failed to turn up, two of them reported sunk by aircraft on their way to the rendezvous. This left only Werner Hartmann's U-37, Herbert Sohler in U-46 and Herbert Schultze in U-48 to carry out what should have been a surprise night attack inflicting heavy casualties on the British convoy.

Sohler was first on the scene, and dazzled by the sight of the great armada of unescorted ships stretching from horizon to horizon, he yielded to temptation. Surfacing just after dawn on the 17th, he opened fire on the 10,138-ton Bibby Line ship *Yorkshire,* with his 88-mm deck gun. The *Yorkshire,* under the command of Captain Victor Smalley, was carrying general cargo from Rangoon to Liverpool, along with 151 passengers, mainly military families being repatriated to Britain. Armed with a 4-inch gun on her poop, she was acting as commodore ship for HG 3. To Sohler's great consternation, he found his fire being returned, shot for shot. He took U-46 down at a rush.

The abortive attack on the *Yorkshire* alerted the convoy to the danger below the surface, and throughout the rest of the day the ships steered zig-zag courses, with those who had guns keeping them manned at all times.

The U-boats made their next move in the late afternoon, when Werner Hartmann closed the convoy at periscope depth and fired two torpedoes at the *Yorkshire,* both of which found the target. The *Yorkshire* sank, taking with her Captain Smalley, twenty-four of his crew, and thirty-three passengers. Fortunately, the American steamer *Independence Hall* was nearby, and she picked up the 105 crew and 118 passengers who had survived the sinking.

While consternation reigned in the convoy following the sinking of the *Yorkshire,* Herbert Sohler in U-46 made up for his failed attack of the morning by crippling the 7,028-ton *City of Mandalay* with a torpedo in the engine room. The *City of Mandalay,* homeward bound from the Far East with cargo for London and Glasgow, took a heavy list and began to settle. Sohler fired a second torpedo at 1700, but this detonated prematurely. The *City of Mandalay* sank in her own time, which allowed all but seven of her crew of eighty to be picked up by the *Independence Hall* and the Norwegian whaler *Skudd IV.*

The third member of Dönitz's depleted pack, Herbert Schultze's U-48, was not to be denied her moment of glory. Surfacing after dark, Schultze turned his sights on a large, heavily loaded steamer sailing near the head of the convoy.

The 7,256-ton *Clan Chisholm* was a twin-screw steamer, only two years old, and a proud member of the fleet of Clan Line Steamers of London and Glasgow, a crack company widely known as the 'Scottish Navy'. Under the command of Captain Francis Stenson, the *Clan Chisholm* carried 9,950 tons of general cargo, including tea, jute, pig iron, coconuts and cotton, all loaded on the Indian coast. She had a service speed of 14 knots, at which she had completed the long passage from India sailing alone and unescorted. Captain Stenson had not been at all pleased when he was ordered to join the 9-knot HG 3 for the final leg of the voyage.

For some hours following the sinking of the *Yorkshire* and the *City of Mandalay*, Stenson had been debating whether he should break away from the convoy and make a dash for home at full speed, but had finally decided to err on the side of caution and stay with HG 3. It was a decision he was to regret bitterly

Schultze's first torpedo ran true enough, hitting the *Clan Chisholm* amidships. However, it failed to explode. Three minutes later, Schultze fired again, and this time his torpedo blew a fatal hole in the Clan boat's sturdy, Clyde-built hull. Four crew members lost their lives, Captain Stenson and the remainder of his seventy-eight man crew being picked up by passing ships.

The *Clan Chisholm* was the first of the Scottish fleet to be lost in the war, but she was swiftly avenged. Twenty-four hours after she went, the U-boats were still snapping at the heels of HG 3, and one of them – it is not known which – was bold enough to surface and attack the other Clan Line ship sailing with the convoy. She was the 23-year-old *Clan Macbean*, commanded by the fiery Captain Ernie Coultas, also homeward from India with a general cargo.

Having missed with a torpedo, the U-boat began shelling the *Clan Macbean*, which was unarmed and unable to hit back. Horrified that anyone should have the audacity to threaten his ship, Captain Coultas gave a double ring on the engine-room telegraph, and charged at the U-boat, intent on ramming. The *Clan Macbean's* blunt bows were within 100 feet of the enemy submarine when the German commander panicked and crash dived, leaving his gun's crew struggling in the water.

So ended Admiral Donitz's first wolf pack attack. Coordinated by Werner Hartmann from the conning tower of U–37, it had not been a great success. Any future pack action, Donitz vowed, would be controlled from ashore.

Unaware of developments on the other side of the ocean, Convoy SC 2 continued to make its lonely way across the North Atlantic. As with all convoys, its speed was determined by its slowest member. Many of the ships were old and worn out by hard voyaging, and SC 2 could be said to be ambling its way home at little more than a fast walking pace. To add to its vulnerability, despite the Commodore's frantic pleading to 'Make less smoke!' a forest of tall funnels continued to add to the ominous black cloud that hung over the convoy. The only thing that seemed to be in SC 2's favour was the weather. Unusually, the North Atlantic was quiescent; the skies were grey, but the visibility was good, and apart from the ever-present swell, the sea was showing a kind face. The less experienced seamen welcomed the benign weather, but to the older hands it was a mixed blessing. They would have preferred the cloak of invisibility offered by a roaring Atlantic gale.

On 30 August, when SC 2 was 1,000 miles out from Cape Breton, and not yet halfway through the long passage, a lifeline was flung across the Atlantic by the Americans. President Roosevelt cabled Prime Minister Churchill: 'It is my belief that it may be possible to furnish the British Government as immediate assistance at least fifty destroyers.' That the destroyers offered by America were near–obsolete and totally unsuited for the rigours of the North Atlantic was neither here nor there. They represented the guns that the Royal Navy desperately needed to protect the convoys.

Unfortunately, the American destroyers would come too late for SC 2. An entry in Admiral Dönitz's war diary for 2 September reads:

> 2.9.1940: U-124, 65, 47 and 101 to operate against the SC 2 convoy. U-101 reported that she still had 6 torpedoes left and more than half her fuel. Contact is to be made before the convoy is picked up by the inward escort. According to reckoning the convoy should be in square AL 0216 at midday on 6.9. One U-boat will be stationed at this point and the others in quarterline astern of her, so that a certain depth is achieved and a total breadth of 40 miles covered. It can then be expected that, if the convoy proceeds

according to plan, all boats will be able to attack, and if it deviates from the rendezvous, at least one boat. Boats are to keep radio silence except for convoy reports. U-124 is to continue with her scheduled weather reports for the present.

Ideally, Dönitz would have liked at least six boats to take part in this first serious demonstration of his *Rudeltaktik*, but his resources were as limited as those of the Royal Navy. He would have to make do with four boats, but he was comforted by the knowledge that two of these were under the command of his best men.

U-47, a Type VIIB built at Krupps Germaniawerft in Kiel, was commanded by thirty-two-year old Kapitänleutnant Günther Prien, already famous for his audacious penetration of the Royal Navy's heavily fortified base at Scapa Flow in October 1939. Threading his way through the defences, Prien torpedoed the 30,000-ton battleship HMS *Royal Oak*, which went down in thirteen minutes, taking 333 men with her. He was awarded the coveted Knights Cross for this action, and went on to become Germany's top U-boat ace. By the autumn of 1940 he had sent another fifteen ships and their cargoes to the bottom.

Racing in to join Günther Prien was Otto Kretchsmer in U-99, another Type VIIB. Twenty-eight-year-old Kretschmer, also a holder of the Knights Cross, had amassed a staggering score of 102,758 tons of Allied shipping sunk since the outbreak of war.

Only two other boats were at hand to make up the wolf pack. They were U-65, a Type IXB with the aristrocratic *Kapitänleutnant* Hans-Gerrit Adalbert Karl Theodor von Stockhausen in command, and U-28, a Type VIIA commanded by *Kapitänleutnant* Günter Kuhnke. Both commanders had been on operations in the North Atlantic since the outbreak of war and already had an impressive number of sinkings to their name.

When a reluctant dawn broke on 6 September, Convoy SC 2 was south of Iceland, and 270 miles due west of the lonely outpost of Rockall. There was still no sign of the enemy, and escorts from Western Approaches Command were expected within the next twenty-four hours. Home was not yet in sight, but the more optimistic were already hanging out their shore-going clothes to air. 'The Channels', that mysterious anticipatory disease that seamen suffer from when the end of the voyage is near, was spreading from ship to ship. But with the dawn came a marked deterioration in the weather. The wind, which had freshened from the west during the night, began to keen in the rigging, and by sunrise the cloud base was down to mast-top height and it was blowing Force 8.

The gale, accompanied by heavy rain squalls, drew a welcome curtain of anonymity around the convoy, but the wind, having backed, was now directly on the beam. The box-shaped merchantmen, many of them already struggling to maintain the convoy speed of 7 knots, began to wallow in the rising swell, losing what little momentum they had. The more heavily laden were experiencing difficulty in holding their course, and the hitherto orderly columns were rapidly becoming ragged.

It was perhaps just as well that the men struggling to control their ungainly ships did not realize that the foul weather was the lesser of the enemies threatening them. Three miles astern of the rear ships, and hidden from sight by the rain and breaking seas, U-65 was following in their wake. Nine days out of Brest on his fifth patrol, Hans-Gerrit von Stockhausen had struck gold. Directed to the expected position of SC 2 by radio signals from U-boat HQ, he had sighted the pall of black smoke generated by the labouring ships, and had closed in at full speed on the surface. Mindful of the order from Dönitz that he was not to attack alone, von Stockhausen settled down to shadow the convoy, reporting its position, course and speed hourly to Lorient. By the time the sun rose behind the thick cloud cover, he was in touch with U-99 and U-28 using 'schnell signals', coded bursts of morse sent at high speed and so brief that they were unintelligible to the listening ears of the enemy.

SC2, still oblivious to the approaching danger, was then 600 miles and 84 hours hard steaming from the shelter of the North Channel, with the promised local escort force not scheduled to arrive until daylight on the 7th. Commodore Boddman-Whetham, on whose shoulders rested the awesome burden of bringing this great armada of merchantmen to safety, was by now feeling the first twinges of anxiety.

The sighs of relief emanating from the merchantmen were almost audible when, just as night was falling on the 6th, the first of the grey-painted escorts appeared out of the murk.

The escort group consisted of the destroyers HMS *Westcott* and HMCS *Skeena*, the sloops *Lowestoft* and *Scarborough*, the Flower-class corvette *Periwinkle*, and the two anti-submarine trawlers *St Apollo* and *Berkshire*. Commanding the group was Commander Arthur Knapp, RN, who flew his flag in the Grimsby-class sloop *Lowestoft*. This appeared to be a force to be reckoned with, and it certainly cheered the anxious ones in the convoy, but it had serious hidden weaknesses. None of the ships had exercised or sailed together as a group before, *Westcott* was of First World War vintage, and *Periwinkle* was newly commissioned and completely untried in action.

Commander Knapp was not aware that the convoy was already being shadowed, but he accepted as a certainty that U-boats would be in the vicinity. He also fully expected the attack to come that night. Accordingly, he distributed his ships to best advantage. *Lowestoft* and *Scarborough* took up the lead, zig-zagging ahead of the convoy, the destroyers were positioned to port and starboard to protect the flanks, while *Periwinkle* and the trawlers dropped astern to cover the rear. This defensive screens was full of holes, but it was the best Knapp could do with his limited resources. They settled down to wait out the critical hours of darkness.

It was a dark, moonless night, and with the gale rising to its screaming crescendo the merchant ships were suffering. Rolling ponderously in the mountainous swells, the angry breaking seas sweeping their open decks, they were in a fight to stay afloat. Some, loaded in a hurry, and with questionable stability, were at times in danger of capsizing as they corkscrewed their way through the turbulent sea. And if the merchantmen were struggling, then their escorts – the little ships that had steamed more than 500 miles to protect them – were experiencing the torments of Hell itself.

The destroyers and sloops, slim in the beam, and low in the water, were like half-tide rocks, sometimes disappearing from view entirely when the waves broke clean over them. The corvette *Periwinkle*, built along the lines of an Atlantic whaler, fared better, rolling and pitching like a mad thing, but riding the waves from crest to trough with the clumsy elegance of an overweight ballet dancer. Only the anti-submarine trawlers, which had rarely known any other weather in their earlier life while scouring Icelandic waters for cod, seemed to be at home in this spume-filled madhouse.

Responding to U-65's signals, U-28, U-47 and U-99 were also riding the roller-coaster of this violent Atlantic storm. Casings completely awash, with only their conning towers above water, the three boats designated, with U-65, to become Dönitz's 'wolf pack', plunged through the waves, eager to join the coming battle.

Günther Prien, in U-47, was first to make contact with the convoy, sighting the battered outriders of SC 2 soon after midnight. With characteristic boldness, and taking advantage of the atrocious weather, Prien remained on the surface, slipping unseen through the escort screen with ease.

First to come into Prien's sights was the 5,155-ton steamer *Neptunian*, owned by W.A. Souter & Company, and under the command of Captain Alexander Campbell. The fifteen-year-old Newcastle tramp, down to her summer marks with 8,500 tons of sugar from Cuba, and underpowered like all her breed, was valiantly attempting to remain on station at the head of Column Eight. Thus occupied, no one on her bridge saw Günther Prien's two torpedoes narrowly missing their ship, speeding on to sink harmlessly in the deep water.

Prien took more care with his third torpedo, which caught the *Neptunian* squarely amidships. She capsized and sank seven minutes later, taking Captain Campbell, his crew of thirty-five, and her precious cargo of sugar with her.

Aboard the sloop *Lowestoft*, keeping station 2 miles ahead of the convoy with *Scarborough*, Commander Knapp heard two muffled explosions in quick succession, which were followed by a bright flash to starboard. Fearing the worst, Knapp turned *Lowestoft* under full helm, raced across in front of the columns of slow-moving merchantmen, and swept down the starboard side.

Scarborough, commanded by Commander Norman Dickinson, had remained ahead of the convoy, carrying out broad sweeps from side to side. Shortly after *Lowestoft* detached, *Scarborough's* Asdic operator obtained a hard contact, which was identified as a submarine. Calling for full speed, Dickinson at once moved in to attack. Almost immediately, a dark shape closely resembling the conning tower of a U-boat was sighted right ahead. This soon disappeared, leaving only a patch of disturbed water, over which *Scarborough* ran, dropping a single depth charge set to 150 feet. The resulting explosion may or may not have damaged the fleeing U-boat, but it also knocked out the sloop's Asdic. By the time the set was working again, some fifteen minutes later, the contact had been lost.

Lowestoft was off station for two hours, during which she made a complete circuit of the convoy. She saw nothing untoward, and obtained no Asdic contacts. It was only when she returned to her station ahead of the convoy that Commander Knapp learned from *Scarborough* of her brush with the U-boat. Neither ship was then aware of the loss of the *Neptunian*. The unfortunate merchantman had gone down unobserved; she had sent no SOS, nor did she fire rockets. Knapp concluded that a U-boat had attempted to attack the convoy, but had made off after being surprised by *Scarborough*. He did not consider the possibility of a U-boat being inside the convoy, and decided to carry on as before.

U–47 had not gone away. She was still on the surface, but trimmed well down so that only her conning tower showed as a vague shadow in the darkness of this the black hour before the dawn. Prien had moved quickly away from the scene of his conquest, and was passing between the ragged lines of ships. Reaching the port side of the convoy, he selected his next target.

The 5,303-ton *José de Larrinaga*, fourth ship in the port outside column of SC 2, was fighting her own lonely battle with the fury of the storm. The Liverpool-registered steamer, under the command of Captain Arthur Gass, was on passage from New York to Newport Mon. with a cargo of 5,303 tons of steel topped off with drums of linseed oil. By the nature of her cargo, 'stiff as a board' in seaman's parlance, her very low centre of gravity gave her a fast, jerky roll that strained every rivet in her hull as she laboured in the rough seas and swell. Again, as with the *Neptunian*, those on the bridge of the *José de Larrinaga* were too occupied fighting their old enemy the sea to notice Günther Prien's torpedo speeding towards them.

The *José de Larrinaga* broke in two, and went down in eleven minutes, consigning Captain Arthur Gass and his crew of thirty-nine to an unmarked grave in the deep Atlantic. Such was the fury of the storm that she went unseen, even by the ships close to her.

The explosion of Prien's torpedo was heard on the bridge of *Lowestoft*, and Commander Knapp again immediately reversed course, this time sweeping down the port side of the convoy. But once more he saw nothing, and made no Asdic contact. None of the other ships in the vicinity reported seeing anything untoward. Puzzled, Knapp took *Lowestoft* back to her station ahead of the convoy. While the sloop had been away hunting, Commodore Boddam-Whethem had taken evasive action, leading the convoy through two emergency turns, first to starboard, and ten minutes later to port. Remarkably, despite the darkness, the wind and the driving rain, convoy discipline held, and this motley collection of ships managed to maintain a semblance of order.

It was still not apparent to Commander Knapp, Commodore Boddam-Whethem, or anyone else in the convoy that a U-boat was running amok within the columns – and even if they had known, there was very little positive action they could have taken. Meanwhile, Günther Prien was stealthily making his way back through the lines of the convoy, narrowly avoiding being run down on several occasions. By about 0400, he had positioned U-47 between the two outer starboard columns, and was manoeuvring to make his next kill. His target was the third ship in Column Eight, the Norwegian steamer *Gro*.

The 4,211-ton *Gro*, commanded by Captain Paul Brun and owned by Grolle and Hysing Olsen of Bergen, had only three months earlier escaped from Norway to Britain, and was already in service for her adopted country. She had joined SC 2 in Sydney, having loaded 6,321 tons of wheat in Montreal for Manchester. She carried a crew of thirty-two, all Norwegians in exile.

Dawn, which promised to be little more than a greying of the heavily overcast sky, was now approaching, and Günther Prien was anxious to strike before the light gave him away. Taking careful aim, he fired a single torpedo which hit the *Gro* squarely in her engine-room on the starboard side. The Norwegian ship's boilers exploded and she broke her back, sinking ten minutes later. Yet again, the passing of another ship was masked by the cacophony of the storm. No one saw her go, and her absence was not noticed until it was fully light and Commodore Boddam-Whethem was able to make a ship count. Then he was horrified to find that three of his ships were missing, including the *Gro*

Astern of the convoy, another reckoning was taking place. Prien's torpedo had destroyed the *Gro's* starboard lifeboat, and the survivors of the torpedoed Norwegian were crowded into the remaining boat. When the role was called, Captain Brun discovered that eleven of his crew were missing. Eight of these had been in the engine-room, and were most probably killed by the explosion and the scalding steam. The others, Second Mate Johan Myklebust, Third Mate Olaf Monsen and Messboy Anbjørn Astad, appeared to have gone down with the ship.

When full daylight – such as it was – finally came, Captain Brun took stock of the situation in the lifeboat. Although the boat was certified to carry thirty persons, it was already uncomfortably crowded with twenty-one on board. To make matters worse, Herolf Sørensen, the *Gro's* galley boy, who had been at the top of the engine-room when the boilers exploded, had suffered extensive burns, and room was needed to attend to him. Fortunately, the boat was well equipped, having on board sufficient warm clothing and oilskins for each man, as well as an ample supply of water and food. There was also a canvas spray hood, which when erected in the bows protected the survivors from the worst of the breaking waves. Having seen to the comfort of his men, Brun hoisted sail and set course for the coast of Scotland 300 miles to the east.

After sailing east for nearly four days, the *Gro's* boat was sighted by the British steamer *Burdwan* 50 miles off the Outer Hebrides on the evening of 9 September. The survivors were taken on board the *Burdwan* just as darkness was closing in. As the *Burdwan* was on passage to Capetown, they were transferred to a British destroyer, and landed in Liverpool.

Eighteen days later, on 27 September, one of the *Gro's* liferafts was found drifting by the corvette HMS *Periwinkle*. Lashed to the raft were two bodies, one of which was identified as that of Second Mate Johan Myklebust. The other body was believed to be that of either Third Mate Olaf Monsen or Messboy Anbjorn Astad. As all three men were missing, it was assumed that at least two of them had got away from the sinking ship on the raft, which was later identified as having come from the bridge of the *Gro*. As to the third man, Monsen or Astad, his tale will never be told.

Reeling from the shock of the silent attack of the night of the 6/7 September, SC 2 closed ranks and made all possible speed for the safety of British waters. At dusk on 8 September, the convoy was within 40 miles of the Outer Hebrides, and shaping up to enter the North Channel. It seemed that the worst of the voyage was over. However, despite the close proximity of British waters, and the increasing presence of RAF Coastal Command aircraft overhead, the four U-boats Dönitz had managed to muster for his first wolf pack were still there.

Once again, it was the fearless hunter Günther Prien who found the first opening. Breaking through the escort screen after dark, he entered the convoy from the landward side, and half an hour before midnight torpedoed the 3,840-ton Greek steamer *Possidon*. The 31-year-old *Possidon*, loaded with 5,410 tons of sulphur phosphate from New Orleans for Glasgow, went down in just a few minutes. Seventeen of her crew went with her.

It was now that Prien made a mistake that almost cost him his life, and the lives of his entire crew. After torpedoing the *Possidon*, he allowed U-47 to drop back through the columns to the rear of the convoy. It was his intention to slip across astern of the convoy, and reach open water to the north. The weather was moderating, but there was still enough turbulence to drown out the rattle of her twin diesels and U-47 crossed the wakes of SC 2's back markers unseen. Unfortunately for Prien, he was unaware that Column Two, second column in from port, contained not five or six ships like the others, but seven. No.27, rear ship of Column Two, was the Norwegian timber carrier *Mäkefjell*, a latecomer to the convoy. The *Mäkefjell*, a small ship of only 1,567 tons, may not have been visible from U-47's conning tower, and in crossing ahead of her Prien found himself in danger of being run down. Only a double ring on the U-boat's engine-room telegraphs and a sudden burst of speed saved U-47. The master of the *Mäkefjell*, Captain Oywind Meitzner, later reported having collided with a U-boat trying to cross his bows. U-47 escaped unscathed, but it had certainly been a very near-miss.

After his narrow escape, Prien sent a brief message to Lorient reporting that he had sunk four ships, adding that he was down to his last torpedo. He was soon to regret revealing the state of his armament, for Dönitz replied by ordering him to break away from the convoy and relieve U-124, which was then far to the west acting as weather reporting boat.

With U-47 withdrawn from the attack, that left only Otto Kretchsmer's U-99 and Günter Kuhnke's U-28 in contact with SC 2, U-65 having lost touch altogether. Unusually for Kretchsmer, who was the originator of the night attack on the surface inside the convoy, he was yet to fire a torpedo in this action. It was left to Kuhnke to strike the final blow against SC 2.

U-28 had not yet succeeded in penetrating the convoy, and was then loitering on the outer fringes of the port outer column. The leading ship of this column was Ellerman & Papayanni Line's *Mardinian*. The 2,434-ton Liverpool ship, commanded by Captain Joseph Every, had joined SC 2 in Sydney from Trinidad, where she had loaded 3,500 tons of pitch for London. Tall-masted and slab-sided, the 21-year-old *Mardinian* presented an easy target for Kunhke's torpedo. Captain Every later reported to the Admiralty:

We left Sydney, Nova Scotia, on 25th August, in convoy of which

I was the leading ship of the port column. We proceeded without incident until 0350 on the 9th September when in position 56° 37'N 9° 00'W we were struck by a torpedo on the port side, about 120ft from the bow. There was a moderate westerly swell, moderate sea, and visibility was fairly good. We were making 6 knots, but not zig-zagging. I was in my cabin on the port side at the time and was awakened by a soft explosion and the sound of breaking glass. The 2nd Officer, who was on the bridge at the time, sighted the torpedo, but only a second or two before the impact.

I rushed to the bridge, and as the engines were still running I telegraphed for them to be stopped. I knew she hadn't been hit in the engine room because the lights were still on, and I think she was hit in the back end of No.2 hold. There was a large column of water which splashed up over the bridge; the vessel rolled a little and then righted herself. I could see from her position that there was no hope of saving her as she had already started to settle by the head, and so I ordered the lifeboats away. They got away in good order, and I left by the port boat at about 4.20 a.m.

When I was able to contact the starboard boat, and ascertained the number of survivors it was disclosed that 6 of the crew were missing. I questioned a number of the men who all assured me that all quarters were free when they left the ship. I afterwards learned that the Bo'sun, who is amongst the missing, released the raft and followed it over the side, accompanied by 5 others and I can only assume that they were drowned.

I remained in my boat on the spot until daylight, and saw the *Mardinian* sink at 4.40 a.m. She went down slowly by the head.

Whilst waiting for daylight at about 4.30 a.m. I saw in the distance the silhouette of a vessel which I should estimate to be about 1,500 tons, and heard a slight explosion just like the crack of a revolver. She couldn't have been more than a ¼ of a mile away and she disappeared about 10 minutes after my vessel had sunk.

At daylight, the two boats still being in company, searched among the wreckage but failed to find any of the missing men. I then set sail intending to make for the Scottish coast which I believed to be about 90 miles away, but at 8 a.m. I sighted an outward convoy and I was picked up by HM trawler *St Apollo* who, acting on instructions from the Officer commanding the Escort, landed me at Belfast the following morning at 7 a.m.

The *Mardinian's* second lifeboat, under the command of her chief officer, made a landfall on South Uist in the Outer Hebrides, while one other survivor was picked up from the water by the armed merchant cruiser *Aurania*. The six missing crew members, Boatswain Robert Brownfield, Able Seaman Percy Rigby, Ordinary Seaman Richard Furmedge, Ordinary Seaman Thomas Shirley, Trimmer George Miller and Assistant Steward Edward Maher, were never found.

Considering the absence of escorts for much of the Atlantic crossing, and that the U-boats adopted the hitherto unknown tactic of penetrating the convoy on the surface at night, it was something of a miracle that SC 2 lost only five ships out of fifty-three. Admiral Dönitz could not claim that this first attempt at using his *Rudeltaktik* was a triumph, but it did serve to demonstrate that there was a promising future for the pack attack.

Chapter 3

The Deep Atlantic

It was around 10 o'clock on the morning of 9 September that Captain Joe Every carefully eased the *Mardinian's* lifeboat alongside the heaving bulwarks of the armed trawler *St Apollo*. As Every and his men, greatly relieved at being delivered from the ordeal of a long haul in an open boat, scrambled aboard their rescuer, far on the other side of the Atlantic, the sun was just rising over the Canadian port of Halifax, Nova Scotia. And as the warmth of the rising sun took effect, the thin veil of early autumn mist lying over Bedford Basin slowly lifted to reveal a large fleet of merchantmen anchored in the deep-water bay. Convoy HX 72 was preparing for sea.

During the course of the morning, the captains of the twenty-six merchant ships, accompanied by their wireless operators, had gathered ashore in Admiralty House to receive their orders from the Naval Control. In a smoke-filled room overlooking the harbour a grey-haired naval commander welcomed them and without further preliminaries informed them that HX 72 was to maintain a minimum speed on passage of 9 knots and expected to complete the Atlantic crossing in eleven and a half days, weather permitting. This brought audible gasps of incredulity from the assembled master mariners, most of whom were all too well aware that the ships they commanded would do well to work up to and maintain 8 knots, and that given a cooperative chief engineer and decent steaming coal, both of which many lacked.

The convoy commodore, Rear Admiral Hugh Hext Rogers, OBE, RN (retired), took the stand next and, ignoring their scepticism, went on to explain the system of flag and light signals to be used to communicate between ships, emphasizing that complete radio silence must be kept at all times, except in a case of dire emergency. Fifty-seven-year-old Rogers, as with most of his kind, had seen service in the First World

War, retiring with the rank of rear admiral in 1935. When war came again, he had responded to the call for experienced men to lead the large convoys, and was given the rank of Commodore, RNR. He was to sail in the 5,200-ton general trader *Tregarthen*, sharing the bridge with her master Captain Jack Willingham. The *Tregarthen*, only four years old, well appointed, and with a relatively good turn of speed, would lead the HX 72 at the head of the middle column.

The technicalities of convoy discipline being dealt with, Rogers warned the assembled captains of the dangers of the Atlantic crossing, which were increasing with every day that passed. The Admiralty, the Commodore explained, had received reports of four German commerce raiders active in the Atlantic, namely the armed merchant cruisers *Atlantis*, *Pinguin*, *Thor* and *Widder*. Their main targets appeared to be ships sailing alone, but they also posed a definite threat to the convoys. Furthermore, since Italy had joined the war three months earlier, the German Navy now had another 100 U-boats at their disposal, some of them with long-range capacity. As an embarrassing afterthought, Rogers remarked that His Majesty's submarine *Seal*, captured by the Germans while laying mines in the Kattegat, might also might be at large, German manned and with belligerent intent.

The conference dragged on until lunch was looming on the horizon, when Rogers at last said, 'That will be all, gentlemen. You may now return to your ships. We sail within the hour.' His audience filed out, leaving behind them a blue fug of Old Holborn overlaid by the pungent odour of the aromatic cheroots favoured by the Scandinavian contingent amongst them.

As the merchant captains were being ferried back to their anchored ships, HX 72's local escort was already leaving harbour. This consisted of the destroyer HMCS *Saguenay*, the armed yacht *Reindeer*, and the small patrol vessels *French* and *Laurier* of the Royal Canadian Mounted Police. The four Canadian ships – only one of which could legitimately be called a warship – were to patrol to a depth of 16 miles off the approaches to Halifax while the convoy was forming up.

An hour later, with a great deal of clanking of steam windlasses, flashing signal lamps and flapping flag hoists, the twenty-six merchant ships hove in their anchors, and began to leave harbour. Almost immediately, one of their number, the Cardiff tramp *Nolisement*, carrying a full cargo of grain from Baltimore, was ordered to return to the anchorage. It was later revealed that on arrival in Halifax three members of her crew had been hospitalized suffering from an undiagnosed illness. This had now been confirmed to be typhoid, and samples taken from the *Nolisement's* drinking water tank showed the water to be contaminated. This was attributed to an act of sabotage committed by an enemy agent, or agents, while the ship was in Baltimore, and was the first indication that HX 72 may have been compromised.

Led by Commodore Rogers in the 5,000-ton *Tregarthen,* the long crocodile of merchantmen filed out through the narrow channel between McNab's Island and the mainland, through the anti-submarine nets guarding the approaches to Halifax harbour, and out into the open sea. Following close on the heels of the last ship came HX 72's ocean escort, the armed merchant cruiser HMS *Jervis Bay.*

The 14,164-ton *Jervis Bay,* an ex-Aberdeen and Commonwealth liner built in 1922, had spent much of her life in the mundane business of carrying passengers between Britain and Australia. Moderately luxurious, and with a cruising speed of 15 knots, she had fulfilled her peacetime role well. Now, dressed overall in Admiralty grey and armed with seven 5.9-inch guns, she gave the appearance of being a powerful man-of-war. A closer look, however, would reveal her to be dangerously vulnerable.

Commanded by Acting Captain Edward Fogarty Fegen, RN, the slab-sided *Jervis Bay* was too big and too cumbersome to be a serious threat to the enemy. While her seven 5.9s amounted to a formidable armament on paper, in reality they dated from the turn of the century – they had probably seen service in the Boer War – and were fired over open sights. When she passed into the hands of the Admiralty in the autumn of 1939, the majority of the *Jervis Bay's* crew opted to remain with her, being drafted into the Royal Naval Reserve under the T124 agreement. While these men, officers and ratings, were first-class seamen and navigators, none of them lacking in courage or determination, they had received only the most basic training in the arts of war.

In addition to her guns, HMS *Jervis Bay* carried two racks of depth charges for use against the U-boats, but given that she had a top speed of only 15 knots the probabilty is that she would have blown her own stern off had she been called upon to use them. Little wonder that the

Jervis Bay and her armed merchant cruiser sisters, now the mainstay of the navy's ocean escort force, were known throughout the service as 'Admiralty Made Coffins'.

Ironically, as HX 72 sailed out of Halifax, back in Bedford Basin a brief ceremony was taking place to mark the handing over of the first eight US Navy destroyers, so long promised to the Royal Navy by President Roosevelt. Flags were lowered and raised, bugles blared, and USS *Buchanan* became HMS *Campbeltown*, USS *Aaron Ward* HMS *Castleton*, USS *Hale* HMS *Caldwell*, USS *Crowninshield* HMS *Chelsea*, USS *Abel P. Upshur* HMS *Clare*, USS *Welborn C. Wood* HMS *Chesterfield*, USS *Welles* HMS *Cameron* and USS *Herndon* HMS *Churchill*.

The transfer of sovereignty complete, the ex-US ships, which had been handed over in exchange for a 100-year lease on British bases in the Caribbean, required significant modification and working up before they would be ready to enter service with the Royal Navy. On the face of it, they were manna from heaven for the hard-pressed North Atlantic escort force, but on closer examination this much-lauded aid from America seemed less than generous.

The reality was that the new Town-class destroyers, as they had been designated by their new owners, were nothing more than throw-outs from the US Navy's mothball fleet. Built in the First World War, they were small, just over 1,000 tons displacement, with a beam of only thirty-one feet. In contrast, they had a high superstructure and four funnels, the added weight of which made them slightly top-heavy. They were twin-screw ships with a speed of 30-35 knots, but their two propellers rotated in the same direction, making them extremely difficult to handle. Furthermore, their ancient rod and chain steering gear, which ran along the main deck, was extremely vulnerable. In heavy weather, which would be their lot for much of the time in the Atlantic, they rolled excessively, and their decks were seldom dry. The 'four-stackers', as they became known as in the Navy, were totally unsuited to anti-submarine warfare, which required above all stability and fast manoeuvrability. But in spite of all their shortcomings, the American ships were welcomed with open arms by the hard-pressed British Navy.

Once clear of the harbour, the merchant ships dropped their pilots off the fairway buoy and began forming up into orderly columns for the ocean crossing. This complicated manoeuvre was carefully choreographed from the bridge of the *Tregarthen* by Commodore

Rogers and his team of signallers, but it was a painfully slow process. Night was falling before order was finally created out of chaos.

Daylight on 10 September saw Convoy HX 72 some 80 miles out into the North Atlantic. HMCS *Saguenay*, her guns manned and Asdics sweeping ahead, was in the lead. The armed yacht *Reindeer* and RCMP's patrol boat *Laurier* were bringing up the rear. *French*, the other patrol boat, running low on fuel, had left to return to Halifax during the night. HMS *Jervis Bay*, perhaps with her dangerous vulnerability in mind, had been allocated a position within the convoy, between the two centre columns and about one cable astern of the leading ships. The whole great assembly of ships, bravely attempting to maintain a speed of 9 knots, was zig-zagging around an easterly course. Occasionally, aircraft of the Royal Canadian Air Force, already nearing the limit of their extreme range, would appear overhead, circling briefly before flying back inland.

At noon, a latecomer, the 7,199-ton *Tudor Prince* joined the convoy from Halifax, bringing the number of merchant ships to twenty-six. HX 72, now steaming in good order and reasonably well protected, moved confidently into the open Atlantic. By nightfall, however, this happy situation began to change dramatically. The convoy's air cover, such as it had been, had left with the setting sun, never to return, and as the darkness closed in *Saguenay*, *Reindeer* and *Laurier*, having reached the limit of their patrol area, made their farewells and turned back for Halifax. The defence of Convoy HX 72 was now solely in the hands of Captain Fogarty Fegen and his ex-passenger liner masquerading as a warship. Even to the lowliest boy seaman sailing in the most disreputable tramp in the ranks of HX 72 it was obvious that the convoy was dangerously vulnerable. And HX 72 was by no means complete, another eighteen ships, nine from Bermuda, and nine from Sydney, Cape Breton were on their way to join at prearranged rendezvouses.

Commodore Rogers' operational skills were sorely tested when, early on the morning of 11 September, with the Sydney contingent about to join up, the convoy ran into dense fog, which persisted for nearly two hours after dawn. Rogers was unable to use radio for fear of giving away the position of the convoy to the enemy, and had no escorts to spare to seek out and guide the newcomers in. He could do no more than pray that the rendezvous would not end up in a horrendous collision between the two groups of ships. Fortunately, the fog cleared shortly before the Sydney section arrived.

The fog came back again that night, creating another nightmare for those manning the bridges of the thirty-six ships steaming in close company. There could be no communication between the merchantmen, who were reduced to steaming at slow speed, all eyes straining to catch a glimpse of the dimmed blue stern light of the ship ahead, or a darker shadow in the murk that might indicate that a ship abeam was moving in too close.

It was a long, long night, packed with nerve shattering alarms and near-misses. The fog persisted throughout the next day, and the nightmare went on.

On 13 September, when 300 miles south-east of Newfoundland's Cape Race, the ranks of HX 72 were further swelled by the arrival of another nine ships, all British, which had sailed from Bermuda five days earlier. In some small compensation, as the newcomers fitted into the ranks, the 12,062-ton British tanker *Cadillac* pulled out and reversed course, recalled to Halifax by the Admiralty for reasons not explained.

By sunset, HX 72 had assumed its final formation, forty-two ships sailing in nine columns abreast, and covering an area of nearly 10 square miles of ocean. Forty-two ships, mostly coal burners, all trailing black smoke from their tall funnels, which formed a dark cloud high overhead, visible in daylight from far over the horizon. This huge assembly of merchant shipping, thirty-two British, five Norwegian, two Polish, one Greek, one Dutch and one American, carried some 300,000 tons of food and war material for the beleaguered British islands. Two of their number were gunwales awash with heavy cargoes of iron ore – a sure ticket to oblivion when the torpedo came – while the three tankers full to the brim with fuel oil for the Admiralty were potential crew-roasting bonfires. Others had steel in their lower holds, topped off by Canadian sawn timber that spilled over onto their decks, and piled so high that they resembled floating timber yards. They were the safe ones, difficult to sink with a torpedo, and guaranteed to give their crews ample time to get their boats away if they were in danger of sinking. In the midst of this great fleet of merchantmen, some of them armed with a single stern-mounted 4-inch, the majority defenceless, steamed their sole protector, HMS *Jervis Bay*, bravely flying the flag of His Britannic Majesty's Navy, but pathetically inadequate should she be called on to defend her charges.

Sixty-nine years later, the recollections of Stan Walton, who at the tender age of 15 years was sailing as an officer cadet in the Newcastle steamer *Selvistan*, serve to illustrate what life was like aboard a typical British tramp in the 1940s:

So far as I remember we sailed from Curtis Bay, Baltimore with a cargo of scrap metal for Halifax, where deguassing cables were installed, and proceeded to Sydney, Cape Breton for bunkers, going alongside a coaling berth for about 8 hours then off to the anchorage to await the convoy sailing date. We sailed in convoy with a couple of small Canadian Navy escorts who left us when we joined up the other section from Halifax with *Jervis Bay* as ocean escort. She was a fine looking vessel and steamed in the middle of the convoy. At that time the weather I think was fair as we kept daylight lookout in a barrel on the foremast cross-trees and at night on the focsle head until the weather changed and lookout was from the monkey island. I was on watch with two old ABs, ex-RN, the watch system was 4 on 4 off, 4 on then 8 off, then a field day of 4 hours etc., during which time the lookout, wheel and standby duties were shared by the three of us and those in the other two watches. We carried a bosun, ex-Head Line apprentice named, I think, Wills from Whiteley Bay, and an old Norwegian carpenter who were day workers, and that was the deck crowd. I was also sight setter on the old low-angle gun mounted on the poop, as we only had an ex-RN (Ret'd) leading hand gunlayer. The rest of the gun crew were mainly from the deck and catering departments, Second Mate George Miles being the Gunnery Officer, and I think Muloholland, the Ch. Steward was the gun trainer. Bulimore, my mate, was a tray or breech worker. *Selvistan* was a single decker, coal burning, ice box ship, poor feeder with spartan accommodation. The crew lived forward, firemen on the port side, deck crowd on the starboard side of the focsle, each side being equipped with a small coal burning bogey stove for heat in the open sleeping quarters. There was a separate mess room and primitive toilet on each side. The chart room was on the lower bridge forward of the Ch. Officer's cabin, that also opened onto the deck. Our 6' x 6' room was on the port side amidships, opened onto the deck. It contained two bunks with lumpy flock mattresses, a 3ft settee, 2ft wardrobe, a 4-drawer chest, and oil lamp, 40 watt light bulb in the centre of the wooden deckhead that leaked, and a ventilator that was located between the jolly boat and the Old Man's room bulkhead on the lower bridge above. There was a converted wash basin stand that served as our food locker, condensed milk, sugar, coffee, tea, jam and bread. The cook wasn't the best, the daily 1 pound loaf had a crust on each end and a lump of 'sog' in the middle. The tinned Irish butter was very salty/rancid and quite strong smelling that we used to swop it with the West African firemen for jam – generally apple and damson. There was no table, meals were consumed sitting on the settee with the enamel metal kits on your knee while the rod & chain steering gear groaned and clanked overhead. The radio 'shack' was on the after end of the boat deck that was equipped with radial davits and a wooden lifeboat on either side.

In the days of normality, now long forgotten in the fog of war, all these heavily-laden ships would have been sailing alone, on courses dictated by their various navigators, but all heading in the general direction of Land's End. The fall of France, the minefields laid in the south-western approaches to the British Isles, and the arrival of the U-boats at their new bases on the Biscay coast had put paid to such *laissez faire* voyaging. Ships bound for all United Kingdom ports, whether sailing alone or in convoy, were routed to west of Ireland and towards the North Channel. Vessels heading for East Coast ports and London joined coastal convoys at Loch Ewe or off Oban, before proceeding around Cape Wrath, through the Pentland Firth, and into the North Sea. This added a considerable number of miles to the Atlantic crossing, but even the masters of the merchant ships, so used to going their own way, agreed that the diversion was a necessary evil.

While HX 72 made its way across the Atlantic, three of Dönitz's top U-boat 'aces' were making ready to put to sea from Lorient, namely Günther Prien and Otto Kretchsmer, both fresh from the assault on SC 2, and Joachim Schepke.

Thirty-one-year-old Günther Prien, commanding U-47, was the senior of the trio. An ex-merchant ship's officer, he had joined the U-boat service in 1935, receiving his baptism of fire in the Spanish Civil War whilst serving as a watch officer in U-26. He was given command of U-47 shortly after the outbreak of war in 1939, and lost no time in proving his worth. As a grand opening to the war, Prien penetrated the heavily defended British naval base at Scapa Flow, sinking the 29,000-

ton battleship *Royal Oak* and, moreover, reached the open sea again without a scratch on U-47's paintwork. His hat trick of sinkings in the attack on SC 2 brought his score to twenty-one Allied ships totalling more than 120,000 tons.

Otto Kretchsmer, younger by three years than Prien, entered the regular navy straight from school, and served in the light cruisers *Emden* and *Köln* before transferring to the U-boats in 1936. In his first command, U-35, he patrolled Spanish waters during the Civil War. Although he had failed to make his mark on SC 2, his record in this war, having already sunk 93,000 tons of Allied shipping, was more than promising.

Joachim Schepke, commanding U-100, had missed SC 2, being at the time fully occupied with the outward bound convoy OA 204, of which he sank five British ships, adding another 21,000 tons to his already considerable total of 28,000 tons. Born in 1912, the son of a naval officer, Schepke had followed his father into the Navy in 1930, transferring to the U-boat Arm in 1935. Tall and handsome, he was described as being 'full of confidence and aggression'. Like Prien, an enthusiastic Nazi, Schepke had also found favour in high places.

As the war progressed, a friendly rivalry had grown up between these three commanders, each eager to outdo the others as they plied their dangerous trade against the slow, and largely unprotected, ships of Britain's Atlantic lifeline. The night before they sailed against HX 72, like true brothers-in-arms, they met in a small village outside Lorient, and drank until dawn.

Out in the Atlantic, Commodore Rogers was experiencing difficulties with the ships under his command. Few of them, in spite of the huge amount of black smoke pouring from their funnels, were able to maintain a consistent speed, and their station-keeping left a lot to be desired. Furthermore, they were a mix of nationalities, and he was already experiencing language difficulties when communicating with some of them. Complete radio silence was essential, but from time to time, whether by accident or intent, unauthorized transmissions were being made. Commodore Rogers did not question the loyalty of the British ships, but he was wary of the foreign-flag ships. A few days earlier his suspicions had been aroused concerning one of them, the 6,031-ton Norwegian steamer *Simla*, by a message from the Admiralty, which read:

S.S. Simla has had crew trouble and conflicting reports about the reliability of Master have also been received. He is reported as stating that he has run the British blockade and he will do so again. Suggest ship and Master be watched.

The *Simla*, leading ship of Column Three, was carrying a load of steel for an East Coast port, and the inference was that she might make a run for German occupied Norway when she was in the North Sea. So far as Rogers was concerned, the Admiralty's message may have been the result of careless talk in a dockside bar, but it was another worry to add to his already considerable burden.

Admiral Dönitz, forewarned of the sailing of HX 72, was meanwhile busy arranging a reception party for the eastbound convoy. His best men were to hand. Günther Prien, in U-47, Joachim Schepke, in U-100, Otto Kretchsmer, in U-99, and Heinrich Bleichrodt, in U-48, were all patrolling in the vicinity of Rockall, carrying out successful hit-and-run attacks on passing convoys. Hans Jenisch, in U-32, had just left Lorient, U-43, with Wilhelm Ambrosius in command, was passing to the north of Scotland after sailing from Bergen, Engelbert Endrass, in U-46, was in the approaches to the Channel, and Han-Gerrit Stockhausen, in U-65, was off the Outer Hebrides.

U-47, by this time down to her last torpedo, Donitz ordered into the mid-Atlantic to act as weather reporting boat for the Luftwaffe's bombers, then busy raiding Britain's towns and cities. Günther Prien, who had been hoping to replenish his torpedoes from one of the 'Milk Cows' on station in the Atlantic, and then re-enter the fray, did not welcome his new assignment. In his opinion, rolling in the Atlantic swells while sending in twice daily reports of temperature, pressure, wind direction and speed, was a criminal waste of a good U-boat.

The other U-boats, although alerted for the pending arrival of HX 72, meanwhile went about their trade. Bleichrodt, in U-48, attacking the eastbound convoy SC 3 as it passed north of Rockall, sank the convoy's only escort, the sloop HMS *Dundee,* then set about the unprotected merchantmen, sending four of them to the bottom. Otto Kretchsmer and Hans-Gerrit von Stockhausen, working only a few miles to the west, picked off three stragglers from HX 71 before answering the Admiral's call.

When he lost contact with SC 3, Bleichrodt moved further to the west, where late on 16 September he sighted the Canada-bound convoy OB

213. He tucked U-48 in behind the rear ships of the convoy, and waited for the opportunity to attack.

Bleichrodt's opening did not come until the early hours of 17 September, when OB 213's escort of a destroyer and two sloops turned for home, having reached the safe limit of their fuel tanks. The convoy sailed on alone into the teeth of a rising north-westerly gale. The rain squalls accompanying the gale gave Bleichrodt the cover he had been seeking, and slipping between the slow-moving columns of ships, he worked his way to the head of the convoy. Leading the centre column he saw a large, two-funneled liner; a worthy target for his torpedoes.

Nudged off course by the rough seas, U-48's first two torpedoes missed the target completely, but the third went home in the stern of the liner, exploding with a flash and a dull thud. The stricken ship began to settle by the stern at once.

Bleichrodt had torpedoed the commodore ship of OB 213, the 11,081-ton Ellerman passenger liner *City of Benares*. On the face of it, this was a legitimate target, but it was a ship Heinrich Bleichrodt was to regret sinking for the rest of his days. On board the *City of Benares* were 191 passengers, ninety of them children being evacuated to Canada to escape the dangers of the German air raids on Britain. Seventy-seven of these innocent youngsters died on that awful, storm-filled night in the Atlantic. Later in life, one of those lucky enough to survive, Edward Stokes, described his ordeal:

> The night was absolutely horrendous. It was the blackest of nights, and it was raining and the wind was blowing at gale force. The lifeboat's keel was the only thing available, so our hands locked onto it. There was a row of hands alongside mine, on my side of the keel – and another row of hands on Beth's side, facing me. Bit by bit the rows of hands grew less and less as people lost their grip, or lost their will to live – and let go.
>
> We knew that if we could hang on until daylight things would be better. We made up our minds – we were just going to go on hanging on, despite everything. Obviously in the later stages we were fantasizing. We saw what we thought were enormous fish, we saw icebergs, we thought we saw ships, we thought we saw planes. We had had nothing to drink and nothing to eat, and we were suffering from severe exposure – I think we were very near death.
>
> It was getting dark (on the evening after the sinking), and Beth

and I had both made up our minds that this was probably going to be our last day. But there, coming towards us, at a very creeping speed, was a black dot on a previously blank horizon seen over the crests of the waves. And unlike the other things we had seen this was definitely moving towards us. This one was real. I croaked to Beth, 'Beth, there's a ship'. When we were finally rescued they had to prise our hands off the keel.

The loss of the *City of Benares* and her young passengers provoked outrage in Britain. Prime Minister Winston Churchill, who had forbidden the sending of young children across the Atlantic, was furious when he discovered that his orders had been circumvented by unknown civil servants within the Home Office. Consequently, the evacuation of children overseas was suspended until sufficient naval escorts were available to protect them.

While the westbound Convoy OB 213 was under attack, its opposite number HX 72 was 400 miles to the south-west, and feeling the effects of the same north-westerly gale. With the wind and sea square on the beam, the deep-laden merchant men rolled and yawed wildly, often resembling half-tide rocks as the seas broke clean over their open decks. Station keeping became impossible, and gradually the once orderly ranks of the convoy descended into chaos. Lifeboats were smashed in their davits, deck cargoes washed overboard, and ships began to fall astern as they adjusted course and speed to avoid damage by the mountainous seas. Eventually, Commodore Rogers was forced to reduce speed to allow the stragglers to catch up. This they did, one by one, all except the *Mount Kyllene*, back marker of Column Eight. The Greek tramp, her cargo adrift below decks, developed a heavy list, and could do little to help herself. She dropped further and further astern, and HX 72 had no spare escort to stand by her. The *Mount Kyllene* must fend for herself. And she did exactly that, reaching her destination, battered, but otherwise unharmed.

At sunset on 20 September, when HX 72 was within 500 miles of the Irish coast, HMS *Jervis Bay* was ordered to return westwards to meet Convoy HX 84, due to sail from Sydney on 27 September. The AMC reversed her course, dipped her ensign in salute, and steamed off into the gathering gloom at full speed. She was sailing into immortality.

On 5 November, Convoy HX 84, consisting of thirty-eight loaded merchantmen with the *Jervis Bay* occupying her usual position in the middle ranks, had reached halfway across the Atlantic, when over the horizon steamed the German pocket battle ship *Admiral Scheer*.

The 12,000-ton *Admiral Scheer*, with a top speed of 28 knots, her hull and decks protected by a foot of armour, and mounting six 11-inch and eight 6-inch guns, would have been a formidable foe for any British warship to meet; for the *Jervis Bay* she was the end of the road.

Captain Fogarty Fegen, although well aware that he and his men were looking death in the eye, did not hesitate. Ordering the convoy to scatter, he hoisted his battle ensigns, and steamed straight for the *Admiral Scheer*.

The result of this encounter was inevitable. Before Fegen could bring his puny 5.9s within range, the *Jervis Bay* ran into a hail of 11-inch shells from the enemy battleship. The liner's bridge was hit, her forward guns were knocked out, and her engine-room turned into a blazing charnel house. Captain Edward Fogarty Fegen died with his face to the enemy, as did 189 of his men. Their ship, crippled and ablaze, but with her ensigns still flying proudly, capsized and sank before her guns could wound the enemy.

The gallant sacrifice of the *Jervis Bay* bought time for the merchantmen of HX 84, allowing most of them to escape into the cover of darkness. Thirty-one of the thirty-eight ships survived to continue their voyage to Britain.

After the *Jervis Bay's* departure, HX 72 faced the prospect of steaming for the next twenty-four hours unescorted, before making a rendezvous with its local escort late on 21 November. At the time a howling gale with poor visibility would have been welcomed by the ships, but, perversely, the North Atlantic was in a kindly mood. By the time darkness fell, the wind had dropped to little more than a moderate breeze, just sufficient to set the white horses running, while overhead a full moon shone down through broken cloud, bathing the sea in a brilliant light. The visibility was excellent, with isolated rain squalls providing patches of cover. Conditions could not have been more ideal for a U-boat attack.

As the night closed in around the convoy, Commodore Rogers took the only defensive actions open to him, first making a bold alteration to the south under the cover of darkness, after which he ordered the ships to steer a pre-arranged zig-zag pattern.

Chapter 4

The Pack Attacks

To be condemned to the non-combatant role of weather observer 750 miles deep in the Atlantic was a bitter pill for Günther Prien to swallow. U-47's lonely assignment would win no glory for Prien and his men. Furthermore, they had been at sea for three and a half weeks, during which they had expended all but one of their torpedoes and deprived the enemy of 35,000 tons of his merchant shipping. It was time, they argued – amongst themselves, of course – to go home, to return to hot baths and soft beds, if only for a short while.

Admiral Dönitz would have none of it. While he appreciated that U-47 had already made a very valuable contribution to the Atlantic campaign, a close watch on the weather brewing up at sea was essential for Luftwaffe operations against Britain. Dönitz also had an ulterior motive for condemning U-47 to her lonely station. She was lying square in the path of eastbound Allied convoys, and would, he hoped, provide him with further advanced warning of the enemy's approach.

For eleven days and nights U-47 made her penance, riding out one howling gale after another, casings awash, corkscrewing from crest to trough, but diligently transmitting her weather reports every twelve hours. Her transmissions must have been heard far and wide, and there should have been ample opportunity for the source of these signals, brief though they may have been, to be plotted by high frequency direction finding stations ashore in Britain. The distance involved was great, and substantial errors might be expected, but an approximate position of U-47 should have been obtainable. It beggars belief, then, that HX 72 was not warned that it was steaming into danger. There is no indication that Commodore Rogers had received any such warning, and so he unwittingly took his forty-one unescorted merchant ships straight into the trap being laid by Dönitz.

The German admiral's foresight in posting one of his best U-boats as lookout in mid-Atlantic paid off just as the sun was setting on the 18 September. Günther Prien, salt spray streaming off his oilskins, was keeping vigil in U-47's gyrating conning tower, when he saw the mast-tops of Convoy HX 72 on the distant horizon. He immediately radioed news of the sighting to Dönitz.

Lorient, where Dönitz had now established his headquarters in a chateau overlooking the Kerneval River, was buzzing like a well organized beehive. U-boats coming in from patrol were handed over to harbour crews, who supervised routine maintenance and repairs, took on provisions and refueled. Meanwhile, the sea-going U-boat crews, accommodated ashore, enjoyed a well earned spell of rest and recreation, but rarely longer than a few days. As soon as a boat was ready for sea, it was thrown out into the Atlantic battleground, where there was such a rich harvest for the reaping. This was the U-boats' 'happy time', and Admiral Dönitz was determined to make the most of it. With another big eastbound convoy in the offing, he began to gather a wolf pack.

Two of the other participants in the attack on SC 2, Otto Kretschmer in U-99 and Hans-Gerrit von Stockhausen in U-65, were close to hand, while Heinrich Bleichrodt in U-48, Engelbert Endrass in U-46 and Wilhelm Ambrosius in U-43 were within 380 miles of the approaching convoy.

Twenty-eight-year-old Otto Kretschmer was the senior and more experienced commander, although he had not been designated as leader of the pack. The lesson of HG 3 had been learned, and Dönitz now preferred to control all pack operations from the shore by radio.

When he commissioned the new Type VIIB U-99 in June, 1940, Kretschmer soon realized that his command was superior in speed and manoeuvrability than many of the sloops and frigates the British were using to escort their convoys. This led him to form a bold plan of action which eventually all but brought these convoys to a halt. Attacking at night on the surface, U-99's low silhouette allowed him to penetrate the ranks of the convoy unseen, and in his own time pick off the unsuspecting merchantmen at will. In the event of the convoy's escorts realising what was happening and coming to the rescue, Kretschmer simply slipped back into the darkness from whence he had come, leaving the British ships chasing their own tails. By the time the war was a year old, Kretschmer and U-99 had accounted for nearly one hundred thousand tons of Allied shipping.

Von Stockhausen, Bleichrodt, Endrass and Ambrosius had not yet equalled the success of Kretchsmer, but they were all potential 'aces', and Dönitz was confident they would make their mark on HX 72.

Dönitz instructed the five boats to form a north–south line on the surface, 5 miles apart and across the anticipated track of the convoy. Each boat would thus be in visual contact with its neighbours, given reasonable visibility, the whole line covering some 30 miles of the horizon. They would soon be joined by two more boats, Hans Jenisch's U–32 and Joachim Schepke's U–100. Jenisch, having been in U–32 since her commissioning in April 1937, as First Watch Officer and later in command, had already amassed a total of 40,000 tons of Allied shipping sunk, including the British cruiser HMS *Fiji*. Twenty-eight-year-old Schepke, described as 'tall and cheerful, the fortunate possessor of great charm and fair good looks that attracted the admiration in which he revelled', was already on his way to becoming the idol of the German media.

Meanwhile, Dönitz ordered Prien to shadow the convoy, reporting its position, course and speed every four hours. The scene was set for the next wolf pack attack.

At dusk on the 20th, HX 72 was 250 miles due west of Rockall, and the clock was ticking for Dönitz's hastily formed wolf pack. If they were to create the maximum havoc, they would need to strike that night while the convoy was still without escorts, and strike hard. As it was, Commodore Rogers' unexpected bold alteration to the south under the cover of darkness resulted in HX 72 avoiding the trap set for it, sailing unseen past the southern end of the line of U-boats.

Shortly before 1900, in the last of the twilight, U–47 radioed in the convoy's position, course and speed for the last time. Conditions for the attack were now as good as they would ever be, with a moderate south-westerly wind, the moon giving excellent visibility, and passing showers providing good cover. U–43, U–46, U–48, U–65 and U–99, were then all within striking distance of the convoy, and Dönitz gave the order to close in and attack.

Otto Kretchsmer in U–99 was first to arrive at the interception position given by Dönitz, but although conditions were excellent, he failed to sight the convoy. To avoid aimlessly cruising on the surface, he took U–99 down to periscope depth and set a listening watch with hydrophones. Before long, the operator reported faint propeller noises to the south, indicating a number of ships, probably merchantmen, under way. Kretchsmer returned to the surface, and motored at full speed along the bearing obtained. His tactics bore fruit when, at about 2230, he sighted the back markers of HX 72. He altered course to pass astern of the convoy.

As U-99, bowling along at a good 17 knots, crossed the wakes of the rear ships, the moon went behind the clouds, Kretchsmer suddenly became aware that he was not alone. U-47, HX 72's shadow, was lying almost stopped on the surface astern of the ships. With the attention of Prien and his lookouts focused on the convoy a disastrous collision between the two boats was only narrowly avoided.

Words were exchanged between the two U- boat commanders before they went their separate ways, after which Kretchsmer claimed to have sighted a destroyer zig-zagging astern of the convoy. This must either have been a trick of the light, or a figment of Kretchsmer's overwrought imagination, for at that time HX 72 was still without a single escort.

If Kretchsmer had known that HX 72 was unprotected, he undoubtedly would have thrown caution to the winds and made a bold attack. As it was, he made a cautious approach, selecting the rear ship of the port column as his first target. She was a big ship – around 10,000 tons Kretchsmer estimated – and her silhouette, with funnel aft and bridge amidships, marked her out as an oil tanker, and fully loaded at that. She was a priority target.

Leaving nothing to chance, Kretchsmer moved in closer, intending to approach within 500 metres of the darkened ship before firing. Perversely, when U-99 was just under a mile off the tanker, the moon came from behind the clouds, bathing the stalking U-boat in brilliant light. Kretchsmer was still convinced that an enemy destroyer was nearby, and feared that at any moment a hail of armour-piercing shells would be coming his way. He fired one torpedo, and quickly turned away, racing for the cover of the nearest rain squall.

On the bridge of the British motor tanker *Invershannon*, Captain William Forsyth was holding the fort while the Third Officer had gone below to call the watch. At the wheel was Chinese quartermaster Lee Ah Chung, his weathered face dimly lit by the light of the compass binnacle as he eased the spokes of the wheel to hold the ship on course. The war forgotten, it might have been any uneventful night in the North Atlantic.

The 9,154-ton *Invershannon*, owned by Andrew Weir's subsidiary Inver Tankers, and registered in Glasgow, was on passage from Caracus

Bay, in the Dutch West Indies, carrying 13,241 tons of fuel oil to Scapa Flow for the Admiralty. Manned in the Andrew Weir tradition by a crew of fourteen British officers and thirty-four Hong Kong Chinese ratings, the *Invershannon* had been built at the renowned Bremer Vulkan shipyard on the River Weser just before the outbreak of war. She was a strong ship with a good turn of speed, yet here she was bringing up the rear of a 7½ knot convoy. At the very least, in the opinion of Captain Bill Forsyth, as a loaded tanker she should have been in the middle of the convoy, with the other ships affording her some protection. Although the night was quiet, the visibility was too good for comfort, and Forsyth feared for the safety of his ship.

Captain Forsyth's fears were realized at thirty minutes before midnight, when Otto Kretschmer's torpedo slammed into the *Invershannon's* hull, and exploded with a roar and a blinding flash. Fortunately, probably because it was fired at long range, instead of inflicting a death blow in the tanker's engine-room, which had been Kretschmer's intention, the torpedo hit right forward in her small dry cargo hold, which was then empty.

With the sea pouring into her cargo hold, the *Invershannon* began to settle by the head at an alarming rate, and Captain Forsyth gave the order to abandon ship. Three lifeboats were used, and the entire crew, none of them injured, left the ship in good order, and rowed clear. It could be clearly seen by the light of the moon that the *Invershannon* was still afloat, so Forsyth decided to lay off until daylight. Then, if the ship was still afloat they would attempt to re-board her.

The drama of the attack on the *Invershannon* had been played out unseen by the rest of the convoy, for moments before she was struck, a heavy rain squall swept across her, completely hiding her from view. The crippled tanker and her lifeboats, their plight unnoticed, were rapidly falling astern of the convoy and already fading away into the darkness.

Kretschmer, still expecting an avenging British destroyer to come bearing down on him at any moment, had by this time headed back across to the far side of the convoy at full speed. There he made a stealthy approach to the rear ship of the starboard outside column, which he described in his War Diary as a 'heavily-laden freighter'. She was the 3,668-ton *Baron Blythswood*, an Adrossan-registered ship owned by Hogarth's Baron Line.

Under the command of Captain John Davies, and manned by a crew of thirty-three, the Clyde-built *Baron Blythswood* was carrying a cargo of

5,450 tons of iron ore from Newfoundland to Port Talbot. Like so many ships in this war, she was far heavier in the water than she should have been, and when Otto Kretchsmer's torpedo blasted open her hull amidships she snapped like a rotten twig, and was on her way to the bottom in 40 seconds. Only one man – his name unknown to this day – survived the sinking to find himself alone in the dark, cold waters of the North Atlantic.

Momentarily shocked by the speed of the demise of the *Baron Blythswood*, Kretchsmer moved deeper into the convoy, and was soon singling out another target. He settled on the third ship of Column Nine, which also appeared to be carrying a heavy load. She was another of Andrew Weir's, the 5,156-ton motor vessel *Elmbank*, under the command of Captain Harold Phillips. The *Elmbank*, with a total complement of fifty-six, was on her way to Belfast with a cargo of steel and timber from British Columbia. With the end of an 8,000 mile voyage via the Panama Canal and Halifax in sight, the atmosphere on board the Glasgow ship was tense. Watches were doubled up, and those lucky enough to be off duty slept fully clothed and with lifejackets close to hand.

Kretchsmer approached to within half a mile of the *Elmbank*, then fired a single torpedo, which exploded amidships with a muffled bang, sending a great column of water and baulks of timber high in the air. The *Elmbank* immediately stopped, and began to drift astern. U-99 stayed with her, attacker and attacked dropping apparently unseen out of the convoy.

U-99 and the stricken *Elmbank* remained within sight of each other for the rest of the night, Kretchsmer watching and waiting while the British ship's crew took to their lifeboats. He was not aware that 35-year-old Captain Harold Phillips had died s a result of the torpedo blast.

Two hours later, with the first pale streaks of the coming dawn showing on the eastern horizon, the *Elmbank*, although noticeably lower in the water, had still not sunk. She lay there passive and forlorn, with the four lifeboats containing her leaderless crew drifting within easy rowing distance.

Given the chance, the *Elmbank's* men would no doubt have re-boarded their ship, but Otto Kretchsmer denied them the opportunity. The other ships of HX 72, apparently still unaware that three of their number had been savaged during the night, were now well out of sight, and Kretchsmer considered it was safe to administer the *coup de grâce* to the *Elmbank*. Opening fire with his 88-mm deck gun at close range, he poured shell after shell into the helpless ship, aiming to blast a hole below her waterline, and send her to the bottom.

After using up nearly ninety rounds of 88-mm, Kretchsmer had succeeded in blowing a large hole in the *Elmbank's* hull, but when planks of timber came floating out through this hole, he realized he was wasting his time and ammunition. Although the ship was carrying a heavy weight of steel in her lower holds, this was topped off with thousands of board feet of Canadian sawn timber, sufficient to keep her afloat indefinitely.

Kretchsmer, nervous now, and fearing the imminent intervention of HX 72's escorting destroyers, decided to use one of his two remaining torpedoes to finish off the *Elmbank*. It was a futile gesture. U-99's torpedo was on target, but exploded harmlessly when it collided with the baulks of timber floating in the water around the ship.

By this time it was fully light, and the thoroughly frustrated Kretchsmer was joined by Günther Prien in U-47, who had been attracted by the gunfire. Both U-boats now turned their guns on the *Elmbank*, finally setting her on fire with phosphorous shells. U-47, having expended all her ammunition, went back to her appointed task, which was to shadow and report on HX 72.

It was then, in the early afternoon, that Kretchsmer discovered that the *Invershannon* was still afloat. He used his last remaining torpedo to sink the tanker, then returned to the *Elmbank*. On his way back he came across a survivor clinging to a wooden liferaft. This man – the only one to survive the catastrophic sinking of the *Baron Blythswood* – was taken aboard U-99, where he was given dry clothes and warm drinks. Kretchsmer, all his torpedoes exhausted, had by this time decided to return to Lorient, and as the British survivor appeared to be concussed, he had no wish to take the man with him. A simple solution would have been to put the survivor back on his raft and abandon him to the sea, but Kretchsmer, like so many U-boat men, had an affinity for his fellow-seamen, even those who were his enemies. He searched around for the *Invershannon's* lifeboats, and when he located them, handed his prisoner over to them. Second Officer H.T. Payne, of the *Invershannon*, later made a statement to Commander E. Ford, RNR at Londonderry, who reported as follows:

A man, who was found to be the sole survivor of the S.S. *Baron Blythswood* and had been rescued from a raft by the submarine, was placed in the Chief Officer's boat. The man had been given dry clothing while on board submarine, also a packet of American cigarettes. The 2nd Officer states that the cigarettes were the same as the stock on board M.V. *Invershannon*. If this man was transferred from submarine on second contact it seems very definite that enemy boarded ship and made search. I find it impossible to establish whether this man was transferred to Chief Officer's boat on first or second contact with enemy submarine. 2nd Officer further states boats became separated three days later when, during night, weather deteriorated.

The name and rank of the lone survivor from the *Baron Blythswood* have never been established, but he is believed to have been one of the ore carrier's firemen/trimmers. He was handed over to Chief Officer Thomas Evans of the *Invershannon*, whose lifeboat, containing sixteen men, including the unknown survivor, later disappeared, and probably foundered in bad weather. Ironically, Otto Kretschmer's humane gesture had ended in death for the man he saved.

When a merchant ship or her cargo suffers damage at sea, it is incumbent upon her Master to register a protest in front of a Notary Public at the first possible opportunity, otherwise the underwriters may refuse to cover the loss. Strange as it may seem, this still held good in the early days of the war, and one of Captain Forsyth's first calls after being landed in Londonderry was to note a protest, which is reproduced below:

SHIP PROTEST, in consequence of Attack

(1/- Stamp) By this public Instrument of Protest BE IT KNOWN and made manifest to all people that on Friday, the 4th day of October, 1940, before me JOSEPH G. O'KANE of 27 Shipquay Street, in the City of Londonderry, in Northern Ireland, NOTARY PUBLIC, by Royal Authority duly admitted and sworn, personally came and appeared WILLIAM FORSYTH Master of the Motor Vessel "INVERSHANNON" of the burthen of Nine thousand one hundred and fifty-three tons gross register, registered in the Port of Glasgow, Scotland; LEE AH CHUNG Quartermaster of the said Vessel, who did severally duly and solemnly declare and state as follows, that is to say:

(1) That on Friday the 20th day of September 1940, the said

vessel was proceeding (in convoy) on a voyage to the Port of Scapa Flow, from Caracus Bay, Dutch West Indies, with a Cargo of Fuel Oil. At about 11.30 p.m., (ship's time) the Master and the Quartermaster were on the bridge, the Quartermaster being at the wheel, when without any warning whatever the said vessel was torpedoed forward on the Port bow. She started to settle down by the head and the Master gave the order for all to take to the vessel's three lifeboats. The ship's position was then 56 degrees North 23 degrees West.

(2) After getting clear of the ship, the three lifeboats kept in the vicinity of the ship until daylight. She was then further down by the head. When the Master was returning to the vessel to salve the ship's papers a German submarine surfaced between the lifeboat the Master was in charge of and the "INVERSHANNON". The Commander of the submarine went alongside the lifeboat that the Chief Officer was in charge of and transferred from the submarine to his boat a survivor from another ship.

(3) The submarine then proceeded to the Port side of the "INVERSHANNON" and remained in that position for half an hour or so. Then there was a terrific explosion which appeared to come from the engineroom. The "INVERSHANNON" then commenced to settle by the stern and was sinking slowly when we last saw her.

The Master then hoisted the sail in his lifeboat and set a course for the North of Ireland. He and the members of the crew that were in his lifeboat were picked up by H.M. Motor Vessel Torpedo Boat at about 6 p.m. on Sunday the 29th day of September, 1940 sixty miles or thereabouts West of Tory Island, and were landed at the Port of Londonderry.

On arrival at Londonderry it was found that the Master and the greater number of the crew were suffering from injuries due to exposure and had to be removed to the City and County Hospital, Londonderry, where they still are receiving treatment. Owing to the said injuries, the Master and the Quartermaster were not in a condition to make this Protest any earlier.

And these Appearers DO PROTEST, and I, the said Notary DO ALSO PROTEST against the said torpedoing and the destruction of the said Motor Vessel "INVERSHANNON" and the cargo therein and all loss and damage caused by reason of said incidents and occurrences aforesaid; and for all and every loss, cost, detriment, damage and expense both to Ship and Cargo and the said Master, Officers and Crew that hath, can or may arise therefrom to the end that the same may be had, borne, sustained and recovered by those to whom of right it doth, can or may appertain, such losses and damages having happened and occurred as aforesaid, and not having been occasioned by or through the neglect of any of the Vessel's company.

Thus Declared and Protested at the City and County Hospital, Londonderry, Northern Ireland.

IN WITNESS whereof the said appearers have hereunto set their hands, I, Joseph G. O'Kane, Notary Public, hereunto subscribing my hand and affixing my Seal, and R.T. Payne, Master Mariner. 134, Victoria Road, Dartmouth, and J.A. Traynor, P.O., R.N., Hama S.C., No.9 G.P.O. London (both being presently patients at the City and County Hospital at Londonderry) also subscribing in testimony of the premises.

Witnesses to the signature
of William Forsyth and
Lee Ah Chung:

R.T. Payne, Master Mariner   W.FORSYTH
134, Victoria Road.,
Dartmouth.

J.A. Traynor, P.O., R.N.   LEE AH CHUNG
Hama/S.C. No.9
c/o., G.P.O. London

IN TESTIMONY whereof I have hereunto subscribed my name and affixed my Seal of Office this 4th day of October, in the year of Our Lord, One thousand nine hundred and forty.

JOSEPH G. O'KANE
Notary Public.

SEAL

WE, WILLIAM FORSYTH and LEE AH CHUNG, Master and Quartermaster Respectively of said vessel, do herby solemnly and sincerely declare that

The contents of the foregoing Declaration and Protest are true, and we make

This solemn Declaration conscientiously believing the same to be true and

By virtue of the provisions of the Statutory Declarations Act 1835.

(2/6 Stamp)	DECLARED at the City and County Hospital, Londonderry, Northern Ireland, on this 4th day of October,
W.FORSYTH	One thousand nine hundred and forty, before me a Commissioner to Administer Oaths at Londonderry in and for the High Court of Justice
LEE AH CHUNG	in Northern Ireland and I know the Deponents.

JOHN A. DOHERTY
Commissioner for Oaths.

Having played the Good Samaritan by handing over the only *Baron Blythswood* survivor into the care of the *Invershannon's* Chief Officer, Otto Kretchsmer pumped a few more shells into the burning wreck of the *Elmbank*, and headed for home.

Soon after U-99 had disappeared over the horizon, U-48 arrived on the scene. Heinrich Bleichrodt, on his first patrol in command, had the bit between his teeth, and for good reason. Since sailing from Lorient a week earlier he had already sent more than 30,000 tons of Allied shipping to the bottom, including an 11,000 ton cargo/passenger liner and a British sloop. His run of luck looked set to continue.

The weather was squally, with a moderate sea running affording good cover when, at about 0300 on the morning of 21 September, U-48 caught up with the rear ships of HX 72. It was very dark, but Bleichrodt had no difficulty in choosing his first victim. She was the 4,409-ton steamer *Blairangus*, the rear ship of Column Four, and was lagging behind the others.

The *Blairangus,* owned by George Nisbet & Company of Glasgow, and commanded by Captain Hugh Mackinnon, was on her way from Botwood, Newfoundland to an, as yet, undisclosed port on the east coast of England with a cargo of pit props. It was a relatively simple matter for Heinrich Bleichrodt to approach and line up his sights on the isolated ship.

The middle watch of the night, midnight to 0400, is often known as the 'graveyard' watch, as it is in these hours that the human conscious is at its lowest ebb. It is a time when the unwary are caught off guard. Be that as it may, there was certainly no lack of vigilance aboard the *Blairangus* in the small hours of Saturday 21 September 1940. The Second Officer, who had the watch on the bridge, had been joined by Captain Mackinnon, and both were fully alert, and sweeping around the horizon with their binoculars.

It was Captain Mackinnon who first became aware of the approaching danger. At 0330, he was standing in the port wing of the bridge peering into the darkness ahead, when he heard an unfamiliar humming noise coming from the port side. He swung round and, as he did, he saw the track of a torpedo racing past the stern of the next ship to port, and heading straight for the *Blairangus.*

Mackinnon made a dash for the wheelhouse, at the same time calling for the helmsman to put the wheel hard to port. He was too late. As the *Blairangus,* her rudder hard over, began to cant to port, Bleichrodt's torpedo slammed into her No. Five hold. Captain Mackinnon later wrote in his deposition to the Admiralty:

> There was a terrific explosion and a column of water and smoke shot up in the air. The engines stopped, the lights went out and the vessel settled by the stern. Deponent sounded the alarm to summon all members of the crew to emergency stations and ordered the 2nd Officer aft to examine the damage. The 2nd Officer returned and reported that the stern of the vessel had been cut off by the after end of the poop deck house and that the crew's accommodation in the poop was completely shattered. The 2nd Officer also reported that he could hear shouts but did not know whether these were coming from the poop or the water. In case the men should be in the water, deponent ordered the port boat to be lowered and rowed aft. Deponent went aft and shone his torch in the water but there was no sign of any men in the

water. By this time all the men of the watch on duty came aft and several men went down an opening where the deck had parted from the ship's side into the crew space accommodation of the poop, and recovered 6 firemen and one A.B. all more or less seriously injured. It was found that the whole of the accommodation was smashed and part of it missing, and the following men were missing, 1 Donkeyman, 2 A.B.s, 1 O.S., and 2 Cabin Boys. The vessel was now settling bodily and the Chief Engineer reported that the engine room and tunnel were flooded. (The tunnel door was closed immediately the explosion occurred). The water appeared to be coming through the after engine room bulkhead.

Reluctant to abandon his ship before daylight, Mackinnon did what he could for the injured men, then put them in the port lifeboat, which was already in the water. An SOS had been sent out when the torpedo struck, which had been acknowledged by another ship, which it was assumed was now coming to their rescue.

No rescuing ship appeared during the night, and at first light, it was obvious that the *Blairangus* had not long to go. At 0800 Mackinnon ordered the starboard boat into the water. Two hours later, with the sea lapping over her main deck, the ship was abandoned. Soon afterwards, Ropner's 3,683-ton *Pikepool*, recently dispersed from the westbound convoy OB 217, steamed over the horizon, and all twenty-eight survivors from the *Blairangus* were taken on board. The *Pikepool* also picked up fifty-five men from the *Elmbank*. Unfortunately, Charles McGaulay, one of the *Blairangus'* badly injured firemen, died on board. The other survivors were landed at St. John's, Newfoundland a week later.

Chapter 5

Help Arrives

It was an hour before dawn on 21 September before Commodore Rogers became aware that all was not well with his convoy. The rain squalls were becoming more infrequent, and with a bright moon breaking through the clouds visibility had increased to more than 3 miles. As Rogers, warming his hands on a mug of hot cocoa, leaned on the after rail of the *Tregarthen's* bridge, a brilliant flash lit up the horizon astern, followed by the rumble of an explosion. He was witnessing the death throes of the *Blairangus*, torpedoed by Heinrich Bleichrodt in U-48.

Rogers immediately ordered an emergency turn to port, and as the ships, showing remarkable discipline, swung to port in unison, he called for an increase of speed to 10½ knots. It may well have been that the *Tregarthen*, a comparatively new ship, had the capability, when pressed, to deliver a burst of speed, but the same could not be said for the majority of ships in the ranks of HX 72. Many of them, built at the tail end of the First World War, and worn out by years tramping, were already struggling to maintain the convoy's current speed of 7 knots. Firemen bent their backs to the ravenous boiler furnaces, but apart from the extra half a knot or so, the Commodore's call did little more than increase the cloud of black smoke hanging over the convoy.

The first light of the day brought Rogers the sobering news that at sometime during the night another four of his ships, Andrew Weir's *Invershannon* and *Elmbank*, Hogarth's *Baron Blythswood*, and George Nisbet's *Blairangus* had been sunk. It had been a disastrous night for the Scots, and for Commodore Rogers it brought the realization that the enemy's wolves were snapping at his heels, and there was little he could do about it.

In desperation, Rogers signalled the *Pacific Grove*, two ships astern of the *Tregarthen*, and in the middle of the convoy, to drop one of her smoke floats. The canister created a great deal of black smoke, but with a freshening south-westerly blowing, the cover provided by the smoke was short-lived. Once more cruelly exposed, the convoy steamed on. The local escort promised by Western Approaches Command was not due to join HX 72 until 4 o'clock that afternoon – another ten hours of nail-biting suspense for the unprotected merchantmen.

It was a long and harrowing wait, hours of agonizing anxiety and anticipation, then a cheer went up when, at 1400, the Royal Navy arrived two hours ahead of schedule. Led by Commander Arthur Knapp in the sloop *Lowestoft*, who twelve days earlier had defended Convoy SC 2 against the first organized U-boat pack attack with some success, HX 72's escort turned out to be another makeshift group 'borrowed' from various outward-bound convoys. *Lowestoft* and the Flower-class corvettes *Heartsease* and *La Malouine* had been detached from Convoy OB 215, which sailed from Liverpool on 17 September. The fourth member of Knapp's command, the 1918-vintage destroyer HMS *Shikari*, had left the Mersey two days earlier escorting the troop convoy OL 3, which was bound for the Cape. A third corvette, HMS *Calendula*, also with OB 215, was to join Knapp later that evening, while the destroyers *Scimitar* and *Skate* were to leave the southbound OL 3 during the day, and steam at full speed to arrive on 22 September. On paper, this was a force to be reckoned with. However, none of these ships had ever exercised or sailed together before and, in fact, Commander Knapp, who was to lead them, had never even had the opportunity of discussing tactics with their various commanders. Over the next fifteen hours Arthur Knapp's powers of command were to be tested to destruction.

Despatching *Shikari* to search for survivors from the torpedoed ships, Knapp distributed his resources to best advantage, stationing *Lowestoft* ahead of the convoy, while the two corvettes covered the flanks. *Shikari* was ordered to bring up the rear when she had finished picking up survivors. Knapp had no way of knowing how many U-boats he faced, but he knew from experience that with every hour that passed the enemy would multiply.

One of those called in to join the pack hunting HX 72 was Joachim Schepke in U-100. Schepke had been patrolling to the north of Rockall when, just after midnight on the night of 18/19 September, he received an urgent signal from Lorient instructing him to home in on the convoy. The enemy ships were reported to be heading south-east at 8 knots. He immediately set off to the southwest with the object of intercepting the convoy before it entered the North Channel

In the early hours of the morning of 20 September, U-100, having covered some 350 miles, most of it on the surface, was 90 miles to the east of Rockall, and heading westwards at all possible speed. The weather was fair, with a light northerly wind and a slight sea, overcast and with good visibility. Ideal conditions for a U-boat on the surface, but the complete cloud cover troubled Schepke. U-100 was still within range of the RAF's Coastal Command Sunderlands, and there was always the possibility that one of these big flying boats might drop out of the cloud and rain depth bombs down on them.

Just before noon, Schepke received a radio signal from U-47 giving the convoy's position as some 450 miles to the west, and steering east at a slow speed. Schepke altered course to due west, and increased speed. An hour later, another U-boat was sighted, which turned out to be Wilhelm Ambrosius's U-43. Ambrosius was inward bound for Bergen after a long patrol, and only too willing to bring Schepke up to date on the situation in the North Atlantic. The two boats lay alongside each other while Schepke and Ambrosius exchanged news. Then they both went their separate ways.

At 1715, when his calculations showed that the convoy should be about 380 miles to the west, Schepke sighted a ship heading in towards the North Channel. At first, he thought that U-47's report of the position of HX 72 must be in error, and he was meeting the first of the British ships. But when the stranger drew near, she was seen to be a two-funneled passenger ship of about 22,000 tons, heading east and zig-zagging at high speed. Her size and speed indicated that she was sailing independently.

The unescorted liner presented a very tempting target for Schepke's torpedoes, and he dived to commence the attack. Unfortunately, the enemy ship was moving too fast, and despite Schepke's best efforts, he was unable to manoeuvre into a favourable position to attack. When he came back to the surface an hour later, the liner was 8 miles off, and showing her stern to the U-boat. Accepting defeat, Schepke resumed course to the west.

It was therefore a frustrated Joachim Schepke who, as darkness fell on 21 September, faced another miserable night in the conning tower of U-100. The weather was deteriorating, the wind freshening, and the passing showers becoming vicious rain squalls that brought more misery to Schepke and his lookouts. Hourly position reports from Günther Prien, who continued to shadow HX 72 in U-47, showed the convoy to be maintaining its easterly course. At 0430, with daylight fast approaching, U-48 also reported she had the convoy in sight. The wolves were gathering.

Although Schepke estimated he was closing the convoy at a combined speed of 18 knots, HX 72 was still more than 200 miles to the west, and he was resigned to another day on the surface exposed to the weather and patrolling enemy aircraft.

The agony was prolonged into the next night, and at 2200, not having seen even a wisp of smoke indicating the presence of the convoy, U-100 ran into heavy and continuous rain. At 2209, assuming he must now be very close to the convoy, Schepke wiped his binoculars, and took one last look around. It was a futile gesture, for the slanting rain beating at his face and streaming off his oilskins had reduced the visibility to zero. He decided to submerge and try another tack.

Schepke's persistence was rewarded. At periscope depth, U-100's hydrophones immediately picked up propeller noises some 15 miles on the port bow. It took only moments to confirm that they were listening to a large number of ships steaming in close company. Schepke returned to the surface, and began to run down the bearing given by the hydrophones. An entry in U-100's War Diary for the time reads:

> 2258. The first shadows are sighted. My boat is on the southern side, i.e. on starboard. About 20 shadows are sighted at first. It is then noted that the convoy contains several columns. My boat is between row 2 and 3. To get into the convoy I decide to shoot my way in.

HX 72 was now on a south-south-easterly course, and making 7 knots towards the northern end of the North Channel. U-100 approached the convoy on its starboard side, coming within 1½ miles of the leading ships of Column Nine without being seen.

Schepke trimmed the boat down so that little more than her conning tower was visible, and moved in closer, then with typical audacity, he set about blasting his way into the convoy. Three large ships bunched together had caught his eye. They were the 4,608-ton *Dalcairn* in Column Six, the 8,286-ton *Canonesa* in Column Five, and the 10,364-ton tanker *Torinia* in Column Four. The *Dalcairn* was slighty ahead, with the stern of the *Canonesa* in the next column just visible behind her, and on the other side of the *Canonesa*, the stern of the *Torinia* was just showing. It was the perfect three-in-one shot.

Schepke wrote in his War Diary:

> On the first run in I fire from the three bow tubes into the three largest ships in the middle of the 3rd row, then turn away and fire the aft torpedo tube. All 4 shots are hits.

Schepke's stern torpedo missed its target, but the result of his brutal thrust into the heart of HX 72 was spectacular.

Steaming in Column Five immediately astern of Commodore's ship *Tregarthen*, and with ships all around her, the *Canonesa*, in the opinion of her master, Captain Fred Stephenson, occupied a reasonably safe position in the convoy. And on that evening of 21 September, for the first time since leaving the St. Lawrence River, he felt able to relax his vigilance. The convoy was at last under the protection of the ships of Western Approaches Command, and the safety of the North Channel lay only forty-eight hours away. Despite the savage attack of the previous night, there now seemed good grounds for optimism.

Owned by Houlder Brothers of London, the *Canonesa* was a 8,286-ton refrigerated ship built in 1920 as a replacement ship for tonnage lost in the 1914-18 war. With oil-fired boilers driving steam turbine engines, she was a substantial ship, employed for most of her life on Houlder's Argentinian meat trade. On her current voyage, however, the necessities of war had taken her to the Canadian port of Montreal, where she had loaded, in addition to 3,358 tons of general cargo, 2,258 tons of bacon, 955 tons of cheese, 379 tons of fish and 250 tons of ham. The hungry citizens of Manchester and Liverpool eagerly awaited her arrival

At 2000, Captain Stephenson visited the *Canonesa's* bridge where the Third Officer had just taken over the watch. The weather was fair, with a choppy sea, and good visibility. Having spent some time in the chartroom checking the courses, Stephenson wrote up his night orders, took one last look around, and went below to his cabin. He had no intention of turning in, but with a mug of hot tea at hand, he sank into his comfortable old armchair. Within minutes, the untouched drink cooling, he entered the somnolent state of half awake, half asleep that he had grown used to on the Atlantic crossing.

Stephenson's rest was short-lived. At 2105, not more than half an hour after he had sought the solace of his armchair, he was jerked back into reality by a muffled explosion as Joachim Schepke's torpedo tore into the *Canonesa's* starboard side, blasting open her hull just abaft the funnel. Her engine room began to flood immediately, she lost all power, and came slowly to a halt.

By the time Stephenson, catapulted from his armchair by the shock of the explosion, reached the door of his cabin, all the lights had gone out, and a deathly silence had descended on the crippled ship.

Captain Stephenson made his way first to the wireless room, where he ordered the radio officer to send out an S.O.S. By the time he reached the bridge, the *Canonesa* was settling by the stern, and it was obvious that she would not stay afloat for much longer. Giving hurried instructions to the Third Officer to get everyone on the boat deck, and to clear away the lifeboats ready for lowering, Stephenson then went aft to assess the damage. As he had feared, the enemy's torpedo had delivered a death blow to his ship. Her after deck was in ruins, the deck plates buckled, and No. Five hold was open to the sea, stripped of its tarpaulins and hatchboards by the explosion. An inspection of the engine room from the top showed the water rising rapidly. Satisfied that there was nothing to be done to save his ship, Captain Stephenson returned forward to the boat deck to supervise the lowering of the boats.

Peter Tingey, one of the *Canonesa's* deck apprentices, who had been on watch on the bridge, later gave a vivid account of the torpedoing:

> I was sent down on deck to ensure that all of our crew were complying with the blackout regulations and I had just finished checking and having a laugh with the ship's carpenter just aft of amidships, when a thunderous and horrific explosion occurred. A torpedo blasted its way into the starboard side of the engine room where my good and respected friend Tom (4th Engineer Tom Purnell) was apparently unable to survive the engine room's immediate engulfment by the thunderous water. However, two on-duty greasers apparently in the boiler room were luckier and in an astounding feat of survival thrashed and wriggled their way up to the top of a thin ventilation shaft slightly aft of the funnel and were covered in oil from head to foot. It was obvious that the two men were assisted by the lubrication effect of the oil because the ventilation shafts were noticeably thin in diameter . . . .
>
> . . . as I went out on deck I could see that the canvas deck cover of hatch number four had been blown sky-high and had come to

rest over the wireless aerial, all this being accompanied by the sound of falling cheeses in their oval containers with an amusing 'plomp, plomp, plomp', although I was not laughing at the time...

One of the *Canonesa's* four lifeboats had been destroyed by the explosion, but Captain Stephenson and his crew, with the exception of Fourth Engineer Tom Purnell, successfully abandoned ship in the remaining three boats. As they pulled away from the *Canonesa*, her main deck was already awash. When the dawn came she was gone from sight below the waves.

Schepke's second and third torpedoes had raced past the *Canonesa's* stern and one found a home in the 10,364-ton motor tanker *Torinia*, second ship of the next column to port. Although less than a year old, even at a convoy speed of 7 knots, the tanker was lagging behind, her stern overlapping that of the *Canonesa*.

Owned by the Anglo-Saxon Petroleum Company of London, and commanded by Captain Henry Jackson, the *Torinia* was carrying a cargo of 13,815 tons of fuel oil from Curacao, destined for the Admiralty's storage tanks on the Clyde. Fortunately for Captain Jackson and his crew of fifty-four, the nature of their cargo was such that it did not easily ignite, and no fire broke out on board when the torpedo hit. And, as far as Jackson could ascertain, although the tanker's engines were disabled, she was in no danger of sinking. She slowly drifted astern, the other ships in the column altering course to get out of her way as she bore down on them.

Schepke's fan of three had been a snap shot, fired with the object of destroying the *Canonesa*, but having already hit two ships, he lived up to his reputation of being 'full of confidence and aggression' by striking gold again with his third torpedo.

The unlucky recipient of Schepke's third torpedo was the Newcastle tramp *Dalcairn*, which had dropped back even further than the *Torinia*, so that her stern was exposed.

The 4,608-ton *Dalcairn*, a Clyde-built ship owned by the general traders Campbell Brothers of Newcastle, had also loaded in Montreal, and had on board 8,000 tons of wheat for Hull, a cargo desperately needed in a Britain under siege.

The *Dalcairn's* master, Captain Edgar Brusby, did his best to save his ship, but with her hull broached and the sea pouring in to saturate the grain cargo, he feared she might capsize. He ordered his crew of forty-seven to abandon ship.

Commodore Rogers, helpless to intervene, was now living the nightmare he had feared might come to pass. He watched in horror as the distress rockets soared skywards astern of the *Tregarthen,* and the unearthly wail of the stricken ships' whistles filled the air. In desperation, Rogers signaled the convoy to increase speed to 10½ knots, hoping to spread the ships out over a wider area, so that they presented more difficult targets. In his report to the Admiralty he wrote:

> It was suspected on the previous night that 2 S/Ms had been attacking. It seemed possible one was on each bow. Any turning action would interfere with local escorts' operations, but an increase of speed should open intervals and make further 'browning' productive of less results, also give more room for freedom of action to individual ships.

While Commodore Rogers was attempting to prevent further losses, Captain Fred Stephenson, having lost his ship to the enemy, was intent on saving his crew. Only one man, Fourth Engineer Tom Purnell, had died during the torpedoing of the *Canonesa;* the sixty-two who survived left the ship in three lifeboats. In accordance with the tradition of the sea, Captain Stephenson was last to leave the sinking ship. He later wrote:

> I went to see how they were getting on with lowering the boats, there was no difficulty with the falls, so I went along to the starboard boat. We cleared away and lowered this boat, the men got into it and I waited for about 20 minutes to see that everyone was off the ship, then I too left. We pulled away from her about 300 yards, and as we left I noticed that the after deck was awash to the mainmast. My boat pulled around to the port side and after about three hours we watched the *Canonesa* sink, going down by the stern without listing.

After the *Canonesa* went down, her lifeboats became separated in the darkness. Captain Stephenson and the thirty-two men in No.1 lifeboat were picked up by the corvette *La Malouine* during the course of the afternoon. They were suffering from mild exposure, but were otherwise in good spirits. It seems unfortunate – and perhaps unfair – that the commander of *La Malouine*, Lieutenant Commander R.W. Keymer, later saw fit to claim that Captain Stephenson's conduct left much to be desired. Keymer reported:

Canonesa was abandoned in unnecessary haste and in poor order, her Captain not only leaving his papers on the bridge, but also men trapped in the stokehold and failing to take any sort of charge in the ship or subsequently in the boat.

Lieutenant Commander Keymer's accusations were not borne out by any evidence given by the survivors of the sinking of the *Canonesa*.

An interesting insight into Lieutenant Commander Keymer and HMS *La Malouine* is provided by Frank Hewitt, who served in the corvette:

La Malouine was a French corvette (British built). When France capitulated she was impounded in Portsmouth harbour and the French crew given the option of joining the Free French or being interned as P.O.W.s. Roughly half the crew took the first option and the others were replaced with British personnel under the command of Lieutenant Commander Keymer R.N.

For the best part of 3 months, *La Malouine* was shunted around Britain from port to port, the crew receiving only temporary pay and little shore leave. The ship being French was not deemed to be the responsibility of the Admiralty until she was eventually integrated into the R.N. as part of the convoy escorts operating out of Londonderry.

I joined the *La Malouine* (along with 3 other ratings) in Liverpool on 27th Oct 1940. It was a cold, wet, miserable night. An air raid was in progress. The ship was being refueled and then sailed to Londonderry. 'We're not stopping here,' the skipper was heard to say.

As a young 19 yr old volunteer my first introduction to a ship was nightmarish. Fearsome oaths & dark mutterings about cutting the skipper's throat and throwing him overboard were all around. Was I going to become involved in a mutiny?

We arrived in Londonderry the following morning, took on stores, fuel and ammunition, and were sent out to sea again.

It was cold and snow was falling as we sailed down the R. Foyle. When to my horror the seaman P.O. on the foredeck (in full oilskins and seaboots) shook his fist at the skipper and yelled, 'You might drive the rest of the crew you bog-whiskered old bastard, but you won't drive me any more', and jumped overboard. The river being in full flood, he was swept away, never to be seen again.

'MAN OVERBOARD' signal was made back to Captain (D) Londonderry (Captain Ruck-Keene) and we were instructed to return to port. On arrival Captain (D) came aboard to address the ship's company. 'You are an unhappy ship. I have never had an unhappy ship under my command and I don't intend to have one. An unhappy ship is not an efficient ship. From now on you will be treated like every other ship, x-days at sea and x-days in harbour.

Our skipper, Lieutenant Commander Keymer, being R.N., became Senior Officer 1st Escort Group.

He was not at all happy with a mixed FRENCH/BRITISH crew and within 6 months had replaced the French and we had an all British crew. If anyone was not up to the job or didn't 'fit in' they were quickly replaced, and he built up a really happy and efficient crew, who would do anything for him.

From initially being loathed by the crew, Lieutenant Commander Keymer became trusted and admired by all. A truly great leader and a happy ship. We still flew 2 flags – the White Ensign and the French Tricolour.

The *Canonesa's* other lifeboats were fortunate to be picked up within minutes of being launched by the corvette *Calendula*. Apprentice Peter Tingey, who was in one of them, later said:-

….there was an understandable nervousness among the lifeboat occupants as it was dark and cloudy. We rolled and pitched on mainly in silence, each I presume thinking of what trials lay ahead. Then about 15 minutes later a rather confusing silhouette loomed in the dark distance which immediately led to a cry from one of our survivors that 'it's a bloody submarine!' Fortunately it was not and as the shadowy object crept closer it thrilled our hearts and minds as it proved to be our rescue ship, the corvette *Calendula*. We stood ready to board the corvette which had temporarily secured our boat with a thin heaving line. Each survivor had to judge the peak of the heavy swell and then jump for his life. I was the last to jump and knew as I prepared to make it that it was probably my last chance as one of the sailors on the corvette had cut the heaving line. If I had missed the jump and the boat had fallen down with the swell, I would have drifted away to what sort of fate I had not imagined.

Captain Jackson and his crew of fifty-four stayed with the crippled tanker *Torinia* in the hope that they could save her, but drifting several miles astern of the convoy she was completely helpless. Rather than take the risk of the loaded tanker being captured by the enemy, Commander Knapp ordered the destroyer *Skate,* which by then had joined his group, to sink her. Jackson and his men were taken off, and the destroyer then sank the tanker by gunfire.

The Newcastle tramp *Dalcairn,* Joachim Schepke's third victim, sank during the night, and Captain Brusby and his crew of forty-seven had taken to their boats. They were also picked up by HMS *La Malouine.*

While the battle raged over HX 72, the other member of Dönitz's nine-boat wolf pack, Hans-Gerrit von Stockhausen in U-65, had failed to make contact with the convoy. For five days and nights von Stockhausen had searched the ocean, but had seen no trace of the convoy. Then, just before dawn on the sixth day, 15 September, he came across a ship sailing alone on a zig-zag course towards Rockall. It had the makings of a foul day, grey and rain-swept, a nasty cross sea running and poor visibility, but convinced he had a straggler from the convoy in sight, Stockhausen set off in pursuit.

There was no convoy ahead of the stranger. She was, in fact, a lone runner, the 4,950-ton Norwegian motor vessel *Hird,* bound from Mobile, Alabama for the United Kingdom with general cargo, including a full deck cargo of timber and cans of turpentine. She was commanded by Captain Ansgar M. Fredhjem, and had a total crew of thirty, all Norwegian exiles.

The *Hird* had left Sydney, Cape Breton on 1 September with the slow convoy SC 3, but a fire broke out on board in mid-Atlantic, and she was forced to drop out. By the time the fire had been extinguished, the other ships of SC 3 were well out of sight. Working up to full speed, Captain Fredhjem attempted to catch up with the convoy, but the weather was against the ship, and worsening. The *Hird* seemed destined to complete her voyage entirely alone, ironically, the only protection she had being provided by the cloak of that weather.

Von Stockhausen found her in the early hours of 15 September to the north-west of Rockall, the exhaust valves of her old Barclay Curle engine popping as she strained valiantly towards the safety of the North Channel. Stockhausen followed her patiently for more than an hour, then moved up on her starboard quarter, and fired a single torpedo.

The *Hird* was hit amidships, and immediately developed a heavy list to starboard. The chains on her deck cargo held, but she lay over on her side like a harpooned whale. Fearing that his ship might capsize at any moment, Fredhjem ordered his crew to abandon ship. The list was so pronounced that it was impossible to launch the port lifeboat, and the majority of the men got away in the starboard boat, with Captain Fredhjem and four others taking the small gig.

After lying off until dawn, Captain Fredhjem attempted to reboard the *Hird* to rescue the ship's papers, but this proved impossible, as by this time the ship was surrounded by an impenetrable sea of floating timber from her deck cargo. To have approached any closer would surely result in damage to his boat.

The *Hird* survivors spent an uncomfortable two hours in their boats being thrown around and drenched by the heavy seas, before they were found by the Icelandic trawler *Thorolfur*, which landed them at Fleetwood on 17 September. Coincidentally, it was in the late afternoon of that day that Hans-Gerrit von Stockhausen, quite by accident, finally came across the rearmost ships of another eastbound convoy.

Such was the huge amount of material flowing across the Atlantic, HX 71 had left Halifax only four days ahead of HX 72, and was then just over 100 miles to the north-west of Rockall. The convoy, consisting of thirty-three ships loaded with the usual mix of steel and general, had crossed the Atlantic escorted by the armed merchant cruiser *Ranpura*, which had returned westwards twenty-four hours earlier, being replaced by three corvettes and an armed trawler from Western Approaches Command.

The handover had taken place in continuing bad weather with the once orderly columns of the convoy becoming increasingly ragged. Rear Admiral H.B. Maltby, convoy commodore, sailing in the British steamer *Newfoundland* had done his utmost to keep the ships together, but even with the help of the newly arrived escorts, some confusion still reigned until dawn on 17 September.

HX 71, nine columns wide, covered more than 10 square miles of ocean, and while Commodore Maltby and the escorts were fully occupied restoring order, no one saw U-65 coming up astern.

With his boat ballasted down until only her conning tower was visible, and the rough seas were breaking over her casings, von Stockhausen kept his distance during the daylight hours. Only when it was fully dark did he begin to overtake HX 71 on her starboard side. By 1800, he was abeam of the leading ship of the outside column. No enemy escort ships were visible from U-65's conning tower.

The 5,242-ton *Tregenna*, sister ship to Maltby's *Tregarthen*, was a First World War replacement owned by the Hain Steamship Company of St Ives. She was on passage from Philadelphia to Newport, Mon. with 8,000 tons of steel in her holds, but unlike most transatlantic steel carriers, she had no compensatory cargo of lumber on top to help keep her afloat if torpedoed. Captain William Care and his crew of thirty-six, even with their lifejackets always to hand, had slept little throughout the crossing.

As soon as dusk closed in, von Stockhausen closed in on his prey, firing a single torpedo that caught the *Tregenna* just abaft her foremast in her No. Two hold. The sea roared into the cavernous hold, empty but for the stacks of heavy steel blocks. The watertight bulkhead at the fore end of the hold collapsed under the pressure of water, and the sea rushed into the forward hold.

An eye-witness to the sinking, the second officer of the Cardiff ship *Filleigh*, keeping station close astern of the *Tregenna*, reported that she was burying her bows in an oncoming wave when the torpedo struck. She appeared to 'stand on her head', going down with her stern high in the air and her propeller threshing wildly. In just forty seconds she had disappeared. Captain Care and thirty-two of his crew, unable to save themselves, went to the bottom with her. Four survivors were picked up by the *Filleigh*, and later transferred to the sloop *HMS Fleetwood*.

U-65 never did make contact with HX 72. Von Stockhausen remained at sea for another week, scouring the convoy lanes, but such was the weather that he saw no more of the enemy and made no more killings. Finally, after twenty-nine days at sea, in which he had sunk only 10,000 tons of shipping, von Stockhausen returned to Lorient.

Chapter 6

Chaos Reigns

Amidst all the mayhem caused by Schepke's attack on HX 72, Heinrich Bleichrodt, who had sunk the Glasgow ship *Blairangus* some eighteen hours earlier, arrived back on the scene with U-48. Aware that the convoy was now under escort, Bleichrodt approached from the north with extreme caution, edging in towards the port outside column. Fortunately for him, at the time Commander Knapp's ships were all busy. Four of their number, the corvettes *La Malouine* and *Calendula,* and the destroyers *Skate* and *Shikari* were still searching for survivors, while *Lowestoft* and *Heartsease* were desperately trying to defend what remained of the convoy. This was a high-risk policy, for it divided the defences of the convoy and put the escorts assigned to rescue duty at the mercy of the U-boats while they were slow-steaming or stopped to pick up survivors. Yet there were now so many men in the water, in boats and on rafts, that Knapp felt obligated to commit the majority of his ships to rescue work.

The intention had been for the last ship in each column to act as rescue ship for that column, but the ordinary merchant ships were not equipped for this work. Being deep loaded, they did not manoeuvre well, and they carried no special boats or trained boats' crews. All too often the outcome of one merchantman trying to rescue the crew of another was two ships sunk or damaged, a needless sacrifice that could not be afforded in these dark days.

It would not be until January 1941 that specialist rescue ships were assigned to convoys. They were usually small passenger carrying vessels, often ex-cross Channel steamers. The conversion to rescue work involved providing accommodation, extra provisions and medical facilities for up to 150 survivors. Scrambling nets were permanently rigged overside, and the clumsy standard lifeboats replaced by sturdy motorized boats manned by picked crews. Later versions of the rescue ships were equipped with High Frequency Radio Direction Finding sets, known to the Navy as 'Huff-Duff'. Stationed as they were at the rear of the convoy, they were often able to provide good triangulation bearings for the escort leader usually scouting ahead of the convoy. A number of U-boats were pin-pointed in this way.

By the end of the war, thirty rescue ships, all crewed by merchant seamen, had been involved with nearly 800 convoys, and had saved more than 4,000 men from watery graves. Only six of these ships were lost while in convoy.

While *La Malouine, Calendula, Skate* and *Shikari* swept the sea astern of HX 72 in search of survivors, U-48 came in from the north undetected. Surveying the massed ranks of ships confronting him, Heinrich Bleichrodt finally selected the rear ship of the port outside column as his target. She was the 5,136-ton steamer *Broompark*, owned by Denholms of Glasgow. Although only a year out of the builder's yard, the *Broompark* had already made a vital contribution to the Allied cause.

On 14 June 1940, with Paris already in German hands and France about to sue for peace, the *Broompark*, under the command of Norwegian exile Captain Olaf Paulsen, arrived off the Biscay port of Bordeaux ready to load cargo. The town had been heavily bombed and the entrance to the port mined, but Captain Paulsen, ever mindful of his duty to the owners, decided to anchor off and wait developments. A few days later, Paulsen had a visitor. He was Charles Howard, the British liason officer in France for the Department of Scientific & Industrial Research. Howard, who had succeeded in rescuing France's entire stock of heavy water, was looking for a ship to carry this out of Bordeaux before the Germans arrived. The heavy water, a key ingredient for nuclear research, amounted to only 185 kilograms contained in twenty-six cans, but with it came a number of crates of specialist machine tools, industrial diamonds valued at £2½ million, and fifty French scientists and their research papers.

Paulsen agreed to carry this bizarre and priceless cargo out of Bordeaux for the Allies, and later that day the *Broompark* sailed out of the Gironde estuary with the cans of heavy water on deck and the scientists, their equipment, and the diamonds safely below decks. The heavy water was dropped off at a secret location on the French Channel coast, to be retrieved later by a British submarine, while the *Broompark* put in to Falmouth on 21 June to land her passengers and the balance of her precious cargo.

From Falmouth, the *Broompark* took the long road across the Atlantic and through the Panama Canal to Vancouver. There she loaded 5,130 tons of steel and sawn timber for Glasgow, joining Convoy HX 72 in Halifax for the homeward passage. On 21 September, three months to the day after she reached Falmouth from Bordeaux, the *Broompark* was again in peril.

Unseen by anyone on the British ship, U-48 crept up on the *Broompark* until she was very close on her port quarter. Then Bleichrodt fired his last remaining torpedo, which at such short range could not fail to find its mark. It exploded in the *Broompark's* after hold with a deafening roar, and the wounded ship took on a heavy list to port as the sea poured into her hull.

Commander Knapp's report serves to illustrate the confusion prevailing at the time:

> The night was light with a bright moon but with periodical rain showers and low visibility. The sea was calm. About 2220/21 a bright light was sighted which appeared to come from the starboard side of the convoy. This was followed shortly by a ship hoisting a red light. This light appeared to come from the starboard side of the convoy but no explosion was either seen or heard. . . I immediately turned to starboard, thinking that the attack had come from that side. I tried to signal *La Malouine* but could not see her and after signalling around the horizon I gave up and called the Commodore instead. I asked the Commodore for information regarding the direction of the attack. He acknowledged the signal but gave no reply.

Only one man died as a result of Bleichrodt's torpedo and the *Broompark*, buoyed up by her cargo of timber, did not sink. She was, however, listing heavily, but after an inspection of the damage, Captain Paulsen decided that she might still be saved. He called for volunteers, and seven men agreed to stay with him. The remaining thirty-one he ordered to take to the boats. They were quickly picked up by the corvette *La Malouine*.

Throughout what remained of that night Paulsen and his seven volunteers, driven by the precariousness of their situation, worked desperately to restart the engines and pumps, eventually bringing the ship upright again by shifting water ballast. By dawn on 22 September, the *Broompark* was under way again, and as far as Captain Paulsen could ascertain, was no longer in danger of sinking. He retrieved the rest of his crew from *La Malouine* and set course for the North Channel.

The *Broompark's* ordeal was not yet over. As she limped into the Firth of Clyde three days later, she was spotted by a patrolling Focke-Wulf Condor, which immediately pounced on her. Once again Olaf Paulsen's extraordinary luck held good, and although he lost one of his crew to the enemy, the *Broompark* fought off her attacker and reached her home port safely.

For his part in snatching the irreplaceable French supply of heavy water from under the noses of the advancing Germans, Captain Paulsen was awarded the Order of the British Empire. The extreme leadership and bravery he showed in saving the *Broompark* and her crew when she was damaged in HX 72 was recognized with the award of Lloyd's War Medal for Bravery at Sea.

The *Broompark*, then under the command of Captain John Sinclair, continued to run the gauntlet of the U-boats in the North Atlantic for another two years. Finally, in July 1942, she was crossing in the westbound convoy OB 113 when she was torpedoed by U-552. Despite extensive damage, however, she remained afloat and was taken in tow by the US Navy tug *Cherokee*. But the *Broompark* had come to the end of her short but eventful life, and three days later she went down off St John's, Newfoundland. Sadly, Captain Sinclair and three of his crew lost their lives with her.

Ironically, six days after the *Broompark* sank, U-48, commanded by *Oberleutnant* Siegfried Atzinger, was caught on the surface by the Canadian corvette *Sackville*. Atzinger, who had used up all his torpedoes, immediately crash-dived, but as she was going under the *Sackville* scored a direct hit on U-48's conning tower, damaging her schnorkel. The corvette followed up with depth charges as the U-boat disappeared below the waves. Oil and debris came to the surface shortly afterwards, and it was assumed, wrongly it seems, that U-48 had sunk. Ten days later, Atzinger brought his command into St Nazaire, battered, but able to return to sea after repairs.

The torpedoing of the *Broompark* signaled the end of any cohesion in the ranks of HX 72. Communication between Commander Knapp in HMS *Lowestoft* and Commodore Rogers in the *Tregarthen* had become almost impossible, with the result that neither was sure of the intention of the other. The heavy thump of the enemy's torpedoes going home, the flares, rockets, and starshell turning the night sky into day, all contributed to what was now a state of near-panic amongst the merchantmen. A vivid picture of the horrors of the night was painted in his book *Atlantic Roulette* by Radio Officer Morris Beckham, who was sailing in the British tanker *Venetia*:

> On that wet cold miserable boat deck we stood, leaned and squatted, all eyes and ears, senses sharpened by fear. Now, our benighted cargo was very much on our minds (the *Venetia* was carrying a full cargo of highly volatile paraffin). Cigarettes would have relaxed taut nerves but smoking was out of the question. Attempts at laboured humour only irritated. A ship was torpedoed and her crew were lost. Her neighbour got away and her crew lived. A U-boat captain's whim could give life or death. Bravado dared not raise its hypocritical head. We were all afraid and were unashamed about showing it. Many had been shipwrecked before and knew what they were coming back to face. At this moment they vowed that they would never sign up again. But they would, all of them. Talk died away as each man hunched into himself, keeping his own thoughts to himself.

Commodore Rogers, horrified by the sudden disappearance of the escorts as they hared off in pursuit of real and imagined enemies, was convinced that the convoy was under attack by a horde of U-boats. Deciding it was time to give the merchant ships a chance to save themselves, he ordered the convoy to scatter.

Rogers' decision to scatter proved to be premature. In fact, U-48 having exhausted her torpedoes, only Joachim Schepke in U-100 was still in contact with the convoy, and he was busy reloading his empty torpedo tubes. An entry in his War Diary made at the time reads:

2341. Bright and clear, moon behind	We are now in the middle of row 2 of the convoy, close behind row 1. Lots of steamers in front, beside and behind us.
clouds, shining through in places NW 2, Sea 1-2, Light swells.	Closest distance is 500 to 600 meters Steamers are now beginning to get closer to each other so our freedom of movement is restricted. There are about 8

> to 10 ships in a row. During the whole
> Time torpedoes were reloaded. At about
> 2400 3 tubes Are ready to fire.

With his bow tubes once more armed, Schepke moved in on the disorganized and unprotected ships shortly after midnight. His first target was the 6,586-ton *Empire Airman*.

The *Empire Airman* was a ship with a chequered history. Built in 1915 at Trieste for the Austro-Hungarian Navy as the *Teodo*, she was handed over to the Italian Government as a war reparation in 1921 and renamed *Barbana*. Two years later, she became the *Barbana G.*, sailing under the house flag of Società Anomima Co-operativa di Navigazionne Garibaldi, of Genoa. On 9 June 1940, she slipped out of Newcastle under the cover of darkness, only to be stopped and boarded by the Royal Navy the next day within hours of Italy declaring war on the Allies. The *Barbana G.* became the *Empire Airman*, owned by the Ministry of War Transport, and managed by Mark Whitwell & Sons, of Bristol.

Commanded by Captain John Raine, and manned by a British crew of thirty-six, the *Empire Airman* joined HX 72 in Halifax, having loaded a full cargo of iron ore in Conception Bay. She had originally been built for 14 knots, but the years had taken their toll, and in that autumn of 1940 the best she could achieve was an indifferent 8 knots. Given that the *Empire Airman* was carrying 7,900 tons of iron ore stowing at 15 cubic feet to the ton, and therefore had the floatability of a lead coffin, it was the ultimate folly for her to be sailing in an exposed position at the head of the outside starboard column of HX 72. The order to scatter came as a welcome relief to Captain Raine.

Joachim Schepke's supply of torpedoes was dwindling and he used them sparingly, firing one at the elderly ore carrier, and a second at what he described as 'a large freighter' close by her. The first torpedo ran true, blasting a large hole in the *Empire Airman's* hull in the region of her engine room. The second shot missed its target completely.

Although badly holed, the *Empire Airman* showed no immediate signs of sinking, a credit to her Italian builders, who had made no concessions to economy. No one was more surprised than Captain Raine to find his ship still afloat after the grievous blow she had received. An investigation of the damage showed that although the ore carrier's engine room was awash, she was in no danger of sinking. With the nearest British port, Londonderry, less than 250 miles away, Raine decided to stay with her and await a tow. The *Empire Airman*, an inert and anonymous hulk in the darkness, dropped out of the convoy and drifted astern.

The other ships were now in complete disarray, and Schepke was able to choose his targets at will. Seeing another ship crossing astern of him, he snapped off a shot from his stern tube. It ran true. U-100's War Diary recorded:

> 0050. Torpedo fired from tube V, G7e. Relative bearing to target 80°, target speed 8 knots, depth 2 meters, distance 53 sec.
>
> After 53 seconds hit forward. Steamer appeared small at first; therefore depth was set to only 2 meters. Shortly after the hit steamer starts burning. The ship was, as was learned by coming close, 6 to 7000 grt, with 5 holds, numerous winching cranes and aft a high placed gun.

The unfortunate recipient of Schepke's torpedo was the eighteen-year-old *Scholar*, owned by T & J Harrison of Liverpool, and commanded by Captain William Mackenzie. The 3,940-ton *Scholar* was nearing the end of a long trek from Galveston, in the Gulf of Mexico, via Halifax, to Manchester with a cargo of steel, cotton and timber. Schepke's torpedo exploded directly under her bridge with a thunderous roar and a brilliant flash. The ship caught fire and quickly developed a heavy list. As with the *Empire Airman*, Captain Mackenzie and his crew refused to abandon their ship and the *Scholar* slowly fell astern to join the drifting ore carrier. She was later taken in tow by the naval salvage tug *Marauder*, but the tow was abandoned after twenty-four hours, and the *Scholar* was sunk by gunfire from the destroyer *Skate*. Captain Mackenzie and his crew of forty-four were picked up by the *Skate* and landed at Londonderry.

While his torpedo-men worked frantically to reload the stern tube, Schepke, his hunting instinct now thoroughly aroused, looked around for his next target. By 0130, he was up with the front runners of the scattering merchantmen. His War Diary again provides a realistic description of the action:

> It gets brighter and more quiet, the moon is on the edge of a cloud and starting to come out any second.
>
> Approached the front row again at full speed because of the larger steamers there. Convoy is now steering 070°. Due to the increasing daylight things have to speed up. A remarkably large

tanker comes into sight. Beside the tanker is a 7 to 8000 grt heavily loaded freighter. Despite the moon in my rear I position myself between the two. Distance is 6 to 7000 meters to each one.

Schepke had turned his sights on the 10,525-ton tanker *Frederick S. Fales*, which was working up to speed as she followed Commodore Rogers' order to scatter and run. She presented a target eminently worthy of any U-boat's torpedoes.

Another Italian-built ship, the *Frederick S. Fales* was carrying 13,849 tons of fuel oil from Curacao to the Clyde for the Admiralty. She was a new ship, less than a year old, owned and registered in Hong Kong by Oriental Tankers, and under the command of Captain Frank Ramsay.

The *Frederick S. Fales* had a good turn of speed, and following the order to scatter, Captain Ramsay was supremely confident of reaching the shelter of the Clyde before the U-boats pounced. His confidence was misplaced. U-100, running on the surface, caught up with the escaping tanker and Joachim Schepke put two torpedoes into her, the combined explosion of which virtually blew her apart.

Captain Ramsay and his crew of forty-one were in the act of taking to the boats when, just five minutes after she had been torpedoed, their ship capsized and plunged to the bottom. In capsizing, the *Frederick S. Fales* struck one of her lifeboats, killing 53-year-old Captain Frank Ramsay and nineteen of his boat's crew.

Even Schepke was horrified at the suddeness of the end of his victim. He wrote in his War Diary:

> I personally have never seen such a violent and imposing direct hit. The ship sinks stern first very quickly . . . shortly thereafter only a small portion of the bow is recognizable until it too sinks. This tanker had an extreme length, singular bridge and large spaces between the superstructures. The details could be clearly seen in full moonlight. His size is according to general estimates 15 to 16000 grt.

Commodore Rogers, no longer in command of the situation, watched with growing horror as the convoy was ravaged. He later wrote:

> Large explosion abaft beam (think this was the F.S. Fales, who had been seen there about ½ an hour before). This was a terrific explosion and masts and bits of ships were visible up in the air.

Schepke's blood was up, and he wasted no time in putting a torpedo into the next unfortunate ship to cross his path. She was the 6,031-ton Norwegian-flag *Simla,* one of the fleet of Wilhelm Wilhelmsen of Oslo. Commanded by Captain Hans von Krogh, the *Simla* was on her way from Philadelphia to an unspecified port on the East Coast of England with a cargo of 8,100 tons of steel and scrap metal.

Right from the time of sailing from Halifax the *Simla* had been under suspicion as a possible danger to the convoy. While she was loading in Philadelphia it had emerged that Captain von Krogh was suspected as not being entirely loyal to the Allied cause. A coded W/T signal from Naval Headquarters in Ottawa to Commodore Rogers, sent on 12 September stated:

> S.S. *Simla* has had crew trouble and conflicting reports about reliability of the Master have also been received. He is reported as stating that he has run the British blockade and he will do it again. Suggest ship and Master be watched.

The inference was that Captain von Krogh had plans to cross the Atlantic under the protection of the convoy, and then make a dash for the nearest German occupied port. Commodore Rogers kept his own counsel on this and later reported that the *Simla* had not shown any unusual behaviour during the crossing. However, several adjacent ships in the convoy accused the Norwegian ship of showing lights, even when the U-boats were attacking. This may have been a deliberate attempt to signal to the enemy, but on the other hand it could have been simply due to poor blackout enforcement in the ship. The latter seems more likely, for at night the U-boats could hardly be expected to distinguish between individual ships, and to show a light would have been the utmost folly, inviting a swift torpedo. Thanks to Joachim Schepke, the truth of the matter will never be known.

When Schepke's torpedo struck, Captain von Krogh was on the bridge of the *Simla,* with Second Mate Harris Evant in charge of the watch. Able Seaman Willie Larsen was at the wheel, and Able Seaman Jorgen Kieding on the lookout. The torpedo exploded underneath the fore part of the bridge, and such was the shock that von Krogh, Evant and Larsen were killed outright. Jorgen Kieding survived the blast, but was severely injured.

It is probable that Schepke's torpedo broke the *Simla's* back, and under the sheer weight of her cargo of steel she sank so quickly that there was no time to get boats away. Fortunately, one of Captain von Krogh's last orders before he died was for all the crew to don lifejackets, and for those not on watch to muster on the upper deck. This undoubtedly saved many lives. When, an hour later, the corvette *Heartsease* came looking for survivors, she plucked thirty-one men from the water. One of those rescued, the ship's cook Martinius Karlsen, died on board the *Heartsease*.

The only resistance met by U-100 came from the vice-commodore's ship *Harlingen*, commanded by Captain Jack Willingham. The 5,415-ton *Harlingen*, owned by J & C Harrison of London, had scattered with the others on the orders of Commodore Rogers, and at 0200 on 22 September was steaming at full speed with only one other ship, the Norwegian steamer *Snar*, in sight. Captain Willingham later reported:

At 2130 G.M.T. convoy attacked by submarines, apparently in large numbers, attack continuing until 0101 G.M.T. 22nd Sept., at which time we were personally attacked by a submarine which emerged right in the path of the moonlight, approx. position 55 degrees 10' N 17 degrees 53'W.

The wheel was put hard a port, the submarine being on the starboard beam, and was thus brought right astern. The torpedo fired by him passed close on the starboard bow, quickly followed by another which passed on the port side. We were enabled to get three shots at him wih the 4" B.L. gun. The first shot passed over him, and the second shot, fired with the sights set at 1400 yards, was followed immediately by a deep thud, the shot striking just beneath the conning tower, which was still awash. The third shot, fired shortly afterwards, we were unable to either see or hear. We resumed our interrupted zigzag, and saw no further enemy craft.

Joachim Schepke's account of the incident reads:

The weather gets more and more unfavourable for an attack. I have to try one more attack with the last remaining torpedo. I decide, despite the moonlight at my back, to turn to a group of steamers from which the largest one, at about 8000 grt, shall be shot at.

But a smaller steamer of about 3000 grt is in front of him. The attempt to pass close behind the smaller one to surprise the larger one fails. The small one sights us, turns away and howls with the steam whistle. This alerts the large steamer. My boat delivers a good shot.

0257. Tube 1 G7e relative bearing of target 090°, target speed 8 knots, depth 3 meters.

Steamer is turning away; the bubble track misses about 30 meters from his bow. At this time we have stopped behind him in full moonlight. Distance 500 to 600 meters.

Suddenly he starts firing with his gun. It sounds like a hit against a tin can. The shot whistles over the conning tower. I turn away at full speed and full rudder, the steamer fires very slowly. The next shot falls short. The third shot is too high. Thereafter he stops firing.

Captain Willingham broke radio silence to report his brush with the U-boat, and HMS *Lowestoft* gave chase. She carried out an Asdic sweep of the area, but made no contact. Commander Knapp then decided his services would be best used rounding up the scattered ships of the convoy. Meanwhile, Joachim Schepke was making good his escape, but not before inspecting the havoc he had created:

I move outside the range of sight. The 2 destroyers are sighted on both sides which close in on the convoy. Under these visibility conditions my boat can no longer stay in the rear sector.

When after the last attack I drifted rearwards I sighted 6 destroyers. I left with strong zigzags and at high speed because the destroyers came towards me and got bigger all the time. To get more clarification about the hits I searched the position where I hit them. We made contact with a destroyer which fired multiple shots. In the beginning we thought he was shooting at us because the distance was about 6000 meters and because he turned towards us a couple of times. Although we altered course his image got larger.

We closed to about 200 meters of the burning freighter (hit 6) and then had to turn away again due to the destroyer.

I am certain I saw the destroyer firing at the wreck and also firing at the wreck of the tanker (hit 5) to get them out of the way, because I observed high water splashes after a salvo.

0645. When there was no longer a chance to get close to the convoy I sent the following message: 0300/22: Have lost contact AL 6525 – U-100.

At about 0600 on 22 September, with the rising sun turning the eastern horizon to a pale grey, the 7,886-ton *Collegian* was 320 miles west of Malin Head and running for the safety of the North Channel at full speed. The *Collegian*, another member of the convoy flying the house flag of T & J Harrison of Liverpool, although built in 1923, had spent the depression years laid up in a backwater in the Thames Estuary, not coming into service with the Harrison fleet until 1935. She was thus a comparatively new ship, and her engines, twin turbines geared to a single shaft, had never been called upon to give of their best. The time had now come for her to show her worth.

When the sun finally lifted from the horizon, despite her heavy cargo of steel, cotton and timber, the *Collegian* was thrusting aside the Atlantic swells at a good 15 knots. At that speed Belfast was only twenty-eight hours away. Unfortunately, U-32 lay submerged directly in her path.

U-32 had sailed from Lorient four days earlier, and her commander, Hans Jenisch, had been hurrying westwards on the surface, anxious to join in the rout of HX 72. When he saw the very substantial merchantman bearing down on him, Jenisch immediately dived, and waited for the right moment to fire.

The unsuspecting *Collegian* steamed straight into Jenisch's sights, but he misjudged her speed badly, and his torpedo went wild. Frustrated, he brought U-32 to the surface and chased after the British ship. When he had closed the range to about 4 miles, Jenisch opened fire with his deck gun. The *Collegian* was hit at once, but she retaliated with her 4-inch, and a gun duel ensued in which the merchant ship inevitably received heavy damage. She was saved by the timely arrival of *Lowestoft*, which had been attracted by the gun flashes. U-32 dived and the sloop followed her down with a pattern of depth charges. *Lowestoft* was joined by the corvette *Heartsease*, and the two escorts began an Asdic search, which proved fruitless. However, their intervention paid dividends, forcing U-32 to quit the area in a hurry..

Jenisch was not alone in quitting the action: all the other U-boats involved with HX 72, having used up their torpedoes, were heading back to Lorient just as fast as their twin diesels would carry them. Many of their torpedoes may have been wasted, but that Dönitz's wolf pack had scored a very significant victory was beyond all argument. HX 72 had lost eleven ships totalling 72,727 tons gross, along with 150,000 tons of vital supplies from the Americas, 45,000 tons of which was fuel oil destined for the bunkers of the Royal Navy. Furthermore, other than unconfirmed damaged inflicted on U-100 by the *Harlingen's* gunners, the U-boats had emerged unscathed from what had been a ferocious battle.

Joachim Schepke was undoubtedly the hero – or villain, depending on how you view it – of the action. Single-handedly, U-100 accounted for two thirds of the total sinkings – seven ships of 50,340 tons. It is significant that both Schepke and Otto Kretchsmer, who also played a major role in the attack, operated on the surface, penetrating deep inside the convoy before firing their torpedoes. The commanders of the other boats in the pack, who had little or no success, were content to submerge and launch their torpedoes from afar in accordance with normal practice. The lesson to be learned from this did not escape the attention of Admiral Karl Dönitz.

The agony of Convoy HX 72 did not end with the departure of the U-boats. When the surviving ships were nearing the west coast of Scotland they ran into atrocious weather, and they came in for a severe battering before they found shelter in the North Channel. But even then their ordeal was not over. On 23 September, long-range Focke-Wulf Condors of the Luftwaffe swooped on the battle-weary ships, attacking with bombs and machine-guns. Desperately tired, but not beaten, the merchant seamen stood to their guns and fought back. Only one ship, the London-registered *Pacific Grove*, received any significant damage. She was 8 miles north of Tory Island, when a bomb crashed through her deck, but fortunately did not explode.

The story of Convoy HX 72 finally ended on 29 September, when the armed trawler *Fandango*, patrolling 30 miles off Tory Island, came across a lifeboat containing fifteen survivors from the tanker *Invershannon*. The men, who had weathered the storm for eight days in their open boat, were in poor condition, but all alive.

Chapter 7

Slaughter

Joachim Schepke had stirred up a veritable hornet's nest during his clash with the *Harlingen*, the gun flashes bringing HX 72's escorts racing in to investigate the furore. Schepke counted six 'destroyers' bearing down on him and, having run out of torpedoes, he wisely set course for home at full speed. He was aware that he had hit the convoy hard, but he had no idea of the scene of utter devastation he had left behind him. Virtually unopposed, he had laid about him for more than three hours, disposing of seven loaded Allied ships totalling 50,340 tons gross, and in the process had once more demonstrated that he was up amongst the top U-boat aces in what Winston Churchill had now proclaimed the Battle of the Atlantic.

Seventy-two hours after U-100 fired her last torpedo, she sailed into Lorient with her conning tower a riot of colour with victory pennants and her crew standing to their docking stations in their best uniforms. There was a heroes' welcome waiting for them; a military band thumped out a rousing tune, pretty young nurses scattered red roses, and the great man himself, *Onkel Karl*, was on the quay to welcome them home. In his report Admiral Dönitz wrote:

> Very successful, well executed mission. The Commanding Officer has made excellent use of his opportunities at the convoy. When estimating sunken tonnage one must always remember that at night most estimates are too high. Only constant self-restraint along with the identification of the names of the sunken ships can bring experience. The CO has tried that in his estimates. It is not quite clear if all torpedoed ships have sunk. This has to be ascertained by all possible means.

In spite of his expressed reservations, Dönitz had no hesitation in recommending U-100's commander for the immediate award of the

Knight's Insignia of the Iron Cross, Schepke having now passed the magic figure of 100,000 tons of enemy shipping sunk.

U-100 spent seventeen days in Lorient, rather longer than usual for an operational U-boat, this perhaps being due to some undisclosed damage caused by the *Harlingen's* shells. The boat finally left port on 12 October, manned by substantially the same crew, and with Joachim Schepke again in command.

Leaving the shelter of the River Blavet U-100 skirted the rocky shores of Isle de Groix and immediately dug her sharp prow into the first of the long swells rolling in from the west, a sure sign that a storm was raging out in the deep ocean. A thousand miles to the north-west Convoy SC 7 was already locked in battle with the raging elements.

SC 7, the latest in the unending procession of ships hauling their vital cargoes for Britain to leave Canada, was made up of thirty-five merchantmen, the majority of which sailed under the Red Ensign. Predictably, most of them were old – the eldest being the Norwegian tanker *Thorøy* which had spent a staggering forty-seven years at sea – all were slow plodders, hence the designation 'SC' (slow convoy). A not insignificant number were so small that under normal circumstances they would not have been considered for the Atlantic crossing, except perhaps in high summer. But the times were far from normal. The whole of Western Europe now lay crushed under the iron heel of Hitler's *Wermacht*, with only Great Britain remaining unconquered and defiant. That she would remain so depended almost entirely on the tenuous link across the Atlantic to the warehouses of the Americas provided by these ships.

Mercifully for this motley collection of small and underpowered ships, when SC 7 put out to sea from Sydney, Cape Breton on the morning of 5 October, the weather was in a kindly mood. Once clear of the headlands, with a great deal of black smoke and grumbling confusion, they formed up into nine columns abreast, yet another convoy ready to face up to the challenge of the North Atlantic.

Leading the centre column of SC 7 was the Convoy Commodore's ship *Assyrian,* under the command of 35-year-old Captain Reginald Kearon of Liverpool. The 2,962-ton *Assyrian,* an early type twin-screw motor vessel, had begun her long life in the shipyard of Blohm & Voss in Hamburg in 1914, and had successfully served her owners, Woermann Line, throughout the First World War. In 1919, she was seized as a war reparation and handed over to Ellerman & Papayanni Line of Liverpool, who, with an eye to Britain's inexhaustible supply of coal, promptly converted her to steam. In between the wars she carried cargoes to and from the Mediterranean, general cargo outwards, and fruit home. Now, in keeping with the demands of war, she had on board 3,700 tons of grain, a cargo eagerly awaited on the other side of the ocean.

In addition to her crew of thirty-nine and three passengers, the *Assyrian* carried the convoy commodore Vice Admiral Lachlan Donald Ian Mackinnon, RN. Fifty-eight-year-old Mackinnon, who before the war had been Rear Admiral commanding the Second Battle Fleet, had been called out of retirement to serve in this more mundane position, and now, like a number of his pensioner colleagues, sailed in the rank of Commodore, RNR.

Although much of Mackinnon's time in the Navy had been spent in battleships, he was not without experience in his new role. In fact, SC 7 was the eleventh convoy he had shepherded across the Atlantic. On this occasion he had the unenviable task of holding together a fleet of merchant ships comprising twenty British, six Norwegian, six Greek, three Swedish, two Dutch, and one American. In their ranks were two loaded oil tankers and three ore carriers, while the remainder, the majority of them ageing tramps, sagged under a multitude of heavy cargoes ranging from scrap iron to wood pulp. At least three of their number should by no stretch of the imagination have been involved in such an arduous winter crossing.

The *Eaglescliffe Hall* and *Trevisa*, were mere 1,800 tonners, while the *Winona* was slightly larger at 2,085 tons. Built to trade in the relatively sheltered waters of the Canadian lakes, which they had done for many years, they were unsuited to the open ocean. They were grotesque looking ships, with their engines right aft and their navigation bridges perched on the forecastle head just a few feet from the bows, which gave them a clear sweep of deck for loading and navigation in the lakes and rivers. This may have been all very well in the lakes, but the North Atlantic at the approach of winter was a different proposition altogether, as those keeping watch on their exposed bridges were about to find out. This trio of lakers would have had no place in SC 7 were it not for the fact that they were urgently needed in British coastal waters to carry coal.

Commodore Mackinnon carried with him a staff of five naval signallers, who would relay his orders by flag and lamp to the merchant ships – there being no other means of communication. This led to the bridge of the *Assyrian* being rather crowded at times, but the division of command was clear and irrefutable. While Mackinnon was responsible for the direction of the convoy, Captain Kearon was at all times in command of his own ship.

It was not without a certain sense of quiet pride that Reg Kearon walked the bridge of the *Assyrian* as she stood out into the Atlantic at the head of this majestic fleet of old and determined ships. To be chosen as commodore ship for such a large convoy was no small honour. On the other hand, it did occur to Kearon that the presence of Commodore Mackinnon and his staff aboard the *Assyrian* might have something to do with the old-world excellence of the ship's twelve passenger cabins. In the now almost forgotten days of peace the *Assyrian* had been a popular ship with holiday makers – and at £1 per day for a forty-day round voyage to the Mediterranean this was not surprising. Moreover, Kearon had already warmed to Mackinnon, a bluff naval officer of great experience. However, for all his rank and seniority, Mackinnon's position on board the *Assyrian* was purely an advisory one, and at no time could he outrank Kearon in the navigation and handling of his own ship.

SC 7's problems began on its first night at sea, when the *Winona's* main generator began to give trouble, and she was forced to turn back for Cape Breton. Then, forty-eight hours later, the convoy's escort was reduced by fifty per cent.

Escorting SC 7 as the convoy left the coast of Nova Scotia astern was the 14-knot Folkestone-class sloop *Scarborough*, an ex-Admiralty survey vessel, with Commander Norman Dickinson again in command, and the Canadian armed yacht *Elk*, a tiny vessel of 578 tons, armed with one 4-inch, and with a top speed of 11 knots. This ill-matched pair did nothing to inspire confidence in those who manned the vulnerable merchantmen. When, two days out from Sydney *Elk*, having reached the limit of her endurance, turned back for Nova Scotia, leaving *Scarborough* as the sole defender of SC 7, the ripple of apprehension that ran through the convoy was almost visible. *Scarborough* was not fitted with Asdic, so Commander Dickinson's options for defence were very limited. When *Elk* departed, he decided to scout ahead of the convoy, relying on the time-honoured 'Mark 1 Eyeball' of his lookouts to warn of danger, and hoping that the mere presence of a British warship, however inadequate, would scare off the U-boats. It was a forlorn hope.

The convoy's route, as laid down by the Admiralty, would take it into the northernmost reaches of the Atlantic, before turning south-east to enter British waters via the North Channel. It was hoped that this diversion would keep the ships well away from the predatory U-boats until the final stages of the 16-day passage, when escorts of the Royal Navy's Western Approaches Command were due to rendezvous with the convoy. In the meantime, Admiral Dönitz, warned of the sailing of SC 7 by Naval Intelligence, was gathering together his grey wolves.

U–38 and U–123 were already at sea. U–123, a newly commissioned Type IXB under the command of *Kapitänleutnant* Karl-Heinz Moehle, had sailed from Wilhelmshaven on her first war patrol on 19 September, being followed a few days later by Heinrich Liebe's U–38, another Type IX, which left Lorient on 25 September. U–48 (Heinrich Bleichrodt), U–101 (Fritz Frauenheim) and U–124 (Georg-Wilhelm Schulz) all put to sea from Lorient on 5 October, while Joachim Schepke's U–100 had sailed from the same port a week later. The pack was complete when U–46 (Englebert Endrass) left St. Nazaire, and U–99 (Otto Kretchsmer) sailed from Lorient on 13 October. If these eight boats could come together in time to bar SC 7's entry to the North Channel, the scene would be set for more wholesale slaughter.

SC 7 was less than 300 miles east of Newfoundland when, at sunrise on 11 October, the real Atlantic began to make itself known. An ominous reddening of the sky in the west had the 'old salts' in the convoy muttering glumly, 'Red sky in the morning, sailor's warning', and they were soon proved to be right.

By noon, the wind was blowing strongly from the north-west, the clouds were lowering almost to mast-top height, and the sea was beginning to heave and roll. As the day wore on, the wind increased steadily, and by nightfall it was blowing severe gale 9 and gusting to storm force 10. The great heaving swells, topped by angry white breakers, were awe inspiring, and at times frightening even to the experienced Western Ocean hands. There was a very real danger that some of the smaller and more heavily laden merchantmen would be pooped as they wallowed in the troughs. Steering a straight course was almost impossible, and soon the once orderly ranks descended into chaos. Even some of the bigger ships were in trouble, among them the

1918-built, 6,055-ton *Empire Miniver.* Loaded with steel and pig iron, she reported her engines to be faltering. Her master Captain Robert Smith also remarked on the conduct of other ships. In a later report to the Admiralty he said, 'we were peering into the darkness when, to our amazement, we saw a bright light on our port bow. When we drew up we found it was a Greek steamer, it had been visible to us for 6 miles!' The rules, instilled into the merchantmen at the pre-sailing conference, were being dumped overboard.

It came as no real surprise that the first to drop out were the tiny Great Lakes steamers *Trevisa* and *Eaglescliffe Hall*, who found it impossible to keep station. It was something of a miracle that these ships had progressed so far, for they were not built for the deep oceans. Both gradually fell astern of the convoy, and were soon out of sight.

Later in the day, the big ships began to go. The 3,554-ton *Aenos*, built two years before the *Titanic* went down, was loaded with 6,276 tons of wheat in bulk and, not surprisingly, her tired old engines began to give trouble. She dropped astern of the other ships, to be followed later by another relic, the 5,875-ton *Thalia,* also under the Greek flag, and carrying a deadweight cargo of steel, lead and zinc. Her poorly maintained engines were unable to stand up to the strain imposed by the heavy rolling and pitching in the huge quarterly seas. Miraculously, both ships later rejoined the convoy.

The storm, whipped up by a large equinoctial depression moving slowly across the North Atlantic from west to east, blew fiercely without let-up for the next four days. But in spite of the weather, the remaining ships of SC 7, cajoled and threatened by Commodore Mackinnon in the *Assyrian* and Commander Dickinson in *Scarborough*, managed to maintain some semblance of order and continued to steam slowly and determinedly north-eastwards. No ship was suffering more than the gallant little *Scarborough* on her station ahead of the convoy. Narrow in the beam and displacing a mere 1,000 tons, the sloop, her decks awash with foaming seas, appeared to be attempting to emulate an enemy submarine as she struggled valiantly to provide some sort of cover for the merchantmen.

On the afternoon of 15 October, to everyone's great relief, the barometer at last began to rise, and the wind eased. SC 7 was then 570 miles west-north-west of the mouth of the North Channel, and just over twenty-four hours from her rendezvous with her local escort. Unfortunately, Dönitz's U-boats were racing neck and neck with the ships of Western Approaches Command. Only the Atlantic would decide who reached the convoy first.

The first intimation SC 7 had of approaching danger came two hours before dawn on 16 October, when frantic distress signals were heard from the *Trevisa*, straggling some 20 miles astern of the convoy.

The *Trevisa*, commanded by Captain Stonehouse, was a victim of her master's eagerness to make up for lost time. Instead of following the route laid down by the convoy conference before sailing from Sydney, Stonehouse had opted for the shortest way home. The *Trevisa* was, therefore, well to the south when Georg-Wilhelm Schulz in U-124 sighted her on the afternoon of 15 October. SC 7, on the other hand, following the prearranged route, was more than 100 miles to the north, heading for the agreed position 60° N 21° W before altering to the south-east for the North Channel. It could be argued that if the *Trevisa* had been to the north where she should have been, U-124 would not have sighted her, and SC 7 might well have slipped past the line of U-boats Dönitz was setting up.

Schulz had attacked after dark, but miscalculating the little ship's speed, his torpedo missed completely. The *Trevisa*, which was carrying her own weight in sawn timber, much of it piled high on her deck, was taking such a hammering from the seas that she was barely able to maintain steerage way. Schulz stayed with her throughout the night, moving into position to attack again at 0350 on 16 October. This time he made no mistake, his torpedo slamming into the *Trevisa's* engine room. Seven of her crew of twenty-one were killed outright, and when the survivors came to abandon ship, they found that both lifeboats had disappeared, blown away by the explosion. At that point it was also realized that Captain Stonehouse was missing. A search of the ship found him in his cabin, calmly fortifying himself with a glass of whisky before leaving his command to her fate. It was fortunate that by this time the weather had moderated, and there being no shortage of timber on board, Stonehouse organized the construction of two rafts. All fourteen survivors were later picked up by the corvette HMS *Bluebell*.

It did not escape the notice of Schulz that such a small and incongruous vessel like the *Trevisa* was highly unlikely to be crossing the Atlantic alone, and he reached the conclusion that she must be a straggler from an eastbound convoy. He reported his suspicions to Lorient. They were immediately passed on to the other U-boats racing in to bar SC 7's entry to the North Channel.

SC 7 had been discovered, but Dönitz needed time to position his wolves. By midnight, a line of seven U-boats lay across the path of the convoy, namely U-38 (Liebe), U-46 (Endrass), U-48 (Bleichrodt), U-99 (Kretchsmer), U-100 (Schepke), U-101 (Frauenheim) and U-123 (Moehle). U-124, homing in on U-93's signals, was racing in at full speed to join them. When complete, this wolf pack would comprise the cream of Hitler's U-boat Arm.

Meanwhile, some help was at hand for SC 7. That afternoon, *Scarborough* was joined by the sloop *Fowey* (Lieutenant Commander Christopher de Lisle Bush) and the Flower-class corvette *Bluebell* (Lieutenant Commander Robert Sherwood), the first of the promised local escort to arrive. The arrival of reinforcements was a boost for the morale of the convoy, but it was most unlikely that the three ships would pose much of a threat to the huge force of U-boats massing. True to form, none of the escorts had worked together before, and they had no coordinated plan of action in case of attack. Commander Dickinson did what he could, stationing *Scarborough* on the port bow, *Fowey* to starboard, and *Bluebell* astern. The distance between each ship averaged 6 miles, their radio link was tenuous and unreliable, and signalling by flag or lamp was a slow and laborious alternative. There was hope, however. The North Channel was drawing ever nearer, it seemed that the enemy might have stayed his hand for too long. Then the unpredictable North Atlantic sprang another unwelcome surprise. The wind dropped to a mere whisper, the clouds dispersed, and by nightfall the convoy, bathed in brilliant moonlight, lay cruelly exposed on a flat calm sea.

At this point U-48 made her sighting. Ordered to join in the operation against SC 7, Bleichrodt had left Lorient on 5 October after a record turnaround of only ten days. Six days after sailing, he ran into another east bound convoy, HX 77, and found himself faced with an embarrassing array of easy targets. The weather at the time was foul, with gale force winds and mountainous seas, and HX 77, somewhat optimistically designated as a fast convoy, was reduced to a crawl.

On the night of 11 October, in the space of just over two hours, and with little real effort, Bleichrodt sank three ships totalling nearly 22,000 tons. They were the Norwegian motor vessel *Brandanger*, the British refrigerated ship *Port Gisborne*, and the Norwegian tanker *Davanger*.

The *Brandanger*, owned by Westfal-Larsen of Bergen, and under the command of Captain Elling Andresen, had loaded 8,000 tons of general cargo in San Pedro, California for Liverpool, joining HX 77 via Bermuda on 3 October. Bleichrodt's torpedo exploded in her engine room causing complete chaos and killing the two engineers on watch. The blast destroyed much of the amidships accommodation, and the lifeboats on the port side were blown away.

Captain Andresen gave the order to lower the starboard boats, but this was an order easier to give than to execute, as the *Brandanger*, now stopped and beam on to the sea and swell, was rolling violently. In lowering the starboard motor boat it smashed against the ship's side, spilling the five-man crew into the sea. Only one man survived.

Two other boats were successfully launched and cleared the ship carrying twenty-one men. Captain Andresen and Carpenter Sigurd Svendsen had remained behind to lower one boat, and were stranded on board when the boat's line parted. They drifted clear on a raft some twenty minutes later when the *Brandanger* went down. They were fortunate in being picked up early next morning by the corvette *Clarkia*, which already had fourteen survivors on board. A second lifeboat, commanded by First Mate Sigurd Sandø, had set course for Ireland. They were found by the British ship *Clan MacDonald* on 16 October when they were 120 miles off the coast. When they were picked up, Sandø reported having met with two other lifeboats, probably British, on the afternoon of 12 October.

The lifeboats seen by the *Brandanger's* boat were probably those of the British ship *Port Gisborne*, Bleichrodt's second victim. She was torpedoed some twenty minutes after the Norwegian ship and, led by Captain Thomas Kippins, her crew abandoned ship in three boats. One of these was reported to have capsized in the rough seas on launching, with twenty-six men being lost. The other two boats endured a long and uncomfortable voyage, before being picked up on 22 and 24 October respectively by the corvette *Salvonia* and the British merchantman *Alpers*.

The Norwegian tanker *Davanger*, also owned by Westfal-Larsen, was Heinrich Bleichrodt's third victim of that stormy night. Leading ship of HX 77's sixth column, the *Davanger* was carrying 10,000 tons of fuel oil for Liverpool loaded four weeks earlier in Curacao.

Bleichrodt again found the vulnerable engine spaces when he torpedoed the *Davanger* and, most unusually for an oil tanker, she sank by the stern within four minutes. Only two lifeboats were launched, and one of these disappeared into the night, never to be seen again. The other boat that successfully cleared the ship had only four men on board. Nine other survivors jumped from the deck of the *Davanger* and eight of these were pulled from the water by this boat. Captain Elliot Karlsen, true to tradition, was last to leave his ship. This gesture cost him his life, for he failed to reach the boat.

Battered by the breaking seas, lashed by the icy rains, the twelve survivors of the loss of the *Davanger*, led by First Mate Kjell Johnsen, fought throughout the night to keep their small craft afloat. When the grey dawn at last came, the wind relented, and by constant bailing they succeeded in emptying their water-logged boat. Later in the morning, with the oars out and a scrap of sail rigged, they also came across two British lifeboats – most likely the same boats seen by the *Brandanger* survivors, and again assumed to be from the *Port Gisborne*.

The boats came alongside each other, and the Norwegians learned that the British intended to wait in the area until they were rescued by searching naval vessels – this being the standard practice recommended by the Admiralty at the time. Kjell Johnsen had no faith in such optimism, and the Norwegian boats carried on to the east. On the morning of 18 October they had the land in sight and early that afternoon, helped by local fishermen, the *Davanger* survivors landed near Broadhaven, County Mayo.

His accidental sighting of HX 77 brought Heinrich Bleichrodt's score since assuming command of U-48 to eleven ships, totalling 59,670 tons. When he saw SC 7, another great fleet of heavily-laden and vulnerable ships steaming eastwards at a snail's pace he was spoiled for choice. He had just four torpedoes left, and SC 7 offered him an opportunity to make them all count. But first he must report the sighting to Lorient.

Dönitz's War Diary for the day reads:

> 1710   Towards 0300 U 48 made contact with an inward bound convoy in square AL 3380 (25 ships, 3 gun boats).
> The order was given: Attack the convoy reported by U 48. This order could not be carried out by: U 38, 93 because of enemy action elsewhere (A little before sunset on the 16th, Claus Korth in U-93 had sighted a large west bound convoy and was giving chase).

At last the true position of SC 7 had been discovered, and now Dönitz needed time to bring in the other members of the pack. By

Deck cargo of timber being loaded in the Canadian port. *(The Ace, Montreal)*

Convoy assembling in Bedford Basin, Halifax, Nova Scotia. *(Manitoba Library Association)*

A typical British cargo ship of the 1940s. *(Clan Line)*

Armed Merchant Cruiser HMS *Forfar* anchored off Funchal, Madeira in her pre-war cruising days. *(Marcel Gommers)*

A four-stacker Town-class destroyer, ex-US Navy. *(Vallejo Naval Historical Museum)*

Flower-class corvette. *(Navy Photos)*

The Wolf Packs Gather. *(Walter Friebolin)*

A torpedoed Norwegian freighter takes her last dive. *(Salvdos Jorge)*

Death Blow. Very few ships survived a direct hit on the engine-room. *(Collier's Photographic History)*

Survivors on a liferaft come alongside a Navy ship. *(Source unknown)*

U-boat approaches a boatload of survivors. *(Bundesarchiv)*

HMS *Sturdy* ended up on the rocks off Tiree. *(An Tinsdeach)*

Bloody Foreland, County Donegal. *(Tourism Ireland)*

A warm welcome on return from a North Atlantic patrol. *(Kramer, Bundesarchiv)*

Joachim Schepke. One of Dönitz's top 'aces'. *(Charles McCain)*

The Author. Second Officer/Navigator with the Scottish Navy. *(The Author)*

midnight, a line of seven U-boats lay across the path of SC 7, namely U-38 (Liebe), U-46 (Endrass), U-48 (Bleichrodt), U-99 (Kretchsmer), U-100 (Schepke), U-101 (Frauenheim) and U-123 (Moehle). U-124, homing in on U-48's signals, was racing in at full speed to join them. When complete, the wolf pack would comprise the cream of Hitler's U-boat Arm.

Bleichrodt curbed his impatience for another three hours, following closely behind the convoy, keeping a close eye on the movements of the corvette *Bluebell*, which was zig-zagging astern of the rear ships. Then, with dawn less than an hour away he could stay his hand no longer and, trimmed right down to offer the smallest possible silhouette, he slipped past *Bluebell*, and entered the convoy between Columns One and Two. He was immediately presented with a target hard to miss.

Keeping station as third ship of SC 7's second column from port, revealed for all to see by the bright light of the moon, was by far the largest and most vulnerable ship in the convoy. She was the 9,512-ton motor tanker *Languedoc*. Built in Copenhagen in 1937 for Societe Francaise de Transports Petroliers, the *Languedoc* was seized by the Royal Navy after the fall of France and taken into service by the Ministry of War Transport. Managed by John L. Jacobs of London, she carried a British crew commanded by Captain John Thomson. On this, her first voyage under the Red Ensign, she was carrying 13,700 tons of fuel oil to the Clyde for the Admiralty.

There were other ships visible ahead and on each side of the tanker, and using the *Languedoc* as his central aiming point, Bleichrodt fired a spread of three torpedoes from his bow tubes.

Bleichrodt's first torpedo caught the *Languedoc* in her engine room, exploding with a dull roar and throwing up a tall column of water and flame. She immediately began to settle by the stern. Miraculously, none of the tanker's crew of thirty-nine were hurt.

The second torpedo of Bleichrodt's fan sped on past the crippled *Languedoc* to hit the lead ship of Column Four, the Whitby-registered steamer *Scoresby* of 3,843 tons gross. Owned by Hedlam & Sons, commanded by Captain Lawrence Weatherill, and manned by a total crew of thirty-nine, the *Scoresby* was carrying a cargo of pit props for Sunderland. She had been appointed as vice commodore for the convoy, which, in effect, meant that in the event of the *Assyrian* going down, Captain Weatherill would take operational control of SC 7. The opportunity never came Weatherill's way. In spite of her pit prop cargo, the *Scoresby* sank soon after being torpedoed. Again, there were no casualties. Bleichrodt claimed that his third torpedo hit and sank another merchantman, but he was mistaken. The torpedo missed completely, and disappeared into the night.

This sudden and completely unexpected attack a few hours before dawn seemed to leave the convoy stunned, and several minutes elapsed before the first rocket, probably from one of the torpedoed ships, went screaming skywards. Others followed as the alarm spread amongst the startled merchantmen. The escorts then added to the illuminations with starshell, and night was turned into day, but Bleichrodt was already hiding in the depths.

In an effort to sheer away from the danger, Commodore Mackinnon ordered an emergency turn of 45 degrees to starboard, but this only added to the confusion, and allowed U-48 to slip clear of the convoy undetected. The rearguard escort, HMS *Bluebell* was fully occupied in picking up survivors from the torpedoed ships and, although *Scarborough* came racing back firing starshell, without Asdics she was unable to track the submerged U-boat.

As soon as U-48 was clear of the convoy and hidden in the darkness, Bleichrodt brought her back to the surface and made off at 17½ knots. *Scarborough* sighted her, and it was now that Commander Dickinson made a miscalculation that was to cost the convoy dear. Consumed by frustration, he chased after the fleeing U-boat, but this was no more than a futile gesture. U-48, on the surface, was more than 3 knots faster than *Scarborough*, and the sloop was soon left behind.

Now should have been the time for Commander Dickinson to abandon the chase and return to protect the convoy. Unfortunately, he stubbornly persisted in searching for the enemy throughout that day. The U-boat was once briefly sighted but, again, using her superior speed, escaped unscathed. Meanwhile, *Scarborough* had fallen many miles behind the convoy, so far behind that she was never able to rejoin her charges. *Bluebell* was fully occupied picking up survivors from the *Languedoc* and *Scoresby,* and out of touch with the convoy, which left the defence of SC 7 totally in the hands of the sloop *Fowey.* It was just as well that none of the other U-boats in the pack had yet made contact.

Languedoc was still afloat, and there was a possibility that she might be brought into the Clyde under tow, but a boarding party from *Bluebell* established that, despite her large and valuable cargo, she was beyond saving. Lieutenant Commander Sherwood made the decision to sink the crippled tanker by gunfire, a procedure that required some considerable time and a great deal of ammunition.

U-48 by this time was well out of sight of the convoy to the west, but she still had one torpedo left, and Heinrich Bleichrodt was loath to carry this home. He decided to attempt another attack but, as he altered course to return, a Sunderland of RAF Coastal Command dropped out of the sun and swooped down on the surfaced submarine.

U-48's alert lookouts saved her, and Bleichrodt took her down in a record-breaking crash dive with the Sunderland's depth charges exploding all around her as she sank out of sight. Lights failed, gauge glasses shattered, and water spurted out through strained hatch seals, but Bleichrodt's'guardian angel was still with him, and there was no serious damage. Wisely, Bleichrodt took U-48 deep, and stayed there until the danger was past. When he surfaced again, SC 7 was out of sight, and he was unable to regain contact.

For a while it seemed that Commodore Mackinnon's decision to press far to the north might have paid off. Blessed with fine weather and good visibility, the convoy was making excellent progress towards the North Channel, and by mid morning was 90 miles due north of Rockall and steering south-east at 8 knots. Another 24 hours would see them in safe waters. Then Heinrich Liebe in U-38 sighted the persistent pall of smoke that continued to advertise the convoy's presence.

Liebe, who had sailed from Lorient three weeks earlier, had scored a significant victory on 1 October by sinking Royal Mail's 14,172-ton *Highland Patriot*, homeward bound with a cargo of refrigerated meat from Argentina, but had since seen nothing but an empty horizon.

Racing to investigate the smoke cloud, Liebe came across the 3,554-ton Greek steamer *Aenos*. The 30-year-old tramp, burdened by 6,275 tons of wheat for Manchester, was straggling well astern and out of sight of the rear ships of SC 7, offering a target that would be hard to miss. Liebe submerged and approached at periscope depth, but in his eagerness to make up for all those lost days spent searching an empty ocean he miscalculated, and his torpedo went wide.

Unwilling to risk another torpedo, Liebe surfaced and opened fire on the *Aenos* with his deck gun. There was no resistance from the Greek ship, and she was soon on fire and sinking. Four of her crew died in the attack, the others took to the boats, and were picked up later by the

Canadian lakes steamer *Eaglescliffe Hall*, which was still struggling to catch up with SC 7. This, fortunately for her, she never did, arriving safely in the Clyde the next day, having completed most of the Atlantic crossing on her own. It had been reported that at the Convoy Conference before sailing from Sydney some naval officers had complained about the 'bloody minded skippers' who considered they would be better off on their own. In the case of the *Eaglescliffe Hall* they had been proven right.

Chapter 8

Rout by Moonlight

W hen word reached London that SC 7 was under attack, it was agreed that the convoy's meagre escort force must be reinforced without delay. Ideally, the situation called for destroyers, but all the Admiralty could come up with was a sloop and a corvette. Already at sea were the Grimsby-class sloop HMS *Leith* and the Flower-class corvette HMS *Heartsease*, both lightly armed and with a top speed of 16 knots. In command of *Leith* was Commander Roland Allen, RN, while *Heartsease* was under the command of Lieutenant Commander Edward North, RNR. Both commanders were experienced in North Atlantic convoy work, but on this occasion neither was fully aware of the situation with SC 7. Commander Allen, who had orders to take over as Senior Officer Escort of SC 7, wrote in his log:

Friday 18 October.

0115: In Company with Heartsease. Course 129° speed 14, sighted SC 7 ahead in position 58° 50' N 14° 12' W. Wind SE force 2, moon behind cloud, visibility good, sea calm.

0134: Red light observed in direction of convoy.

0138: An unknown ship astern of convoy signalled he was hit on the port side.

The arrival of *Leith* and *Heartsease* had coincided with U-38's attack on the main body of the convoy. Having set the straggler *Aenos* on fire and left her in a sinking condition, Heinrich Liebe had set off in pursuit of the convoy, finally coming up on the rear ships late that night. Making a cautious approach on the surface, he moved up on the port side of Column One until he was abreast of the high-sided timber carrier *Carsbreck*. The 3,670-ton, Glasgow-registered, *Carsbreck*, bound for

Grimsby with her holds tight-packed and her decks piled high with Canadian timber, a ship as difficult to sink as a barrel of cork, as Liebe soon discovered. At 0204 he fired two torpedoes, only one of which hit the *Carsbreck*, striking her amidships on the port side.

Predictably, the *Carsbreck*, much to Liebe's annoyance, showed no sign of sinking. He watched and waited for another twenty minutes, then fired another torpedo. This missed its target, and the *Carsbreck* sailed serenely on. Disillusioned, Liebe withdrew from SC 7 and turned westward looking for fresh pastures.

Although Heinrich Liebe had not succeeded in sinking the *Carsbreck*, he left his mark on SC 7. At daybreak, Commander Allen, who had taken over as SOE, reviewed the situation, and as the *Carsbreck* was still afloat, able to steam at 6 knots, and eminently salvageable, ordered *Heartsease* to escort her into the Clyde. Allen's judgement proved sound, for after repairs the *Carsbreck* was back at sea within two months. However, in saving the damaged ship SC 7 had been robbed of a quarter of its effective escort force. This was to have very serious consequences in the hours to come.

Commander Allen rearranged his remaining ships which, with *Scarborough* still missing, consisted of his own command, *Leith*, the sloop *Fowey*, and the corvette *Bluebell*. He stationed *Bluebell* on the port beam, from which direction Allen judged the attack was most likely to come, while *Fowey* swept astern of the convoy. *Leith* continued to zig-zag ahead of the convoy, and later in the day she sighted two rafts containing nineteen survivors from the Estonian ship *Nora*.

The *Nora*, thirty-eight years old and just 1,186 tons gross, had been crossing the Atlantic alone with a cargo of timber for Belfast, when in the early hours of 13 October she had been sighted and stalked by Viktor Schütze in U-103. Schütze missed with two torpedoes, finally scoring a hit with his third, which blew a hole in the *Nora's* side and sent her timber deck cargo, along with both her lifeboats, soaring high in the air. Some of the heavy baulks of timber crashed into the sea around U-103, and she narrowly escaped damage. With that, Schütze decided to look for new pastures, and left the *Nora* to her fate. Both the Estonian's lifeboats had been destroyed by U-103's torpedo, and her survivors escaped on two makeshift liferafts, which were then sighted by HMS *Leith* after five days.

After torpedoing the *Carsbreck*, Heinrich Liebe had reported to

Lorient and all U-boats within range, giving the position of the convoy as 90 miles north-west of Rockall and steering a south-easterly course for the North Channel. Now was the time for Dönitz to strike in force, and he began by ordering U-46, U-99, U-100, U101 and U-123 to set up a patrol line close south-east of Rockall, and directly in SC 7's path.

Otto Kretchsmer in U-99 was last to join the patrol line. An entry in his War Diary reads:

> 1745: Wind southeast, force 3; sea 3; moderate cloud. U-101, which is two or three miles north, signals by searchlight: 'Enemy sighted to port.'
>
> 1749: A warship is sighted bearing 030°, steering east. Soon afterwards, smoke to the left of her. Finally the convoy. While hauling ahead to attack, we sight steamship in the southeast, apparently on a westerly course.

Kretchsmer began stalking the lone merchantman, which appeared to be romping ahead of the convoy. Another two hours elapsed before he was in a favourable position to attack. His War Diary reads:

> 1928: Submerge for attack.
>
> 1950: Surface, as ship is making off slowly to the east. Haul further ahead: at 2000 pass within a few hundred metres of a U-boat on the surface, apparently U-101 again.
>
> 2024: Another U-boat has torpedoed the ship. Shortly afterwards exchange signals with U-123.

The object of the unwanted attentions of the three U-boats was Christian Salvesen's 5,458-ton *Shekatika*. Kretchsmer classed her as a 'romper', and having originally been the rearmost ship of SC 7's Column Eight, she was very far off her station, but this may have been deliberate. The *Shekatika*, built in 1936 at the Caledon yard in Dundee, was a comparatively new ship with a fair turn of speed, and it is possible that her master, Captain Robert Paterson, had decided to leave the convoy and make a dash for the North Channel alone.

Karl-Heinz Moehle's torpedo caught the *Shekatika* amidships, sending up a tall column of water and slowing her down to a crawl. Seven minutes later, Moehle fired what he thought would be a *coup de grâce.* The torpedo went home, but to his consternation and annoyance, the British ship remained stubbornly afloat and upright.

When the *Shekatika* loaded in the Gulf Of St Lawrence, she had achieved a rare balance, full deadweight, full cubic, and full deck cargo – every shipowner's dream of perfection. Distributed in the bottom of her holds she had 2,000 tons of steel ingots, which gave her maximum stability, and on top of that 6,000 tons of wooden pit props, which filled every remaining cubic foot of her holds, and spilled onto her decks stacked 12 feet high. This ship was virtually unsinkable, and U-123's torpedoes did little to change that state.

Annoyed at having his intended prey snatched from under his nose, Otto Kretchsmer stood by in sight of U-123, and watched as Captain Paterson and his crew abandoned ship. When the survivors were clear, Moehle, by this time more than a little frustrated, used a third torpedo on the *Shekitika*. As with the others, much of the shock of this was absorbed by her cargo of pit props and, although she seemed lower in the water, she showed no obvious signs of sinking. Both Kretchsmer and Moehle now decided to look around for more likely victims, leaving the abandoned *Shekatika* to her fate.

Dönitz's grey wolves were now gathering in force, among them U-46, with Oberleutnant Englebert Endrass in command. An ex-merchant seaman, Endrass had been Günther Prien's First Watch Officer in U-47 when Prien wrote a new page in the history books by penetrating Scapa Flow to sink the battleship *Royal Oak*. This earned Endrass an early command, and he made two highly successful voyages in U-46, sinking ten ships totalling 62,000 tons, including two British armed merchant cruisers. Now, with the ribbon of the Knights Cross at his throat he was back in the thick of the action.

U-46 also approached SC 7 from the north, and shortly after 2100 was abreast the leading ships on the port side of the convoy. In the brilliant light of the moon Oberleutnant Endrass was presented with a solid mass of slow moving shipping; targets he could not fail to hit. Almost carelessly, he fired a fan of four torpedoes from his bow tubes, and waited to see what mayhem they might cause.

Aboard the Cardiff steamer *Beatus*, port outrider of SC 7 leading Column One, Assistant Steward Frank Holding had finished work for the day, and was taking a breather on deck. Years later he wrote, 'That night I went to look over the side, there was a big white patch going from the side of the ship right out to the horizon. Moon on water, and you're thinking "someone's out there". You took your lifejacket around with you all the time, on deck or wherever you were going.'

The 4,885-ton *Beatus* had a similar load to that of the ill-fated *Shekatika*, with steel ingots below and timber above and stacked on deck. Silhouetted in the light of the moon, she was an easy target for anyone with a torpedo to hand. Nevertheless, Endrass's first torpedo missed her, skimming across within feet of her bows to find a home in the second ship of Column Two.

Ironically, the unfortunate recipient of U–46's torpedo was one of the two neutral ships sailing in SC 7, the small Swedish steamer *Convallaria*. Loaded with 2,000 tons of pulpwood from Newfoundland, she stayed afloat just long enough for her crew to take to the boats.

Aboard the *Beatus*, Frank Holding, roused from his contemplation of the moon on the water by the boom of the explosion as the *Convallaria* was hit, looked up in time to see the little ship on fire and listing. Reminiscing, he wrote, 'I went back to my cabin and I said to my mates. "We'd better keep ourselves handy here". The next thing I heard was this explosion and a sound like breaking glass coming from the engine room. The ship stood still.'

On the bridge of the *Beatus*, Captain William Brett had sighted the attacking U-boat off his port bow, and had instructed his radio officer to send out an SSS message. But as the ship's radio hummed into life, Endrass's torpedo struck the *Beatus* amidships. The sea poured into her engine room, all her lights went out, and she slowly lost way through the water. An inspection of the damage satisfied Captain Brett that the ship would not stay afloat for long, and he ordered his crew to take to the boats.

The *Beatus* carried two lifeboats, easily capable of accommodating her crew of thirty-seven, and as she was settling on an even keel, with the sea a flat oily calm, the evacuation should have presented no problems. However, in common with many coal burners of her day, the Welsh ship carried a large Indian engine room crew. These men panicked and attempted to lower one of the boats in a hurry. Disaster struck when they mistakenly cut through the rope falls, and the boat up-ended and crashed into the sea. It was so badly damaged as to be totally unseaworthy, leaving the *Beatus's* crew with just one lifeboat and a small jolly boat. Frank Holding commented, 'We knew we were sinking. While we were standing on deck by the funnel, all this wet ash came down over us, the sea was in the engine room.'

When both boats were in the water and ready to cast off, it was discovered that one Indian fireman was missing. Captain Brett and the DEMS gunlayer carried out a search of the accommodation, and eventually found the man hiding at the top of the engine room. He was paralysed by fear and it took a great deal of persuasion by Brett and the gunner to get him into the boat.

The slaughter was now beginning in earnest. U–46 and U–123 had been joined by U–101 and Fritz Frauenheim, approaching the disorganized convoy on its starboard side, wasted no time in joining the fray. He was immediately presented with an easy shot.

Clinging tenaciously to the outskirts of the convoy, the 3,917-ton London tramp *Creekirk,* sagging under 5,900 tons of iron ore, was steaming hard, but barely making way through the water. Choosing his moment, Frauenheim closed in on the unfortunate ship, and despatched her with a single torpedo. The explosion broke the 28-year-old *Creekirk's* back, and in a matter of seconds she was gone, taking Captain Elie Robillard and his crew of thirty-five with her.

After the waves had closed over the *Creekirk,* SC 7 enjoyed a brief respite, during which Commodore Mackinnon tried in vain to impose some sort of order on his charges. Then, just after 2200, U–99 joined in the action.

With characteristic verve Otto Kretschmer penetrated the ranks of SC 7, entering from the rear and weaving in and out of the columns of ships looking for the plumpest target for his torpedoes. He finally settled on the leading ship of Column Eight the 6,055-ton *Empire Miniver.*

The *Empire Miniver,* another survivor of the First World War, had begun life as the *West Cobalt,* built in Portland, Oregon for the United States Shipping Board. In the inter-war years she had sailed for Lykes Lines of New Orleans, being sold to the Ministry of War Transport in 1940. Managed by Andrew Weir's Bank Line of London, and commanded by Captain Robert Smith, she was on her first voyage under the Red Ensign, loaded with 4,500 tons of pig iron and 6,200 tons of steel.

When the attack began, Captain Smith, having in mind the huge deadweight of cargo he was carrying, had already decided to leave the convoy and try to escape alone under the cover of darkness. Unfortunately, he had left it too late. Kretschmer's torpedo exploded with a resounding bang and a flash, all the lights went out, the *Empire Miniver* slowed to a halt, and she lay drifting helpless in the water. A quick inspection of the damage showed that all the wooden hatch covers had been blown off, and the holds were rapidly filling with water.

In the scramble to abandon their doomed ship, three of the crew of the *Empire Miniver* lost their lives, while Captain Smith and thirty-four others were taken on board HMS *Bluebell,* joining all the other survivors crowding the corvette's decks.

On the bridge of the Commodore's ship *Assyrian,* leading the convoy at the head of Column Five, Captain Reginald Kearon had been a witness to Kretchsmer's bold penetration of the convoy. He wrote in his report to the Admiralty:

> . . . I saw a torpedo approaching quite fast from the port quarter, it crossed my stem, missing us by about a foot, and this caught the *Empire Miniver* who was away ahead out of station, being the leading ship of the 8th column.
>
> We looked around for H.M.S. LEITH which had been zigzagging across our stern. We could not see her. A little later I saw what I thought were flares descending from the sky, they were being fired from abeam of the convoy. I saw the flash of a gun and afterwards discovered the flares were being fired by H.M.S. LEITH. Some more ships, the names of which I could not distinguish, were torpedoed on our port side. We now made several turns, 40° to starboard, then another 40° to starboard, waited a while and then returned, 40° to port, then a further 40° to port, bringing us back on our course. While we were making these turns there were no more torpedoings. We proceeded at a speed of 9 knots.

While Commodore Mackinnon was taking this frantic evasive action Englebert Endrass, who had been away reloading his torpedo tubes, brought U-46 back into the action. His target was the 1,572-ton Swedish steamer *Gunborg,* bound for Glasgow with a cargo of pulpwood on board. One well-aimed torpedo was sufficient to put an end to her voyage. She remained afloat long enough for her crew to take to the boats.

Another witness to this wholesale slaughter of helpless merchantmen was 54-year-old Captain James Walker, commanding the 4,155-ton *Blairspey.* Vice Commodore ship of SC 7, and leading Column Three, the Glasgow-registered steamer was carrying 5,400 tons of Canadian timber consigned to Grangemouth, in the Firth of Forth. Captain

Walker wrote in his report of the voyage:

> We were making emergency turns the whole time, following the Commodore. About 10 p.m. a torpedo just missed us coming again from astern on the starboard side. The BOTUSK gave us the warning as the torpedo passed on her port side and on my starboard side.
>
> At 10.30 p.m. when in position 57° 55' N 11° 10'W, about 200 miles from land we were struck by a torpedo on the port side in way of No.1 hold about 50-60ft from the bow. There was not a very loud explosion – just a dull thud – and at first I did not realize that we had been torpedoed. There was a large column of water thrown up on the bridge, but there was no flame, smoke or smell. The ship gave a slight stagger and took a small list to port and then straightened up. In the meantime a joint blew out in the engine room and the engine room became full of steam and the ship stopped. An escort ship came and circled round, inquiring our name and what had happened. We informed the escort that we would try to get the BLAIRSPEY to Loch Swilly, but the commander of the escort ship suggested the Clyde.
>
> Later this escort ship returned with another escort vessel and asked us where the convoy was. I said that the convoy had gone to the east.
>
> About this time there were quite a number of flares going up and it looked like moonlight. I think these flares came from the submarines. The two escort ships went off and we never saw them again.

The two escorts sighted by Walker were most likely *Leith* and *Bluebell*. In his report to the Flag Officer in charge, Commander Allen gives some idea of the confusion reigning:

> 20:20 – A ship torpedoed on port side of the convoy in position 57 22N 11 11W. Altered course 120° to port, and increased to full speed firing star shell. Proceeded 10' and then turned towards the convoy.
>
> 21:30 – Sighted *Fowey* who had been 5' astern of the convoy when attack took place. Stationed *Fowey* abeam 3,000 yards and searched up wake of convoy at 14 knots.

22:05 – Sighted two horizontal red lights then some miles ahead. They burnt for about 15 seconds. Heard explosion ahead.

22:10 – Heard explosion ahead.

22:20 – Heard explosion ahead. Increased to 15 knots and sighted several ships.

22:37 – Heard two explosions ahead.

22:40 – Sighted a "U" boat on surface straight ahead steaming fast on the same course. Distance 3000–4000 yards. Opened fire with star shell. The "U" boat and her wake were clearly visible but not sufficiently for the Gunlayer of "A" gun to get his sights on before she submerged a few minutes later. Contact by echo was obtained at about 3000 yards range and was held on the run in up to 800 yards.

22:55 – Contact was then lost. Meantime *Bluebell* who was in the vicinity had been ordered to join the hunt, which continued until 23:55. About the time the "U" boat was sighted a sheet of flame was seen on the starboard bow. It was assumed to be a tanker exploding.

Commander Allen remarked on the confusion:

With regard to the series of attacks that commenced at 20:20/18 events moved so rapidly and over such a large area that the report must only be a portion of this unfortunate night's action. The reports of *Fowey* and *Bluebell* will no doubt complete the picture. I am however convinced that the convoy was the victim of a well organized attack.

How well organized the attack on SC 7 was Commander Allen was yet to realize. In fact, no fewer that six U-boats were involved, causing such confusion that the frightened merchant ships were already scattering, most intent on making a dash for safety. In view of the fact that the escorts appeared to have deserted them and were away chasing shadows in the darkness, it was not surprising that the merchant captains preferred to go it alone. Commander Allen later admitted that his actions may have been hasty. In his report to the Admiralty he wrote:

It is noteworthy that at 20:20 only one ship was struck. This ship was on the up-moon side. It was an unfortunate coincidence that at that moment *Leith* happened to be at the extreme starboard limit of her station ahead and that *Fowey* was away searching astern.

Further, when *Leith* and *Fowey* had been drawn away they never again caught up with the convoy in spite of every effort.

In amongst the madhouse that had once been a tightly organized convoy, Otto Kretchsmer had another helpless victim in his sights. The 3,854-ton Greek-flag *Niritos*, worn out by thirty-three years hard steaming in the cross trades and sagging under a full cargo of sulphur, was making a gallant, but futile, effort to escape the slaughter. In the brilliant moonlight she presented an easy target, but although Kretchsmer approached within 700 yards of her, his first torpedo missed, but four minutes later he fired again, this time scoring a hit on the *Niritos* forward of her bridge. Her volatile cargo of sulphur went up in a sheet of flame, and she disappeared from sight in less than half a minute.

Far astern of the other ships the abandoned *Shekatika,* cruelly savaged by three torpedoes from U-123, stubbornly remained afloat. She was drifting aimlessly in the full light of the moon when Joachim Schepke, anxious to join in the rout of SC 7, found her. Schepke moved in close before firing a single torpedo, which went home in the hull of the doomed ship with a resounding thud, but again the *Shekatika* refused to surrender to the deep. Disgusted, Schepke left her to her fate and hurried towards the sound of the guns far ahead.

Meanwhile, U-99, having blasted the *Niritos* into oblivion, was sighted by the Commodore's ship, Ellerman & Papayanni's 2,962-ton *Assyrian*. Under Commodore Mackinnon's guidance the *Assyrian* had just completed leading what remained of the convoy through a series of wide sweeps to port and starboard alternately. Captain Kearon wrote in his report to he Admiralty:

At about 2100 on the 18th I noticed a submarine 4 points on my port bow, 200 yards distant. I altered course and increased my speed to intercept and ram him, but the submarine took evasive action, altering ahead of me, afterwards adopting the course the convoy was steering at the moment, which was approximately 150°. (We had altered course at 2000 that night). I chased the enemy for 7 minutes and worked my speed up to 10 knots. We could plainly see his periscope and the track it made, and it is my opinion that during those 7 minutes the submarine definitely made a good 10 knots during which time he was submerged. At the end of the 7 minutes we saw the conning tower rise out of the water, and smelt the exhaust fumes when he started up his diesel engines. When he surfaced his position was dead ahead of me, about 400 yards away. Once he had surfaced he rapidly drew away, but we were sending out wireless signals that we had him ahead and were keeping him ahead, so that the escort could come up and attack. He altered course gradually round to starboard, we followed, eventually losing him on the starboard quarter of the convoy. At that time we were heading 270°. We turned away and fired a shot to indicate his approximate position.

Otto Kretchsmer's account of the incident is less forthcoming:

Boat is soon sighted by a ship which fires a white star and turns towards us at full speed, continuing even after we alter course. I have to make off with engines all out. Eventually the ship turns off, fires one of her guns and again takes her place in the convoy. I now attack the right flank of the last formation but one.

In all, the *Assyrian's* pursuit of U-99 lasted some forty minutes, during which Captain Kearon attempted to vector in the escorts on the U-boat, but his calls for help went unanswered. *Scarborough* and *Heartsease* were still absent, while *Fowey* was 4 miles astern of the convoy and *Bluebell*, with more than 100 survivors already on board, was still busy plucking unfortunate victims of U-boat torpedoes from the sea. HMS *Leith* was also somewhere astern attempting to ward off an elusive enemy. If the Admiralty had not been so keen to implement the terms of the Geneva Convention to the letter, and the *Assyrian* had been allowed a gun mounted forward, the careers of Otto Kretchsmer and U-99 might have been brought to a sudden end.

Amongst the pathetic wreckage strewn in the convoy's wake was the abandoned Cardiff steamer *Beatus*. She took some 40 minutes to go down, and while she was inching her way below the surface, the Dutch timber carrier *Boekelo*, unofficial rescue ship of SC 7, sighted her two lifeboats. Captain Jan de Groot, rather unwisely under the circumstances, slowed down and then stopped engines ready to take the survivors on board. De Groot later reported:

I told my officers that being the rescue ship, although we stood a good chance of being torpedoed ourselves, we had to stand by to pick up the survivors. We stopped the ship and after about 20 minutes one of the lifeboats of the *Beatus* reached the side of the vessel and the other one could be seen approaching.

We were in position 200 miles west of Ireland, visibility was very good and the sea smooth. We had just managed to take the mess boy from the *Beatus* on board when we were torpedoed on the port side by No.4 hold. The explosion was not exceptionally loud but seemed like a dull boom. There was a big sheet of flame as high as the mast, volumes of smoke, but no water. There was a great deal of debris, all the planks and rafts having been blown high into the air. The vessel took an immediate list to port and the after rail was soon level with the water.

I knew it would not take long for the vessel to sink, and so I ordered the lifeboats to be launched and, as everyone had already prior to the explosion been mustered amidships to assist the survivors of the *Beatus*'s crew, they were able to get away . . .

While engaged on her mission of mercy the *Boekelo* had fallen victim to Joachim Schepke in U-100. The Dutchman's cargo of timber kept her afloat, but her engine room was soon awash, and unless she was taken in tow, which was very unlikely, she had come to the end of her voyaging.

For Captain Ebenezer Williams, surveying the carnage erupting around him, a long dreamed nightmare was coming true. Some four weeks earlier, in the port of Three Rivers on the St Lawrence estuary, when the two Cardiff tramps *Beatus* and *Fiscus* were loading at adjacent wharves, Williams had confided to his fellow Welshman Captain Brett that he had a strong premonition that the coming voyage would be his last. Both ships were loading 5-ton steel ingots, but whereas the *Beatus* would load timber on top giving her ample reserve buoyancy, the *Fiscus* would carry only steel below decks, with a number of crated aircraft on deck. In the words of one of her crew members she was 'a floating brick', her lifespan measured in seconds should an enemy torpedo find her. Ebenezer Williams, who had survived the trauma of the First World War, had good reason to fear that he would never see his home on the island of Anglesey again.

In complete contrast to their captain's pessimistic outlook, to Ken and Ray Lewis, two brothers aged 14 and 15 respectively serving in the *Fiscus*, the coming Atlantic voyage presented a challenge they looked forward to with the supreme confidence of the young. In reality, their place was in the classroom ashore, and not in the midst of this cruel and bloody war. Yet so eager were they to get away to sea that they are believed to have forged a letter from their father giving his permission for them to join the ship in Cardiff. They would pay the ultimate price for their youthful enthusiasm.

When he saw the explosion that destroyed the *Boekelo*, Captain Ebenezer Williams, like others in the convoy, decided the time had come to take matters into his own hands and escape from this dreadful catastrophe overtaking the convoy. The *Fiscus* was surging forward at 10 knots when Otto Kretchsmer blew her out of the water.

Forty-eight-year-old Ebenezer Williams' premonition had come true. He died with his ship, as did the young Lewis brothers and thirty-five of the *Fiscus'* crew. Only one man survived to tell the story of the last minutes of the Welsh ship. He was Ordinary Seaman Edward King, who later testified before the Admiralty in Cardiff:

> . . . Deponent was lying dozing in his bunk when a violent explosion occurred and the ship took a heavy list to starboard. One packing case was lying alongside No.2 hatch. It was not lashed to the deck. Deponent got on to the packing case, when the sea washed him into No.2 hold, the hatches of which had been blown off by the explosion. Evidently, the torpedo had struck No.2 hold, starboard side, blowing off beams and hatch covers. The hold was full of water. Deponent sank and rose to the surface when he grabbed the rope lashing around the packing case. The case floated away, the fore deck of the ship being by this time under water. The packing case swept clear of the ship and when the deponent looked around the ship had disappeared, and the sea was a mass of wreckage. In deponent's opinion vessel sank within a minute of the explosion. After about two hours on the packing case deponent sighted three Indian firemen clinging to the ice box about 20 yards away. He called to them and helped them on to the packing case. They died from exposure the next morning. Deponent did not see any other members of the crew. He remained on the packing case until picked up on 21/10/40 by a lifeboat full of survivors . . . The boats of the *Fiscus* were swung out ready for launching. One raft was in the starboard fore rigging and two others aft in main rigging, one on each side. Master had given strict orders on 17/10/40 that every man was to wear his lifesaving waistcoat continuously and deponent knows that all deck personnel wore them accordingly.

Chapter 9

Running the Gauntlet

It would be too indulgent to speculate that the little *Assyrian's* aggressive pursuit of U-99 caused the attacking U-boats to pull back. It is far more likely that they withdrew to reload their tubes. Whatever the reason, for the next hour, as midnight passed and a new day arrived, a strange calm descended on SC 7. This provided a heaven-sent opportunity for Commander Allen's escorts to restore some semblance of order to the shattered convoy. In the space of less than four hours of this dreadful night the U-boats had torpedoed ten ships. Some were still afloat, others loaded down to their marks with heavy steel cargoes had disappeared from sight in seconds taking their men with them. There can be no doubt that, on this occasion at least, Donitz's *Rudeltaktik* was proving to be a resounding success

The lull in the attack also provided a much-needed opportunity to rescue survivors from the multitude of lifeboats and rafts littering the sea astern. This was left to Lieutenant Geoffrey Walker in the corvette *Bluebell,* who achieved a small miracle and ended up with almost 200 wet, cold and shocked survivors crammed into her tiny accommodation and on deck. It was time for *Bluebell* to go home.

In giving chase to U-99 Captain Reg Kearon had given some expression to the angry frustration he felt at being powerless to hit back at the ruthless enemy intent on destroying the convoy. But his gallant action had taken the *Assyrian* some miles ahead of the other ships. She was now out of reach of the few escorts defending SC 7, and dangerously exposed. Kearon reduced speed, and began to fall back on the other ships.

The moon was now well up, clearly revealing the ragged lines of merchantmen in its silvery light. On the advice of Commodore Mackinnon, Kearon burned a smoke float on the *Assyrian's* after deck which for a while blurred the outlines of the ships.

The uneasy peace that had descended on SC 7 lasted for almost an hour, during which the merchantmen had time to put their ships in order. But the U-boats were still out there in the darkness, reloading their torpedo tubes and positioning themselves for another onslaught. U-99 was still ahead, and Kretschmer had been joined by Fritz Frauenheim in U-101.

Frauenheim, who had already torpedoed the *Blairspey* and the *Creekirk*, had worked his way around ahead of the convoy, and was now lying in wait for the opportunity to increase his mounting score of Allied ships. When he saw the *Assyrian* approaching, and some way behind her the leading ships of SC 7, Frauenheim grasped the opportunity for a multiple strike. Lining up his sights on the shadowy outline of the *Assyrian,* he fired a spread of three from his bow tubes, then reversed course under full helm and fired his stern tube in the same direction.

Standing side by side on the bridge of the *Assyrian*, Captain Kearon and Commodore Mackinnon watched in horror as two of U-101's torpedoes swept by the ship, one passing close ahead of the bow, the other crossing the stern. There was no time to take avoiding action before Frauenheim's third torpedo found its mark. Kearon wrote in his report:

> . . . I saw another torpedo coming towards us which hit us in the stokehold, 166 feet from the bow. There was only one explosion, which was a dull report, the ship was lifted but no water was thrown up as far as I know; the Chief Engineer said the water came up through his cabin floor, his room being at the after end of the engine room, 40-50 feet further aft than where we were hit. There was no flame or smell, but a good deal of smoke. The top sides of the ship on the starboard side were opened up right to the boat deck, there was quite a large hole, and the decks were broken so that we could not use the starboard side of the deck at all.
>
> Up to this time, including the ones I have already mentioned, I had had 4 torpedoes fired at me, 3 missed their mark....

The fourth torpedo seen by Kearon, and fired from U101's stern tube, went on to hit the Dutch steamer *Soesterberg,* which was leading Column No. Three. The 1904-ton *Soesterberg,* carrying a cargo of pit props from New Brunswick, was stopped in her tracks, the explosion of the torpedo blowing four men overboard and wrecking the starboard lifeboat. The surviving crew left the ship in the port lifeboat, and when the roll was called it was found that the men of the engine room watch were missing. The Master and the First Mate reboarded the ship, but no more survivors could be found.

The *Soesterberg* was then abandoned, but she remained afloat, eventually drifting down to collide with the crippled *Assyrian*. The Dutch ship then suddenly rolled over and sank, her deck cargo of pit props breaking loose as she went. It was unfortunate that as the heavy lengths of timber went shooting into the water, Captain Kearon was engaged in getting most of his crew away from his sinking ship. He described the disaster that followed:

> I could see the "ASSYRIAN" was not going to last very long. The starboard boat was smashed by the explosion, also one raft, so I put the port lifeboat in the water with 15 of the crew in her, and was getting the rafts over the side when the Dutch vessel was torpedoed, all her cargo of pit props came sweeping along our ship's side, knocking men off the rafts into the water, carrying away the lashings we had fixed to keep the rafts together, holing the port boat, and carrying all beyond the ship. I was still on board directing operations. We pulled all the men we could back in to the ship, but some of them were badly hurt by the timber. We put the remainder of the rafts in the water and finally there were 18 of us left on board. The vessel was tilting slightly down by the head but with no list. I saw there was nothing for it but to make a new raft and stay on the ship as long as possible. This we did, Admiral Mackinnon giving us great help. He worked like a Trojan, and so did his Yeoman of Signals and my Wireless Operator, but these two men were both dazed, having been knocked off one of the rafts by the pit props; my 2nd Officer and Bo'sun also helped.

Bringing up the rear of Column Five in the *Empire Brigade*, Captain Sydney Parks watched with increasing anxiety as the horizon ahead of him erupted in smoke and flame. The 5,184-ton *Empire Brigade*, well into her second world war, had been built for Court Line of London in 1912. She was sold to Italian owners between the wars, and came back under the Red Ensign when she was seized by the Royal Navy as a war prize in June 1940.

Captain Parks had good cause to worry. The 28-year-old *Empire Brigade* was carrying a very heavy cargo, namely 750 tons of copper, 129 tons of ferrous alloys and 980 tons of steel – and all this without the usual compensatory buoyancy of timber on top. When Otto Kretchsmer, operating on the surface and inside the convoy, crept up on her, it required only one torpedo to end *Empire Brigade's* long years of sailing the oceans. She went down in a matter of minutes, taking five of her crew of forty-one with her.

So long as he had torpedoes left, Kretchsmer had targets to shoot at. He next turned his sights on the Greek steamer *Thalia,* which was desperately trying to escape from the hell she was caught up in. But the 23-year-old tramp, also weighed down by a heavy steel cargo, was almost running to stand still. No matter how hard her ageing triple-expansion steam engine thumped, her bow wave showed no urgency.

U-99's war diary recorded the end of the *Thalia* in just a few words:

0155: Fire bow torpedo at the next large vessel of some 7000 tons. Range 975 metres. Hit abreast foremast. Ship sinks within 40 seconds.

Only four survived from the *Thalia's* crew of twenty-six.

While Kretchsmer was disposing of the *Thalia,* a few cables ahead of the doomed Greek ship Sir Robert Ropner's *Sedgepool* was also doing her utmost to get away. Under the command of Captain Robert Witten, the 5,556-ton *Sedgepool* was fully loaded with 8,720 tons of wheat destined for Manchester. It was another priceless cargo that would never come within reach of the dockside cranes. Moehle had been stalking the West Hartlepool tramp for some time, and by the grace of God and some skillful manoeuvring by Captain Witten, she had already avoided one torpedo. When he gave the order to fire again, Moehle was so close to his victim that he felt the blast when the torpedo exploded deep in the *Sedgepool's* hull. The heavily loaded steamer went down with an indecent rush, and when she went Captain Robert Witten and two of his men went with her.

When the alarm bells first rang out, *Sedgepool's* chief engineer, James Aves, had gone below to take charge in the engine room. The engineer on watch was killed when Moehle's torpedo struck, and it was left to Aves to shut down the engines when the word came from the bridge to abandon ship. But when he returned on deck he found that all the lifeboats had left the ship, except one, which was empty, and seemed to be jammed alongside. He struggled for some time to free the boat, but he was forced to give up when he crushed his hand badly between the boat and the ship.

The *Sedgepool* was going fast and Aves just had time to jump overboard before she went. Luck was with him, for after swimming around for a while he was picked up by a liferaft, on which several other men had escaped.

The crippled *Assyrian* was by this time also living out her last moments. Eighteen men were still on board, including Captain Kearon, his Chief and Second Officers, the wireless operator, and Commodore Mackinnon and his staff. Their makeshift raft was ready for launching, but still mindful of the dreadful slaughter he had witnessed when the *Boekelo* shed her deck load of pit props into the sea amongst the *Assyrian's* liferafts, Kearon was unwilling to put the raft over the side until he was certain that his ship was going down. He wrote in his report:

> We had two large wooden spars on the starboard side and I had these cut adrift in case we were washed off the raft. Then the ship began to tilt more rapidly so we launched our makeshift raft and started to man it. The bos'un held on to a line from the raft so that it would not float away, we got the Admiral and his staff on to it, and there were the bos'un, AB Jones, the Chief Officer and myself left still in the ship. I slid the Chief Officer down the rope, then the ship started to go and I could not get down. Jones jumped overboard but hit his head on a log and was killed instantly, the bos'un I did not see go, but apparently he jumped and he was still all right. The ship was down by the bows with her stern 50 feet in the air, she went end-on, practically upright, her stern continued to rise, and gradually she turned right over and disappeared. As her propeller rose out of the water it caught the raft, tilting it so that some of the men were thrown into the water, but fortunately one of the planks of the raft snapped and the raft cleared. I myself floated off the ship, I was sucked down and after coming to the surface several times I found myself beside the spar; a fender then came alongside me and I hung on to that too. I noticed my Chief Officer on the other end of the big spar, he edged along to me and I lashed him to the opposite side, as he was an elderly man and I thought he might have become too tired to hold on.

As Kearon and Chief Officer John King clung to their life-saving spar with the tenacity that only men facing death can summon up, their situation worsened as the wind began to keen, whipping up an angry sea that lashed at them with icy fingers. Elderly John King, who like

Commodore Mackinnon had been enticed out of retirement to help fill a gap in the ranks of British merchant officers who were facing complete annihilation at the hands of the U-boats, was already suffering from exhaustion and exposure. If he had not been lashed to the spar he would probably have given up hope and slipped beneath the waves. In an effort to save him Kearon discussed their chances of being picked up, displaying an optimism he did not feel. While he talked, they were joined by two other survivors, Able Seaman Price-Rees and Yeoman of Signals Hall, one of Commodore Mackinnon's staff. Cold and miserable, the four men were resigned to waiting for daylight before rescue came – if it came then, which as the hours went by seemed more and more doubtful. Captain Kearon described the wait:

> Then we saw a steamer, she appeared to stop and we thought perhaps she was the rescue ship sent by the escort to stand by to pick up survivors. We shouted and signalled, but received no reply. Later on we saw a sloop come by which proved to be HMS *Leith*, she steamed towards us, we signalled, but she went away again, much to our disappointment. The Chief Officer and Hall by this time were shivering and moaning from the cold. Later the *Leith* returned, but once more turned away, although we were continually flashing the torch, but afterwards I found that she was picking up men from all over the place. When she came towards us for the third time and stopped, one of my ABs, Price-Rees, left the spar crying for help; he swam about 300 yards to the escort, was pulled on board but collapsed and died almost immediately. Hall started to swim after Price-Rees but I told him to come back and stay with us, as at least we had a light and would very soon be seen. He returned and stayed with me by the spar. The escort eventually came alongside the spar, threw me a line which I made fast to my wrist. The Chief Officer was still alive but I was not strong enough now to untie the lashings for him, I was too far gone. It was very cold, and the wind was force 4 with a slight sea. By the time we were alongside the *Leith* the Chief Officer was dead. Hall was pulled on board and taken to hospital as he was only just alive. I was the last man picked up by the *Leith*; this was at 0245 on the 19th. I was pulled on deck, then taken to the Captain's cabin where I soon recovered, but I am sure I should not have lasted another 10 minutes in that water.

Despite the catalogue of disasters that attended her sinking, nineteen of the *Assyrian's* total complement of thirty-six survived that terrible night. Among them was 58-year-old Commodore Lachlan Mackinnon, who was thrown into the icy water when the raft he had helped to construct was smashed by floating pit props. He survived by clinging to a plank of timber until HMS *Leith* found him. He was then so exhausted that his rescuers hoisted him aboard in a net. Sadly, the ordeal left him in poor health, and he died seven years later without returning to the sea he loved.

Some miles astern of this dramatic rescue scene, the *Blairspey*, with her No.1 hold flooded as a result of Fritz Frauenheim's torpedo, was not only still afloat, but she was under way again. The explosion of the torpedo had caused a joint to blow in the main steam pipe in the engine room, and she had lain stopped for four hours while her engineers had worked under appalling conditions to repair the joint. It was just as well that when she was hove to and completely at the mercy of any attacker, the U-boats were busy elsewhere. This happy situation was not to last, for Joachim Schepke, having failed to put the *Shekatika* down, had brought U-100 in astern of the convoy looking for another victim. Captain Walker related the events that followed in his report:

We were torpedoed again at 1 a.m. on 19th October on the starboard side between No.1 and No.2 holds about 100 ft from the bow. We were all at stations at the time. A column of water and some timber was thrown up. I then gave orders to abandon ship. The explosion sounded like a dull thud and there was no flame. While abandoning ship we were again torpedoed on the port side amidships about 150 ft from the bow. There was about a 5 minute interval between these two torpedoes. I think there were two submarines firing at us, because the ship had stopped and was drifting to leeward.

The Mate's boat had got away on the port side and he told me afterwards that he thought the torpedo passed under his boat and that he saw an orange colour in the water when the torpedo exploded.

About ¼ hour later when we were in the boats, the submarine came up alongside us. There were four men in the conning tower and one of them came forward to speak to me. He asked us in perfect English the name of our ship and then he backed away.

About 10 minutes later he came back again and asked the same question. I do not know if it was the same submarine which returned; it was very dark at the time and I cannot remember if it was the same voice speaking.

The *Blairspey's* cargo of timber kept her afloat, and she was later taken in tow by a salvage tug, which brought her into the Clyde on 25 October. Captain Walker and his entire crew survived without injury, and their ship would sail again. She was taken into dry dock, where her damaged fore part was cut away, and a complete new bow section was built and fitted. She was then taken over by the Ministry of War Transport, renamed *Empire Spey*, and handed back to her original owners for management. She returned to service in March 1942 and continued to defy the U-boats, sailing in three more Atlantic convoys. She survived the war.

In the midst of the chaos of this bloody battle for SC 7 the small Norwegian steamer *Snefjeld* had come across survivors from the Greek ship *Thalia* struggling in the water. Without thought for his own ship, Captain Finn Skage stopped and lowered three boats to the water.

The *Snefjeld*, 1,643 tons and manned by a crew of twenty-one, was a veteran of the timber trade and the oldest ship in the convoy. She was built at Rotterdam in 1901, when sail still dominated the seaways and the new-fangled steamship with her tall funnel belching forth black smoke and cinders was considered to be a foul abomination. Thirty-nine years later, under the ownership of Harald Grieg Martens of Bergen, *Snefjeld* was involved in her second world war, and still ploughing a furrow across the Atlantic.

The *Snefjeld's* boats found only four survivors from the *Thalia*, and as they were coming back alongside their ship U-99, hidden in the darkness to starboard, put a torpedo into the Norwegian's No. Two hold. Three men, the Second Mate, the Steward and the Messboy, were injured by the explosion.

First Mate, Hjalmar Hægland, who had been in charge of the rescue operation, was bringing his boat alongside the *Snefjeld* when the blast of Kretchsmer's torpedo blew him out of the boat into the water. Luckily, he was not injured, and when he came to the surface he struck out and was able to reboard the ship on the after deck. He went immediately to the bridge, but found it engulfed in flames.

With the sea pouring into her breached No. Two hold, the *Snefjeld* took such a heavy list to starboard that the lashings securing the cargo on her foredeck parted under the strain, and the whole lot cascaded into the sea. The heavy planks of timber swept aft, destroying the two lifeboats lying alongside. Fortunately, the motor lifeboat was clear of the ship, and was able to take off most of the sinking ship's crew. The rest left in the jolly boat.

The *Snefjeld*, still burning fiercely, remained afloat for another six hours, finally breaking in two and sinking at about 0800 on 19 October. All twenty-one crew, three of whom were injured, got away in the two undamaged boats. In accordance with Admiralty advice, the boats remained where they were overnight in the hope that rescue might come. But when by noon next day no ship or aircraft had appeared Captain Skage decided to make for the nearest land. This was the Outer Hebrides, 120 miles distant.

The survivors' journey was not to be an easy one. All attempts to start the engine of the motor boat failed, and they were forced to resort to the oars. Progress was painfully slow and later in the afternoon, when the weather worsened, became even slower. Eventually, when despite the immense effort they were putting into the oars it became obvious that they were barely holding their own, Skage decided to lie to a sea anchor until the wind eased.

The boats became separated during the night, but regained contact again at daylight, when the wind began to ease. That afternoon they found themselves passing through the scattered wreckage left by the assault of the previous night. An empty liferaft from the *Thalia* yielded some very welcome provisions and then, like a gift from the gods, they came across an abandoned lifeboat from the *Empire Brigade*, another of Otto Kretchsmer's victims. The boat was undamaged, and fully equipped with food, water, and all the necessary gear. Captain Skage redistributed his men between the three boats.

An hour or so later, the little flotilla found Ordinary Seaman Edward King, sole survivor of the *Fiscus*, who was floating on his now waterlogged packing case. King, who had been stranded on his box for more than forty hours at the mercy of the wind and waves, was completely exhausted and suffering from exposure.

On the morning of 21 October, the *Snefjeld's* boats came face to face with yet more evidence of the bloody harvest being reaped by Admiral Dönitz's U-boats. They met up with another lifeboat heading for the land. This proved to be from the *Port Gisborne,* sunk ten days earlier by Heinrich Bleichrodt in U-48 120 miles west-south-west of Rockall.

It had been blowing a full gale when Bleichrodt's torpedo caught the *Port Gisborne* in the region of her bridge, crippling her. Her crew of sixty-four abandoned ship in three lifeboats, but one of these capsized in the rough seas. Twenty-six men lost their lives.

The weather was moderating when the *Port Gisborne's* boat, carrying twenty-nine survivors, including Captain Kippins, met up with the *Snefjeld's* boats. Kippins and Skage discussed the situation, and it was decided that the three boats would stay together while they steered for the land. However, they lost touch after dark, and did not meet again.

For some time the *Snefjeld's* motor lifeboat had been taking in water, and on the morning of 22 October, Captain Skage decided to transfer all survivors to the jolly boat, which was tight and dry. With twenty-six men on board the little boat was uncomfortably crowded, and her gunwales were only inches above water, but they were afloat and dry. Rowing with great difficulty, they continued to crawl eastwards for another thirty-six hours, being picked up by the corvette HMS *Clematis* on 23 October. They landed in Methil, on the Firth of Forth three days later. Both boats from the *Port Gisborne* were also picked up before reaching land.

The agony of SC 7 was not yet over. Drifting forlornly many miles astern the abandoned Salvesen's steamer *Shekatika,* unfortunate recipient of four torpedoes, and twice subjected to a coup de grâce, was still afloat. With her hull pieced like a colander, she was very much lower in the water and listing crazily, but was still very much afloat, buoyed up by the 6,000 tons of pit props she carried. And that was how Karl-Heinz Moehle, whose torpedoes had done most of the damage, found her again in the early hours of 19 October. Seething with frustration, he brought U-123 as close in to the wreck as he dared, and used another torpedo on it, probably earning the *Shekatika* the accolade of being the most torpedoed ship of the war. At long last she succumbed; a fire started in her engine room, and her list became even more precipitous, her deck chains parted with a series of loud cracks, and thousands of pit props went shooting into the sea. U-123 had by this time moved clear, and Moehle finally had the satisfaction of seeing the British ship capsize and sink. At the cost of five torpedoes it had been a most expensive sinking.

There was one last scene to be played out before the curtain came down on SC 7. It featured the 3,106-ton North East Coast tramp

Clintonia. The 23-year-old *Clintonia,* commanded by Captain Thomas Irving, was on her way from St Francis, Nova Scotia to Manchester with a full cargo of wood pulp. She was the leading ship of Column six when the attack began, but such was the confusion around her that Captain Irving was approached by some of his officers, who suggested leaving the convoy and making a run for it on their own. The discussion was taking place on the bridge when Otto Kretchsmer found the *Clintonia.*

The *Clintonia* did not go without putting up a fight. When U–99 surfaced close to her, Captain Irving adopted the classic defence position for a merchant ship under attack, presenting his stern to the U-boat and taking violent evasive action. The 4-inch gun on the poop was manned, and the *Clintonia's* crew prepared to sell their ship dearly.

This display of defiance was in vain, U–99's torpedo went home in the *Clintonia's* engine room, and the resulting explosion brought down her mainmast. This crashed down onto the wireless room abaft the bridge, smashing all the radio equipment and so destroying all hopes of sending out an SOS. The ship remained afloat, buoyed up by her cargo of pulpwood, but an inspection of the engine room revealed it to be awash. Captain Irving decided there was nothing more to be done, and the *Clintonia* was abandoned.

Irving lost two men in the attack, one killed in the engine room, and another, the ship's chief cook, who was part of the gun's crew, smashed against the breech of the gun by the blast of the torpedo and so horribly injured that, mercifully perhaps, he died.

The 23-year-old tramp was left to drift forlornly at the whim of wind and current. And that is how U–123 found her at daylight. The wreck offered a unique opportunity for a practice shoot, and Moehle's gun's crew disposed of her at their leisure.

The relevant entry in his Otto Kretchsmer's War Diary covering the incident reads:

0356: Fire at and miss a rather small unladen ship, which had lost contact with the convoy. We had just fired as the steamer turned towards us.

0358: Turn off and fire a stern torpedo from a range of 690 metres. Hit aft of amidships. Ship drops astern, somewhat lower in the water. As torpedoes have been expended, I wait to see if she will sink further before I settle her by gunfire.

0504: Ship is sunk by another vessel by gunfire. I suppose it to be a British destroyer, but it later transpires that it was U.123. Some of her shells land very close, so that I have to leave the area quickly. The ship was *Clintonia*, 3,106 tons.

0530: I commence return passage to Lorient . . .

Commenting on the efforts of SC 7's escort force Kretchsmer had nothing but contempt:

Starshell was still being fired on either beam of the convoy in spasmodic bursts, having a curiously ineffective result in the pale light of the moon. The nearest flares were falling 10 miles away and looked to the U-boat crew to be about as effective as a small child playing with matches in the middle of the Sahara Desert.

The *Clintonia* finally went down some 60 miles to the west of Rockall, and only a day's steaming from the safety of the North Channel. Captain Irvine, thirty-three crew members and one naval gunner were picked up by HMS *Bluebell*. The corvette was by this time, in the words of one of her crew, 'heaving with wet, frozen seamen: Lascars from India, Jamaicans, Frenchmen, Norwegians and Swedes. Every square inch of deck was filled, every available blanket and piece of clothing used.' When *Bluebell* eased alongside her berth at Gourock late on 20 October, she had on board a total of 242 survivors. In acting as rescue ship for SC 7, Lieutenant Geoffrey Walker and his crew had done everything that was asked of them, and beyond. However, in doing so, the corvette had taken little part in the defence of the convoy, and with *Scarborough* having lost contact early on, this left too many gaps in the escort screen. In retrospect, it would have made more sense to designate one of the merchantmen as rescue ship, preferably small, without deck cargo, and with experienced boat handlers in her crew.

The battered remnants of SC 7 eventually found sanctuary in the Firth of Clyde; out of the thirty-five ships that had set out to cross the Atlantic sixteen days earlier only fifteen remained, and three of these were badly damaged. And so ended one of the bloodiest battles in maritime history. The U-boats, operating on the surface at night, had made a mockery of the efforts of the few lightly armed escorts with the convoy, picking off the defenceless merchant ships at will. In the space of seventy-two hours twenty ships, totalling 79,646 tons gross, were sunk. With them went more than 100,000 tons of valuable cargo and 135 men. The U-boats suffered no losses.

The great irony of SC 7 was that the tiny *Eaglescliffe Hall*, which had dropped out of the convoy shortly after sailing from Sydney, found her way across the North Atlantic alone and unprotected, reaching Scottish waters unharmed. Furthermore, on her lonely way she picked up twenty-five survivors from the torpedoed Greek steamer *Aenos.*

It is probable that the battle for SC 7 would have carried on right up to the approaches to the North Channel, had not the U-boats run out of torpedoes. Later Admiral Dönitz claimed his men had sunk thirty Allied ships of 196,000 tons in the action. This may have been a gross exaggeration, but the next opportunity for the U-boats to strike would not be long in coming.

SC 7 came under the protection of Coastal Command in the North Channel, and the U-boats made a discreet retreat back out to sea, where less than 200 miles to the west the masts and funnels of yet another large east bound convoy were appearing over the horizon.

Chapter 10

More Lambs to the Slaughter

Even as SC 7 sailed out of Sydney, Cape Breton on 5 October, the nucleus of the next convoy in Britain's transatlantic supply chain was already assembling in Halifax, Nova Scotia.

One by one the salt-stained merchantmen came steaming into the bay to drop anchor in their allocated berths. They were the usual mixed bag: Maclay & McIntyre's 4,966-ton *Uganda* in from Montreal sagging under a colossal 8,000 tons of steel and lumber; Brocklebank's *Matheran* from New York with a mix of iron, zinc, grain and machinery; the tanker *Shirak* up from Aruba with a full load of 'refined petroleum products' – a cargo to send a shiver down the spine in these dangerous days. Eventually, they were all there, swinging lazily to their anchors, drab grey hulls streaked with red rust that spoke of countless battles with the sea. Convoy HX 79, officially designated a 'fast' convoy, was preparing to challenge the North Atlantic.

Nearby, in the naval anchorage, lay HX 79's ocean escort, the 16,314-ton armed merchant cruiser HMS *Montclare*. The 18-year-old ex-Canadian Pacific passenger liner, requisitioned by the Admiralty in August 1939, had a top speed of 16 knots, and was armed with eight First World War vintage 5.5-inch guns. Her accommodation had been stripped of much of its opulent fittings, and her holds were filled with empty drums and timber in order to give her extra buoyancy. A proud ship ready to fight off any threat to her flock, but like all her dual-purpose sisters pitifully inadequate for the job.

Anchored close by, and completely dwarfed by the AMC, was the tiny Royal Netherland's Navy's submarine O-14. Based in Curaçao when Holland was overrun, O-14 was taken under the wing of the Royal Navy, and ordered to proceed to the Clyde. Conveniently, she had been allocated to HX 79 as part of her ocean escort, although it is hard to imagine what role she was supposed to have played in the defence of the convoy in the event of an attack. In reality, the presence of the Dutch submarine was no more than a token show of force designed to boost the morale of the merchant ships. She was sailing with HX 79 more for her own safety than that of the convoy.

HX 79 was twenty ships strong when, on the morning of 8 October, led by the Commodore in the three-year-old Donaldson Line ship *Salacia,* the convoy filed out through the breakwaters of Halifax harbour. Last in line came the high-sided *Montclare,* black smoke trailing astern from her tall twin funnels, and in her wake the diminuative O-14, her Dutch tricolour snapping proudly in the breeze.

Outside, the ships were met by their local escort, the Canadian destroyer *Saguenay* and two auxiliary patrol boats *French* and *Reindeer.* Steaming in loose formation five abreast, the merchantmen then set course to the north-east with *Saguenay* zig-zagging ahead, while the two patrol boats covered both quarters. *Montclare* and O-14 sailed in the middle of the convoy. *French* and *Reindeer,* having reached the safe limit of their fuel tanks, turned back as darkness fell. *Saguenay* remained with the convoy until early afternoon on 9 October, then she too reversed course and headed back for Canadian waters.

The next morning, a rendezvous was made off Newfoundland with a contingent of nineteen ships from Sydney, and later in the day HX 79 was completed by the arrival of ten more ships from Bermuda carrying cargoes from America's west coast and the Caribbean. By the time the sun went down the convoy had assumed massive proportions, consisting of forty-nine ships sailing in nine columns abreast, and covering the ocean from horizon to horizon. A quarter of a million tons of cargo, steel, iron ore, kerosene, pit props, wheat, molasses, aircraft, everything that a nation at war needed, was on its way across the North Atlantic. *Montclare* was in the middle of the convoy, between Columns Four and Five, with the Dutch submarine in close attendance. The agreed speed for HX 79 was 9 knots, but forward progress was considerably reduced by zig-zagging during daylight hours. As the U-boats had not yet reached this far west, it would seem that this precaution, with its inevitable loss of speed and danger of collision between ships, was hardly necessary.

The only credible threat to the convoy on the ocean passage was likely to come from German surface raiders, two of which were known to be at large somewhere in the Atlantic. And these were a force to be reckoned with. Whereas the Admiralty had pressed into service as armed merchant cruisers old passenger liners which were themselves dangerously vulnerable, Berlin had taken a very different approach. German commerce raiders were, in the main, ex-fruit carriers – small, fast, and armed with modern weapons, including torpedo tubes. The maiden voyage of the *hilfskreuzer* (auxiliary cruiser) *Thor* served to illustrate the difference.

Laid down in 1938 as the *Santa Cruz* for the Oldenburg Portuguese Line, the 3,862-ton fruit carrier was requisitioned on the stocks on the outbreak of war and renamed *Thor*. Four hundred feet long and 55 feet in the beam, she had fine lines and was powered by a 6,500 hp oil-fired steam engine that gave her a top speed of 17 knots. When completed, her armament consisted of six 155mm and two 37mm guns, plus four 53cm torpedo tubes in twin mountings. She carried an Arado spotter plane which was to prove invaluable in searching out her prey.

Under the command of *Kapitän zur See* Otto Kähler, the *Thor* embarked on her first war patrol on 6 June 1940, and was an immediate success, cutting a swathe through Allied shipping in the Atlantic that set the alarms bells ringing in London.

The *Thor* met her first serious opposition on 28 July, when she was sighted by the armed merchant cruiser HMS *Alcantara*.

On paper, the 22,181-ton, twin-screw *Alcantara* was a formidable opponent. Built in 1927 for Royal Mail Lines, she was requisitioned by the Admiralty in 1939, when her luxury accommodation, which once housed 1,430 passengers, was gutted, and in the space of a few months she emerged as an armed merchant cruiser flying the White Ensign. She mounted eight 6-inch and two 3-inch guns on deck, the larger guns being relics from an earlier war with a range of only 14,200 yards. Her twin Burmeister & Wain diesels gave her a top speed of 16 knots.

The action between the two merchant cruisers that followed was largely inconclusive. Kähler had the advantage in that his more modern guns outranged the *Alcantara's* by at least 6,000 yards. This led to the *Thor's* gunners scoring three early hits, one of which flooded the British ship's engine room and slowed her down to a crawl. Kähler then made the mistake of closing the range, which gave the *Alcantara's* gunners the opportunity to hit back. A few well-aimed salvoes set the *Thor* on fire and killed three of her crew.

At this point, mindful that his primary duty was to attack merchant ships, Kähler decided to call off the action, and retired under cover of a smoke screen conveniently laid down by the *Alcantara*, leaving the AMC to limp back to port for repairs.

Some four months later, the *Thor* met up with HMS *Carnarvon Castle*, another 20,000-ton ex-passenger liner. Kähler was reluctant to become involved, and presented his stern to the AMC. Not realising that the enemy ship had three of her 155mm guns mounted aft, the *Carnarvon Castle* gave chase. The *Thor's* fourth salvo caused major damage and casualties aboard the British ship, and thereafter the German guns scored another twenty hits on the *Carnarvon Castle*, forcing her to run for the safety of Montevideo.

The *Thor's* third encounter with a British armed merchant cruiser came in April 1941, when she met HMS *Voltaire* in mid-Atlantic. The *Voltaire*, an ex-Lamport & Holt liner of 13,245 tons, had a top speed of only 14½ knots and was armed with the usual array of obsolete guns.

Thor's first salvo went home with devastating effect, and within minutes the *Voltaire* was on fire and steaming in circles, her steering gear apparently hit. Kähler was able to stand off out of range of the *Voltaire's* guns and pound the helpless ship until until she rolled over and sank.

Thus ended the *Thor's* first war patrol, in which she had terrorized Allied shipping in the Atlantic, and swapped shell for shell with three British armed merchant cruisers, coming out on top each time.

Fortunately, the majority of those who manned the ships in HX 79 were ignorant of the threat posed by German surface raiders, and life went on as usual. There was an awareness of the danger, of course, but in war or in peace there is a strict routine to be followed. By virtue of their commercial calling, merchant ships carry minimal crews, and there are no idle hands. They are self-contained communities afloat, and every man has his allotted task. There are watches to be kept, engines to be nursed, galley fires to be stoked, and above all the day-to-day maintenance of the ship to be seen to.

Aboard the Cardiff tramp *Ruperra*, sailing near the rear of HX 79's Column Six, Captain David Davies had a crew of thirty-six to run his 4,548-ton steamer. She was no rust-bucket, but fifteen years in the punishing cross-trades had left their mark on her. Davies and his men had a constant fight on their hands just to keep her at sea and making a profit for her owners John Cory & Sons. On this, her fourth consecutive

Atlantic crossing of the war, the *Ruperra* was loaded to her gunwales with steel billets, scrap iron, and crated aircraft, a high-freight cargo guaranteed to give a good return, should she make port.

In contrast, 3 miles out on the *Ruperra's* port beam, sailing as the rear ship of Column One, was the smart new motor vessel *Wandby*. Only months out of her Sunderland shipyard, the 4,947-ton *Wandby*, owned by Sir Robert Ropner & Sons of West Hartlepool, was on the return leg of her maiden voyage, a long haul of 7,000 miles from Canada's west coast, via the Panama Canal and Bermuda. At the bottom of her holds she carried a layer of 1,700 tons of lead and zinc, which provided a low centre of gravity for the 7,200 tons of timber occupying the rest of the cargo space and spilling out onto her decks to a height of twelve feet. Although at first sight the *Wandby* appeared to be ridiculously top heavy, she was in little danger of capsizing. And having come this far without incident, Captain John Kenny's confidence in his new ship was growing by the hour.

In the van of HX 79, leading Column Six, was Anglo Saxon's motor tanker *Caprella*, 8,230 tons gross, and with a cargo of 11,300 tons of fuel oil on board. Commanded by Captain Percy Prior, the *Caprella* was British officered with Singapore Chinese ratings, her total complement being fifty-three. No shortage of hands here, but Captain Prior was aware that there might be a question of discipline with his Chinese crew in the event of the ship being attacked.

Well placed in the middle of the convoy was Maclay & McIntyre's 5,452-ton *Loch Lomond*, third ship in Column 3. Under the command of Captain William Park, the *Loch Lomond* had a similar load to the *Wandby*, with 1,858 tons of steel below, topped off by 6,000 tons of timber, all loaded in Montreal. Much to Captain Park's amazement, his ship had been designated as rescue ship for the convoy. Her envisaged role in the event of an attack was to drop back and pick up survivors from any torpedoed ships. Later in the war, rescue ships would be a common feature of Atlantic convoys, but these were usually small handy ships, often cross-Channel ferries, specially equipped for the job. They carried powerful motor lifeboats crewed by experienced small boat handlers, were equipped with the best of life-saving apparatus, extra blankets and warm clothing, medical supplies, and in many cases there was a doctor on board. The *Loch Lomond* had none of this, and Captain Park commented: 'I think that it was rather absurd to appoint us as rescue ship. We had only two lifeboats and were not at all a suitable ship. I think the fact that a rescue ship is appointed has a psychological effect on the other ships in the convoy.' In the case of HX 79 Captain Park's words had more than a ring of truth.

Although the Autumnal Equinox was past and winter was drawing near, the North Atlantic was in an unusually benign mood throughout the crossing. The weather was fine, the sky mainly overcast, but visibility was good, with a light to moderate south-easterly wind, and a slight sea. Considering the number and diversity of the merchantmen, and the zig-zag courses being steered, station keeping was excellent, with the convoy maintaining an average speed of 9 knots. The ocean escort had by this time been supplemented by the arrival of HMS *Alaunia*, a 14,000-ton ex-Cunard White Star liner.

During the morning of 17 October HX 79 reached latitude 59°, the furthest point north in its designated route. Iceland was 300 miles on the beam, and the sea and sky were a uniform grey, with the thermometer hovering around freezing. For those unfortunate to be keeping watch on deck in the ships the hours passed slowly and in misery. However, spirits were high, for word had gone round that ships of the Royal Navy were racing to meet them. At noon, course was altered to east-south-east for the North Channel, and home.

Twenty-four hours later, at noon, the armed merchant cruisers *Montclare* and *Alaunia* signalled their farewells, and steamed away to rendezvous with the next east-bound convoy. This left HX 79 without a naval escort of any size or shape. Mercifully, the news that somewhere up ahead Convoy SC 7 was being savaged by a pack of U-boats had not yet filtered through to the ships. However, early that morning a warning had been received from the Admiralty that enemy submarines were in the vicinity, and this was qualified later in the day by a signal indicating that U-boats had been sighted ahead of the convoy.

By sunrise on 19 October it was all over for SC 7, and the surviving ships of the shattered convoy were running for the shelter of the North Channel as fast as their labouring engines could take them. At the same time news of the impending arrival of HX 79 in the operational area of his U-boats had reached Admiral Dönitz, and he was already planning a reception committee. However, the resources at his disposal were limited.

Kretschmer in U-99, Frauenheim in U-101, and Moehle in U-123 had exhausted all their torpedoes, and were returning to Lorient.

Between them they had accounted for 84,555 tons of Allied shipping in less than two weeks. The tumultous welcome awaiting them in Lorient was well earned.

The departure of the three boats left only Englebert Endrass's U-46, Heinrich Bleichrodt's U-48 and Joachim Schepke's U-100 in the path of HX 79, and Bleichrodt's involvement would be short-lived, as U-48 was down to her last torpedo. Further out, and racing to join Dönitz's pack, were Günther Kuhnke's U-28 and Heinrich Liebe in U-38.

Forewarned of the imminent threat to HX 79 by increased radio traffic between Lorient and the U-boats, Western Approaches Command in Plymouth had hastily put together an escort group for the convoy. Led by Lieutenant Commander Archibald Russell, RN, in the Modified 'W' class destroyer HMS *Whitehall*, only two months out of the repair yard after being dive-bombed while evacuating troops from the beaches of Dunkirk, the group was a force to be reckoned with. Under Russell's command were a second destroyer, HMS *Sturdy* (Lieutenant Commander George Cooper, RN), the Flower-class corvettes *Arabis* (Lieutenant Commander B. Blewitt, RNR), *Coreopsis* (Lieutenant Commander Alan Davis, RNVR), *Heliotrope* (Lieutenant Commander John Jackson, RNR) and *Hibiscus* (Lieutenant Commander George Cuthbertson, RNR), the Halcyon-class minesweeper HMS *Jason* (Lieutenant Commander Reginald Terry, RN), and the anti-submarine trawlers *Angle, Blackfly* and *Lady Elsa*.

At first sight, this was a powerful escort force well able to drive off marauding U-boats, but in reality it lacked cohesion and experience. Diverted from the westbound convoy OB 229, which they had just escorted out of Liverpool, none of these ships had any real experience of working with the others as a unit. The corvettes were all recently commissioned, with raw crews and, crucially, there had been no opportunity for any of the commanders to meet to discuss tactics.

Coming from various points of the compass, the ships of HX 79's local escort made contact with the convoy between 0800 and 1200 on 19 October. Unknown to Lieutenant Commander Russell, the enemy had arrived before them.

Following in the wake of the rear ships of HX 79 at a discreet distance, trimmed right down so that little more than her conning tower was above water, Günther Prien's U-47 had been there since shortly after dawn. Prien, directed to the area by Lorient, had been scouring an empty ocean for forty-eight hours, and might well have missed HX 79 if it had not been for the pall of black funnel smoke hanging over the convoy. The weather remaining fair and the visibility unlimited, the pall was visible at more than 30 miles. Prien lost no time in radioing news of his sighting to Lorient , and the call went out to the other boats of the pack to close in on U–47.

Prien shadowed HX 79 throughout the day, taking care not to approach close enough to be seen, all the time transmitting signals for the other boats to home in on. At dusk he was joined by Heinrich Liebe in U–38, and as the darkness closed in the two boats increased speed and began to overtake the convoy. The weather was in their favour, with a light south-easterly wind and overcast sky, from behind which the moon shed a pale, almost ghostly light onto the sea. Occasional patches of thin fog drifted across the horizon, providing more cover for the stalking submarines.

By 2100, Prien and Liebe were abreast the leading ships of the convoy, U–47 being to port and U–38 to starboard. Liebe was first to fire, selecting as his first target the leading ship of the outside starboard column. He chose well; the 12,062-ton Anglo American Oil tanker *Cadillac* was carrying a lethal cargo of 17,000 tons of petrol and kerosene. Had she been hit the holocaust that followed would have been of awesome proportions. Fortunately for her crew, Liebe's torpedo completely missed the *Cadillac*. Her time would come five months later, and in the same area, when the tanker, loaded with aviation spirit, was blown out of the water by U–552. Only five men survived.

The 7,653-ton Liverpool steamer *Matheran*, sailing as lead ship of Column Eight, was the unfortunate recipient of Liebe's torpedo. She was hit amidships, the force of the explosion stopping her dead in her tracks. Weighed down by a cargo of 3,000 tons of iron, 1,200 tons of zinc, topped off by grain and machinery, she went down in minutes, taking Captain John Greenhall and eight of his crew with her.

Sailing immediately astern of the *Cadillac*, and close to starboard of the *Matheran*, was the 6,856-ton Holland-America steamer *Bilderdijk*, carrying 8,000 tons of grain from Baltimore to Liverpool. When the stricken *Matheran* staggered out of line, the Dutch ship was forced to alter course to starboard to avoid a collision. In doing so, she ran straight into Heinrich Liebe's second torpedo with disastrous results. She did not sink at once, but an inspection of the damage revealed that there was no hope of saving her. Her crew took to their lifeboats.

Flushed with success, Liebe lined up his sights on the next ship astern of the *Bilderdijk*. Also deep in the water and with the usual deck cargo of timber from Montreal, the 4,966-ton Glasgow-registered *Uganda* presented a tempting target. But even as Liebe was about to fire, the *Uganda* staggered and a great spout of water, debris and planks of timber erupted from forward of her bridge. Liebe had been beaten to the kill by Günther Prien, who had penetrated the ranks of the convoy and brought U-47 across to starboard.

There had already been some unease in the ranks of HX 79 following the news of the massacre of SC 7. And this sudden vicious attack in which three ships had been hit in as many minutes threatened to throw the convoy into complete confusion. Men who had spent so many days and long nights searching the horizon for an enemy that never came suddenly found themselves under immediate threat of attack. Lookouts were doubled, guns manned, and lifejackets kept close at hand.

When the Commodore signalled for an emergency turn of 40 degrees to port the response was immediate, every ship sheering away from the enemy threat in unison. As they did so, the destroyers *Whitehall* and *Sturdy*, which had been scouting ahead of the convoy, reversed course and came racing back, Asdics pinging and depth charge racks manned.

Narrowly avoiding being run down when the convoy made its emergency turn, U-47 dropped back, and then approached again from astern. There Prien found a likely target in the Baltic Trading Company's tanker *Shirak*, the back-marker of Column Three. The 6,023-ton *Shirak*, loaded with nearly 8,000 tons of kerosene from Aruba, had fallen astern of her position, and she began to burn fiercely when Prien fired one of his stern torpedoes into her. The tanker's crew lost no time in abandoning her, but she was still afloat an hour later, when Heinrich Bleichrodt in U-48 found her. A single torpedo was sufficient to end the *Shirak's* career.

In the words of the old saying, 'one man's loss is another man's gain', the Dutch submarine O-14, which had been keeping station inside the convoy, had missed the Commodore's signal for an emergency turn to port, and found herself outside the convoy. To complicate matters, she then ran into a bank of thick fog, and became hopelessly lost. By pure chance, she was only 300 yards off the *Shirak* when the tanker was torpedoed. The ensuing conflagration acted as a beacon, guiding O-14 back to the convoy.

Captain John Kenny, on the bridge of the motor vessel *Wandby*, rear ship of HX 79's port column, was another involuntary witness to the torpedoing of the *Shirak*. Kenny, twice torpedoed in the First World War, was no stranger to the harsh realities of war at sea, but before the night had been turned into a nightmare by the opening torpedoes of U–38 and U–47, he had been contemplating the successful conclusion of the *Wandby's* maiden voyage.

In the six weeks that had elapsed since the *Wandby* sailed out of the River Wear with the paint barely dry on her superstructure she had traveled far; to the other side of the world and back. Surely, with less than forty-eight hours left to reach British waters, and the convoy protected by no less than ten escorts, nothing could go wrong now.

Unknown to Captain Kenny, as he watched in horror the burning of the *Shirak*, his own ship was next in line of fire. Günther Prien, having crippled the *Shirak*, had now turned his sights on the *Wandby*, clearly visible in the light of the flames on the tanker. Furthermore, the fire had also attracted the attention of Englebert Endrass, who was then bringing U–46 in from the west. Both U-boats fired simultaneously, their torpedoes aimed at the port side of the *Wandby*. It is believed that while one torpedo found its mark – probably that of U-47 – the other missed. Captain Kenny later reported:

> At 2240 the vessel was struck by a torpedo on the port side in the hold directly under the fore end of the bridge, the explosion being very violent. No flash was seen but a considerable amount of smoke was in evidence, and the resulting damage included destruction of the port bridge lifeboat and davits, engine room bulkhead split and fuel pipes to the donkey boiler fractured, the vessel listing to port almost immediately after the impact.

It was typical of the unassuming John Kenny that he failed to mention his own injuries in the report. The force of the explosion had picked him up and hurled him across the bridge wing, slamming him against the bulwark. He was in great pain from leg injuries, yet his greatest concern was for the damage to the donkey boiler, which was used to power the ship's vital auxiliaries, pumps, steering engine and dynamo. Without these essentials, the *Wandby* was helpless. Kenny explained in his report:

> For some minutes the vessel was able to proceed at slow speed until she was prevented from doing so by reason of a flooding

engine room, from which it was impossible to pump water owing to the supply of oil being cut off from the boiler . . .

Although it was likely that the *Wandby's* timber cargo – she had 7,200 tons on board – would keep the ship afloat for some time, she was drifting without power and an easy target for any U-boat in the vicinity. His first thought being for the safety of his crew, Kenny therefore decided to abandon ship for what remained of the night, with the possibility of reboarding at daylight.

The weather was still fair, but there was a nasty chop on the sea, and with all thirty-five men crowded into one lifeboat the night proved to be without comfort. At 0900, Kenny brought the boat back alongside the *Wandby*, which apart from the list and being noticeably lower in the water, was showing no immediate sign of sinking. However, a closer examination confirmed the worst. Kenny's report gives the details:

An examination of the *Wandby* at 0900/20 carried out by the Chief Officer and Chief Engineer, who returned to the vessel for that purpose, confirmed the condition of the ship. The engine room was completely flooded, decks split across the fore side of the saloon and indications were that she would split in half and founder, and a final decision to abandon her was made.

At daylight on the 21st the vessel was again sighted with the after main deck awash. A last report at 1530/21 indicated her to be still in that condition.

The *Wandby's* crew had been prepared to wait out another long night in their crowded lifeboat, but within two hours of abandoning ship for the second time, rescue was at hand. Out of the darkness came the anti-submarine trawler HMS *Angle*, and all thirty-four survivors were soon on a dry deck again. It was while they stood on that deck contemplating their extraordinary luck in be rescued so soon, that the full horror of the night was brought home to them. There was a tremendous double explosion from the direction of the convoy, now some 5 miles ahead, and the whole sky on the horizon was turned blood red. Joachim Schepke in U-100 had caught up with the convoy, and had lost no time in making his presence felt.

It was precisely three quarters of an hour to midnight when Schepke, having penetrated deep into the convoy, fired a spread of two torpedoes and scored a double bullseye.

Anglo-Saxon Petroleum Company's 6,218-ton motor tanker *Sitala*, commanded by Captain John Morgans, and carrying a cargo of 8,444 tons of crude oil from Curaçao, went up in flames when she was hit, and was abandoned at once. All but one of her crew of forty-four escaped, the ship breaking her back and sinking shortly after they took to the boats. Fortunately, the anti-submarine trawler *Lady Elsa* was nearby, and Captain Morgans and his remaining crew were quickly taken aboard.

It was a bad night for Anglo-Saxon, the *Sitala's* sister-ship *Caprella* being the second victim of Schepke's salvo. The 8,230-ton *Caprella*, also loaded with heavy oil, was commanded by Captain Percy Prior, and carried a crew of fifty-two, the officers being British, and the ratings Singapore Chinese.

The *Caprella's* end was a mirror image of that of the *Sitala*, and was later described by 3rd Radio Officer Gerald Whitehead:

> The *Caprella* was torpedoed at 2315. Fortunately the heavy oil cargo did not catch fire but the vessel broke her back. Lifeboats were got away both amidships and aft. All members of the crew survived with the exception of the Chief Officer. He was known to be on the bridge when the torpedo struck between the midships bridge section and the after engine room. I knew that other ships had been hit and a tanker could be seen burning on the port quarter. The lifeboat drifted close to another vessel which appeared to have been abandoned and was settling in the water.
>
> After an hour or two – it was difficult to assess the length of time – we were picked up by an A/S trawler, one of the escorts, the *Lady Elsa*, an ex-deep sea trawler out of Hull and manned by RNVR officers and crew. She picked up survivors from the *Caprella* and *Sitala*.

The 518-ton *Lady Elsa*, commanded by Lieutenant J.G. Rankin, RNR, now had a total of ninety-five survivors on board, and her decks and accommodation were so crowded as to impede her fighting capability. At the same time, her food and water supplies were severely limited. Lieutenant Rankin wisely requested, and was granted, permission to leave the convoy and proceed to Belfast.

Chapter 11

The Turkey Shoot

Into the bloody mayhem that was Convoy HX 79 now came *Oberleutnant* Engelbert Endrass in U-46. Twenty-nine-year-old Endrass, an ex-merchant seaman who had been Günther Prien's First Watch Officer in U-47 when he penetrated Scapa Flow to sink the battleship *HMS Royal Oak*, was well on his way to gaining the coveted Knights Cross with Oak Leaves. In the four months he had been in command of U-46 he had accounted for seventeen Allied ships, totalling 92,574 tons gross. This impressive record included the sinking of the two armed merchant cruisers HMS *Carinthia* and HMS *Dunvegan Castle*.

The *Dunvegan Castle* was a 540ft-long ship of 15,000 tons gross, one of Union Castle Mail Line's fleet that in pre-war days sailed out of Southampton every other Thursday for the Cape packed with sun-seeking holidaymakers. Stripped of her peacetime fittings, painted overall in sombre Admiralty grey, and mounting half a dozen 6-inch guns, she had the trappings of a warship, but nothing could change her high silhouette or put fire into her twin engines designed to cruise at a leisurely 16 knots.

Shortly before sunset on 27 August 1940, U-46 was patrolling on the surface off the west coast of Ireland, when she sighted the *Dunvegan Castle*. Endrass wrote in his log:

> A steamer on the starboard. Steering a general course of 70-90°, large zig-zags, high speed (15-16 sea-miles) . . . Enemy is a large passenger steamer, light grey, 16-20000 tons, armed, probably merchant cruiser. Due to his extreme zig-zags, we can keep up well despite his high speed.

Captain H. Ardill, RN, commanding *Dunvegan Castle*, who was well aware of his ship's vulnerability to submarine attack, ceased zig-zagging after dark and pressed ahead at full speed on a steady course. Unfortunately, the AMC developed a fault in her starboard engine, and was making only 14 knots when U-46 moved in to attack. High-sided, clearly visible against the night sky, the British ship was an easy target.

At 2147, having approached to within 400 metres, Endrass fired a single torpedo, which hit the *Dunvegan Castle* aft. No significant damage was visible, but the liner lost speed and began to steam in wide circles, indicating possible damage to one of her propellers. Endrass prepared to attack again, but the U-boat had evidently been spotted by the *Dunvegan Castle's* gunners, who opened fire. Endrass was forced to dive.

Resurfacing after ten minutes, Endrass found his target still steaming in circles, but at an even slower speed. He decided to use another torpedo. The log of U-46 reads:

22:12 second surface attack, single shot, hit engine-room. We wait a while to observe the results. Nothing special to see, suddenly come under artillery fire, alarm.

Half an hour later, Endrass came back to the surface, noting in his log:

Enemy lies there stopped, but seems to float well under the circumstances . . . Steered closer again, 22:51 third attack, single shot, hit forward quarterdeck Enemy begins to burn, sinks significantly deeper, heavy list. Now I think he's had enough. Not even the best steamer can survive three hits, as well as fire on board.

At about daybreak on 28 August, the destroyers *Primrose* and *Harvester* came racing to the aid of the *Dunvegan Castle.* The stricken ship was still afloat, but burning fiercely. Captain Ardill had lost four officers and twenty-three ratings to Endrass' torpedoes, yet he still managed to abandon the sinking ship in a disciplined manner, the remaining 250 crew leaving in five lifeboats, one of which was holed, and two rafts. In his report to the Admiralty Captain Ardill wrote:

I am satisfied that I remained on board as long as possible . . . I have since ascertained that the actual time of leaving was 0220. The ship was badly on fire, the depth charges and ready use ammunition were exploding at regular intervals liable to set alight to the floating oil fuel. With a waterlogged boat it was just possible to get clear before the floating oil actually took fire.

By the time *Primrose* and *Harvester* arrived on the scene, Englebert Endrass and U-46 had long departed for pastures new. They disposed of three more Allied ships before reaching Lorient on 6 September.

It had been a very rewarding patrol for Endrass, adding another 36,000 tons to his mounting total of Allied ships sunk. His Knights Cross was ensured, but his greatest achievement had been to demonstrate forcefully the utter futility of the Admiralty's policy of sending out vulnerable ex-passenger liners to meet the threat of the U-boat, the most sophisticated weapon yet seen at sea.

Endrass had broken off his attack on SC 7 after dark on 18 August, having exhausted his ready-use torpedoes sending the heavily-laden *Beatus* to the bottom, followed by the two small Swedish ships *Convallaria* and *Gunborg*. Withdrawing into the darkness to reload his tubes, Endrass lost touch with SC 7, but had only to lie in wait until the next eastbound convoy, HX 79, crossed his path twenty-four hours later.

The night visibility was good, with a near-full moon shining down through thin high cloud to reveal the havoc wreaked amongst the once well-ordered columns of HX 79 by the torpedoes of Liebe, Prien, Bleichrodt and Schepke. Seven ships had been hit in the space of three hours, the gaps in the ranks where they had once sailed showing dark and ominous like gaps in a forest of tall trees swept by a lightning storm. Some of the wrecks were drifting astern into the darkness, chased by disorganized escorts which should have been closing the net around the remaining ships. Meanwhile, the Convoy Commodore in the *Salacia* at the head of Column Five was doing his utmost to prevent a panic, which would send the undefended merchantmen scattering to the four winds to become easy victims of the waiting U-boats. The *Salacia's* signal lamp was running hot, her steam whistle reduced to an ineffectual hiss as the Commodore attempted to pass his orders.

The Cardiff ship *Ruperra*, hitherto an impeccable station keeper, had been in the thick of the mayhem, ships being torpedoed all around her, and, not surprisingly, she had fallen out of line and was straggling astern of Column Six. It was there that Endrass, creeping back in to attack from astern of the convoy, found her.

Evening star sights had put the *Ruperra* some 140 miles to the south-west of Rockall, nearing her journey's end, it could be said – and then the wolf pack had moved in, setting the night sky ablaze with the flash of exploding torpedoes.

Sweeping the horizon with his binoculars, 46-year-old Captain David

Davies could see no avenging destroyers racing to defend the exposed rear of the convoy, and knew it was time for a decision to be made. Should he now break ranks and make a run for the North Channel? The *Ruperra*, although fifteen years old, and deep laden, should still produce a credible 12 knots with her boiler safety valves screwed down. Only for a few hours, perhaps, but long enough to get them out of this terrible holocaust.

Davies was sorely tempted, but before he was able to put his ship to the test Endrass' torpedo slammed into the *Ruperra's* engine room and blew the bottom out of the Cardiff tramp.

With her largest watertight compartment breached, the *Ruperra* lost most of her buoyancy, and sank under the sheer weight of her cargo of steel in a few minutes. Captain Davies went with her, as did thirty of his crew, the youngest, Galley Boy William Spiller, aged 15, on his first trip to sea, and the oldest Chief Officer John Ellis, 68-years-old, retired, and returned to sea to fill a gap in the ranks caused by German torpedoes.

The seven men who survived the *Ruperra* were picked up by the Glasgow-registered *Induna* and later transferred to the corvette *Coreopsis* and landed in Methil. The others, those who died, found unmarked graves in the deep Atlantic, with the exception of Captain David Thomas Davies, whose body was washed ashore near the Scottish island of Arran. He lies buried under a plain granite stone in the cemetery at Troon, overlooking the steel-grey waters of the Clyde.

Having torpedoed the *Wandby* shortly before midnight, and watched her drift astern into the darkness, Günther Prien brought U–47 back into the fray, penetrating the rear of the convoy, and sailing boldly between the columns. Regardless of the risk of being seen, he looked around carefully before selecting a target.

The 5,185-ton motor vessel *La Estancia*, owned by Buries Markes of London, was nearing the end of a marathon run, having crossed two oceans in her voyage from Queensland, Australia with a cargo of 8,333 tons of sugar. Commanded by Captain John Meneely, she was a new ship, having left the Sunderland yard of William Doxford in the early part of the year. For a merchantman of her day she was exceptionally well armed, carrying both a 4-inch and a 12-pounder HA/LA gun. Unfortunately, at that time the Admiralty was still adhering strictly to the rules laid down by the Geneva Convention, and both guns were mounted aft, rendering them ineffective in anything but a stern chase.

However, there was not even time to man the guns when the attack came. Captain Meneely wrote in his report:

At 2240 GMT, when in position 57° N 17° W, being 400' off Barra Head, I heard the swish of a torpedo on the port quarter. I think it must have been fired from a distance because it was breaking surface and throwing up a spray of water. It might have been 10 yards away when I first saw the torpedo; I tried to shout out "Hard Over", but it was too late and we were struck on the port quarter by the after end of No.5 hatch. The explosion was not exceptionally loud but sharp; there was no flame or column of water, but plenty of debris in the way of hatches, etc.

I already had my men mustered amidships, and as the vessel immediately began to sink stern first I ordered the boats to be launched. Everyone got into the boats with the exception of the 3rd Officer whom I last saw on his way down a ladder. The vessel was going down so fast that I realized that unless the boats were cut away they would be dragged under so I gave the necessary order and the boats got way just as the vessel sank, 4 minutes after the explosion. I was left alone on the ship and was dragged down, I think through the funnel as that is where I was standing, to a great depth. Then the rush of water forced me up again and I was soon picked up by one of my own boats.

As the ship sank the starboard boat was broken up. A number of the men clung to the wreckage, but 7 of the crew were picked up by the *Induna* which fact I later confirmed. About an hour after the torpedoing we were picked up by the *Coreopsis*, which also had on board 6 men from the *Leferra* (*Ruperra*), and landed at Gourock.

As the long night of 19 October drew to a bloody close, a new chapter in the saga of HX 79 opened. The anti-submarine trawler *Angle*, with the survivors of the *Wandby* on board, was steaming through a sea of oil covered debris on the lookout for more survivors, when she came across the wreck of the tanker *Caprella*. The 8,000-ton *Caprella* had been torpedoed forward of her bridge, and although her bow was noticeably low in the water, she did not appear to be in a sinking condition. Here was an opportunity to save at least one precious cargo, and after consultation between Lieutenant Arthur Blundell, RNR, commanding *Angle*, and Captain Kenny of the *Wandby*, it was decided to attempt salvage the derelict tanker. Third Radio Officer Gerald Whitehead later told of the attempt:

> A crew consisting of *Wandby*'s Chief Engineer, Senior Third Engineer and carpenter, along with eight ratings from the *Angle*, including a signalman, now boarded the *Caprella* and got to work. The ship's donkey boiler was still warm, and after half an hour on the hand pump the two engineers raised enough steam to start the oil burning equipment. Slowly, the Shell tanker began to move off astern of the trawler.
>
> The approach of darkness, however, brought a turn in the weather, the wind freshened from the east and raised a head swell which caused the tanker to pitch ominously – and at 4 am she began to break up. The boarding party, now all gathered aft, could see the focsle head rising and falling between the lower and upper bridge, for all the world as if the ford section was attached to the rest of the vessel by hinges. Then the bizarre moment came when the ford section broke away. As it sank the jumper stay between the two masts did not part until it had forced the top part of the main mast into a crazy angle, and when it did finally part it was like a shot from a 4-inch gun.
>
> Now the boarding party were marooned on the still floating half of the ship with no means of abandoning it. They sent up a distress flare. *Angle* steamed back to the rescue but when her boat was launched it sank to the gunwales; excessive use had made it unseaworthy. All that was left now was a Carley float. *Angle* attempted to fire a line by rifle on the leeward side of the half-ship, so that the boarders could pull the raft across to them. But the wind had risen and this plan proved abortive; the trawler had to steam in circles and could only fire each time she passed.
>
> *Angle*'s coxswain, a deep-sea fisherman, now gave the finest display of ship handling any man there had ever witnessed, as he brought the trawler around in the heavy swell dangerously close under the tanker's stern, so that a line could be thrown over to her deck. It was caught amid a shower of fruity language.
>
> But the men were not out of danger yet. The first party to take to the raft in the dark found themselves unable to paddle it away from the tanker, the angry sea nearly washing them into the torn portion of one of the hulk's midships tanks. *Angle* came in close

again and passed over another heaving line; they now had a line from the raft to the trawler as well as one back to the tanker; and with one line heaved on and the other paid out they were able to get alongside *Angle* and board her, then send the raft back for the remaining men.

Even in these seas the derelict half-ship still remained afloat, apparently the only remaining evidence of the U-boat pack's attack on the convoy. It was a danger to shipping; *Angle* sank the hulk with four shells from her 4-inch. So ended the salvage bid.

The man who opened the attack on HX 79, Heinrich Liebe in U-38, had by now emptied all his tubes. Taking advantage of the chaos reigning in the storm-filled night, he withdrew to the eastwards and began the onerous task of reloading his tubes. In harbour, with a flat calm, handling the 1½ ton missiles was difficult and dangerous enough; out in the open Atlantic with U-38, rolling crazily, her casings awash, it became a life and death contest dominated by iron nerve and sheer physical strength.

While U-38 was thus engaged, her lookouts sighted a loaded tanker on a south-westerly course. She was the 9,432-ton Norwegian motor vessel *Sandanger*, which in the confusion of the night had lost touch with the convoy. Down to her marks with a full cargo of highly volatile kerosene, the *Sandanger* was desperately trying to find and join the other ships.

With the reloading operation in progress Liebe was unable to use his torpedoes on this very tempting target. He resorted to opening fire on the Norwegian tanker with his deck gun, but the violent movement of the U-boat in the rough seas upset the aim of his gunners. No hits were scored, and the *Sandanger* survived to serve the Allied cause for another two and a half years.

While Heinrich Liebe bombarded the *Sandanger* with no visible results, another member of the wolf pack was encountering unexpected success to the south-west of Iceland.

Sailing out of Lorient on 5 October, U-124, under the command of Georg-Wilhelm Schulz, hurried north-westward to join in the attack on Convoy SC 7. Schulz failed to locate the convoy, but in the early hours of the morning of 16 October came across the small Canadian steamer *Trevisa*. Having lost contact with the convoy in bad weather, the *Trevisa* was pluckily attempting to get through to the North Channel on her own. She was easy meat for Schulz's torpedo, going down shortly before 0400 with the loss of seven of her crew.

Schulz searched for SC 7 for some hours without success, finally deciding to move north in the hope of meeting with another Allied convoy. His perseverance was rewarded three days later when the 5,810-ton Norwegian steamer *Cubano* hove in sight, on a westerly course and entirely alone.

The *Cubano*, owned by Wilhelm Wilhelmsen, and under the command of Captain Häkon Martinsen, was on a ballast passage from Manchester to Montreal, and twenty-four hours earlier had been part of the 30-ship convoy OB 229.

OB 229, escorted by the destroyers *Sturdy* and *Whitehall*, the corvette *Heliotrope* and the armed trawlers *Arabis*, *Blackfly* and *Lady Elsa*, had dispersed after dark on 18 October, the hard-pressed escort force then racing west to pick up the more vulnerable loaded ships of HX 79.

Captain Martinsen's orders were to make full speed for longitude 25° W, and from there steer directly for Montreal. The *Cubano*'s 2,900 ihp triple expansion steam engine, although twenty years old, still delivered a service speed of 12 knots, and Martinesen, having completed a number of wartime crossings unescorted, was confident of clearing the danger area before the U-boats pounced.

The chance meeting with U-124 – and it was by pure chance that they met – came half an hour before midnight on 19 October, when the *Cubano* was within a couple of miles of crossing the 25th meridian. (57-55N 24-57W)

Schulz's torpedo hit the *Cubano* squarely amidships, blasting a huge hole in her port side between the after bulkhead of No. Three hold and the stokehold. The blast severed the main steam pipes between the boilers and the engines, filling the engine room with high pressure steam. The main engine and its auxiliaries ground to a halt, and the sea poured into the empty No. Three hold. The *Cubano*, listing heavily to port, slowly lost her way through the water. Her sailing days were over.

Satisfied that the *Cubano* was sinking, Schulz looked around for another victim. This he found half an hour later in the British fruit carrier *Sulaco*. Owned by Elders & Fyffes, the London banana importers, and under the command of Captain Henry Bower, the *Sulaco* had left OB 229, and was bound south for Victoria, British Cameroons. When Schulz's torpedo went home the empty ship sank within minutes. Captain Bower and sixty-four of his crew went down with her. U-124 continued to cast around for further victims, but with OB 229 now scattered far and wide, success eluded her.

Aboard the stricken *Cubano* decisions were being made. Her port lifeboats had been destroyed by the blast of Schulz's torpedo, but the two remaining boats on the starboard side were designed to carry all thirty-one crew. Captain Martinsen ordered his men to man these boats and lower them to the water. This done, Martinsen remained on board to determine whether there was any hope of saving his ship. A brief visit to the top of the engine room was enough to establish that the main engine was already under water. The *Cubano* might not be in immediate danger of sinking, but she would go nowhere under her own steam.

Martinsen now discovered that two men of his crew were missing, and with the help of Able Seaman Roald Kristiansen, who had returned on board, a thorough search of the ship was made for the missing men. They could not be found, and Martinsen assumed they must have been killed in the stokehold when the torpedo struck.

Convinced that there was no longer any hope of saving his ship, Captain Martinsen ordered the First Mate's boat to return alongside, and having collected any provisions and gear to hand, he and Kristiansen at last abandoned ship, going over the side on a rope ladder. Unfortunately, the boat was rising and falling on the rough sea, and in danger of being smashed against the ship's side. Kristiansen boarded safely, but Martinsen fell between the boat and the ship. Only prompt action by the boat's crew saved him from a horrible death.

Both boats now pulled away from the ship, and throughout the rest of the night remained hove to within a mile of the *Cubano*. Four other ships, probably from the dispersed OB 229, were seen to pass close by during the night. But none answered the distress flares burned by the lifeboats.

When the reluctant daylight finally came, the *Cubano* was seen to be still well afloat. Martinsen contemplated reboarding the ship to get more supplies, but the storm was raging with renewed fury, and to try to get back alongside the heaving ship would have been to court disaster.

It was decided to remain in the vicinity of the ship for a while to see if conditions improved. They did not, but during the course of the morning cries for help were heard, and then a small liferaft was sighted. Clinging to the raft was Chief Cook James Harvey, the sole survivor of the British ship *Sulaco*, also sunk by U-124. When he was hauled aboard one of the boats, Harvey told his rescuers that the *Sulaco's* chief officer had been with him on the raft, but overcome by cold and exhaustion, slipped away during the night.

The boats stood off the *Cubano* for a few more hours, but her increasingly sluggish movements indicated that she was sinking. Martinsen now decided to hoist sails and steer for the west coast of Scotland, which he estimated to be 600 miles off. This was an enormous undertaking. By skilful seamanship the two boats managed to stay together throughout that day and the stormy night that followed. Next morning, they were sighted by the Canadian destroyer *Saguenay*, which took them on board and landed them at Greenock on the evening of 23 October.

While U-124 was busy hunting down the unprotected runners from the dispersed OB 229, Günther Prien, who in U-47 had been the first to sight HX 79, had returned to the fray. Having found an easy victim in Buries Markes' motor vessel *La Estancia*, he then penetrated deeper into the convoy. The weather was in his favour, being described by Lorient as: 'The weather is ideal for U-boats. Few waves, little wind (SE 2-3), some diffuse light from the moon, and every now and then a little fog that made it hard to see the horizon.'

Slipping unseen through the now somewhat untidy lines of merchantmen, Prien reached the sixth column and selected a very deep loaded ship near the head of the column. She was the 5,026-ton *Whitford Point*, a London tramp owned by the Gowan Shipping Company. Under the command of Captain John Young, and carrying a crew of forty, the *Whitford Point* had on board 7,480 tons of steel billets loaded in Baltimore for London. Broad in the beam and slow moving, she was the proverbial 'sitting duck' of HX 79. Chief Officer J.N. Marcombe had the watch on the bridge of the British ship. He later reported:

On 20th October at 0001 when we were steering a N course in position 56.38N 16W, proceeding at a speed of 9 knots we were struck by a torpedo right amidships on the port side, about 300 feet from the bow, in the after end of No.2 hold. About half an hour before we were torpedoed two ships were torpedoed on the starboard side, and we then made an emergency turn to port.

I was on the bridge at the time. There was a terrific explosion, but I did not see any flame or smoke, but there was a column of water thrown up on the port side. As soon as the *Whitford Point* was struck, the Captain, who was also on the bridge, ordered us to take to the boats, as he could see the ship was going to sink. I went on to the lower bridge on the port side. I then got hold of an axe ready to slip the boat, but I did not have time to do this, as the ship broke in half and sank in about 15 seconds. I was taken down under the water by suction from the ship and when I came up I saw only 2 men in the water, and they were each hanging on to a small raft. There was a small piece of wood just where I came to the surface, and I held on to this.

I had a whistle in my pocket and kept blowing this all the time. Eventually all the ships went out of sight and after about 3½ hours HMS *Sturdy* came along and I blew an SOS on my whistle and she came over and picked me up. The destroyer circled all around, but no more survivors were seen. We proceeded on board HMS *Sturdy* and were landed at Londonderry.

Chief Officer Marcombe and the two others rescued by *Sturdy* were the only survivors of the sinking of the *Whitford Point*. Captain John Young, thirty-five crew members and one DEMS gunner went down with the ship, which had slipped from under them in a matter of seconds.

For Günther Prien the night developed into a turkey shoot. Having watched the brief death throes of the *Whitford Point*, he remained on the surface, allowing the convoy to flow by him, while HX 79's escorts frantically chased their tails impotently lighting up the sky with starshell. This show of force did little to stiffen the morale of the bewildered merchantmen. The enemy was already within.

Prien dropped back between Columns Six and Seven until he was abreast the rear ships. To port of U–47 was the Swedish ore carrier *Sir Ernest Cassel*, deep in the water with 10,000 tons of iron ore for Glasgow, a tempting target, but to starboard Prien saw an even finer prize. She had the unmistakeable silhouette of an oil tanker, and in accordance with Admiral Dönitz's standing orders she took priority over all other targets.

The ship to starboard of U–47 was in fact the British motor tanker *Athelmonarch*, 8,995 tons, commanded by Captain Thomas Donovan, and manned by a crew of forty. However, contrary to Prien's assessment, she was not carrying a priceless cargo of oil. Her tanks contained 13,141 tons of molasses from the West Indies; a valuable enough cargo, but hardly vital to Britain's war effort. Fifty-four-year-old Captain Donovan later wrote in his account of the attack:

. . . everything went well until the night of the 19th/20th, although we had had one or two scares two days previously. On the 19th October the weather was fairly good, but the sea was rough, wind SE force 3 to 4, sky cloudy and overcast, with flashes of moonlight after dark. At 2230 on the 19th the first ship of the convoy was torpedoed; she was right out on the starboard wing at the time. We kept going and after an hour, at about 2330, two more ships were torpedoed within a few seconds of one another, the *Caprella* who as the leading ship of the 6th column and the *Sitala* the leading ship of our column, the 7th. Five minutes later the *Janus* was struck, then several other ships on our port quarter, the names of which I do not remember, then the *Matheran*, 11 ships within an hour, between midnight and 0100 on the 20th. The last ship to be hit was the *Assyrian* who was right out on the port wing, the leading ship of the port column, at 0200, an hour after us. We never saw anything of the enemy all this time, not even the tracks of the torpedoes.

Donovan was mistaken about the *Assyrian*, as she had been sunk in SC 7 twenty-four hours earlier, but this error was perhaps indicative of the confusion that reigned in Convoy HX 79 on that dreadful night in the Atlantic. The helpless merchant ships, not knowing who, or where the enemy was, were being picked off one by one like plastic ducks in a fairground shooting gallery.

During the attack, the convoy Commodore, leading Column Five in the *Salacia*, gave the ships the only protection he could offer by taking them through a series of emergency turns, swinging sharply from port to starboard, and starboard to port. The general idea was to spoil the enemy's aim, but in reality these wide sweeps only served to slow the ships down further, thereby offering them up to the German torpedoes. It was during one of these emergency turns that Günther Prien found the *Athelmonarch* drifting slowly across his sights. Captain Donovan wrote in his report:

I was on the bridge and saw nothing of the torpedo, there was only one explosion, which was a loud bang, a lot of very strong fumes like cordite, no flame, but tons of water were thrown up over the bridge. I think we were hit in the midships pump room on the port side, just on the tipping centre, 250 feet from the bow. All the tank tops were screwed down but the pump room tops were blown up.

The port forard lifeboat was smashed and there was a hole in the port side about 37 feet deep by 45–50 feet across. The deck itself was set up about 18" near where the explosion occurred, for some 25–30 feet. Immediately after the explosion the ship listed 15° to 20° to starboard, but gradually righted itself again.

Donovan had no means of knowing how badly his ship was hit, but the *Athelmonarch*, built on the Clyde in 1926, was unlikely to go down without a fight. Like most oil tankers of her day, her hull was constructed using the Isherwood system. This involved heavy longitudinal girders running the full length of the ship to compensate for the bending stresses imposed when loading tank by tank. Furthermore, each cargo tank was separated from the other by reinforced watertight bulkheads, so that the *Athelmonarch's* hull was divided into a dozen or more watertight compartments. She also had side tanks, which for much of her length gave her a double skin. Only if torpedoed in her engine room would she be in danger of foundering quickly.

In this case, the *Athelmonarch's* engine spaces had not been breached, and although she had slowed down to a mere crawl, her engines were still turning over, and her steering gear did not appear to be affected. Even with the huge hole blown in her side by Prien's torpedo, Captain Donovan estimated the tanker's chances of survival as high. But firstly, as a precaution against the ship sinking suddenly, he telephoned the engine room instructing the Chief Engineer to stop the engines and bring his men on deck.

Chapter 12

The Rescue Ship

With everyone on deck, Captain Donovan conferred with his senior officers, and after a short discussion it was unanimously decided that the tanker appeared to be in no immediate danger of sinking and there was still a possibility of saving her. Volunteers were called for to man the engine room, and within ten minutes the *Athelmonarch* was under way again. She was slow, extremely vulnerable to the torpedoes of any lurking U-boat, but she was manned by men who were determined to get her home.

While the *Athelmonarch* had been hove to, the convoy had moved on ahead, but the rear ships were still just visible. Donovan commented in his report:

> There were flashes of moonlight at intervals and we could see the smoke of the convoy 3 or 4 miles in front. They were still zig-zagging, making it difficult for us to rejoin them, but we were able to do so at 9½-10 knots, in spite of being torpedoed, and we eventually picked up the convoy at 0400 on the 20th, regaining our proper station at 0700, after which we kept station satisfactorily until we reached Liverpool, where we discharged our remaining cargo. We had jettisoned 250 tons to lighten her, and some cargo was lost from tanks 5, 6, 7 and 8.

Captain Donovan had nothing but praise for the conduct of HX 79's escorts, but he had this to say of the Royal Netherlands Navy submarine O-14, which was sailing with the convoy, ostensibly to supplement the escort screen:

> The Dutch submarine which was with the convoy was a great nusiance. After zig-zagging, at one time we found this submarine on our starboard quarter within 500 yards of us and we trained our gun on her, thinking she was an enemy; we did not open fire,

fortunately, as I could not identify her as being German. She flew the Dutch flag and remained on the surface all the time, but we did not know anything about her, nor who was in her.

Lieutenant Tichelman, commanding O-14, had his own views on the perils of sailing in convoy:

19 Oct 1940 at 21.15 hrs at position 57N–18W. While at a 80° W course the convoy is attacked, forward starboard, by U-boats. At the same time the convoy changes course 40° to port side. This puts O 14 in a position at port of the convoy. Because of the fog the O 14 loses contact with the convoy and has to increase speed.

At 22.37 she is in a position of 250 mtr abeam of *Shirak* (loaded with Kerosene) which is struck (port side aft) by a torpedo. A destroyer sailing half a mile behind O 14 fires flares over the port side of the convoy.

O 14 changes course 90° starboard and at +/– 23.00 hrs she spots, 4° over port side, the convoy in the light of an explosion on board the *Shirak*. O 14 decides to follow the convoy on its general course of 110°. O 14 observes that on the other side of the convoy two ships are ablaze, one of them is a tanker.

The convoy still zig-zags with a general Western (sic) course of 110°. But because of all the course changes the convoy has scattered somewhat.

O 14 has to increase speed several times because she is getting closed in by the merchants.

At 01.00 hrs O 14 sails next to a tanker, possibly the *Sandanger*. The tanker is falling behind and not zig-zagging and O 14 increases speed in order to get ahead of the tanker.

At 01.15 hrs at a distance of 500 mtr from the O 14 the tanker is struck by a torpedo on her port side below the bridge. O 14 turns to port and starts to sail an irregular course.

Lieutenant Tichelman identified the torpedoed tanker as the *Sandanger*, but the Norwegian ship was not involved in the action, and reached Belfast undamaged. The best estimate is that Tichelman had been a close witness of the torpedoing of the *Athelmonarch* by U-47.

In retrospect, it seems that the presence of O 14 in the convoy was of no help to anyone. She played no part in the defence, and was in fact twice mistaken for the enemy and attacked by the other escorts.

The *Athelmonarch* survived to carry many thousands of tons of precious oil for the Allied cause, being finally lost in the Mediterranean on 15 June 1943, when she was torpedoed and sunk by U-97. Four of her crew lost their lives in the sinking. Captain Thomas Donovan was not on board, having died of natural causes in Basra a month earlier. It is most likely that the immense strain of war at sea was a major contributory factor to his death.

In his thwarted attempt to sink the *Athelmonarch* Günther Prien had used up his last torpedo, and was instructed by Lorient to return to port. U-47 arrived there on 23 October, having been at sea for only ten days. In this short voyage she sank four ships totalling 20,124 tons and put a vital oil tanker out of service for many months. Hitler's propaganda machine exaggerated this score to eight ships of 50,500 tons, which took Prien over the 200,000 ton mark. He was called to Berlin to be feted and presented with the Oak Leaves to his Knight's Cross.

When U-47 retired from the battle, she was quickly replaced by Engelbert Endrass's U-46, which a few hours earlier had sent the Cardiff tramp *Ruperra* to the bottom. Approaching the convoy from astern, Endrass came up with the Swedish-flag tanker *Janus*, which was straggling in the wake of the rearmost ships.

The 9,965-ton Swedish motor ship *Janus*, carrying 13,885 tons of fuel oil from Curacao to the Clyde, had been sailing as third ship of Column Six, but in the confusion of the night attack and the evasive changes of course signalled by the Commodore, she had suddenly found herself dangerously hemmed in on all sides, and Captain Larson had been forced to reduce speed and drop back. Eventually, the *Janus* had found herself alone and racing to catch up with the other ships. That she had survived thus far was nothing short of a miracle, for the tanker was still in her peacetime colours, her hull painted a pale grey, and her upperworks a brilliant white. In the bright moonlight she stood out like a glowing marker beacon, much to the discomfort of those ships sailing alongside her.

Straggling astern of the main body of the convoy, although she was making 13 knots, the *Janus* had no escape from Endrass's torpedo, which caught her square in the engine room. Four men were killed by the explosion, and the *Janus*, her back broken, slowly sank. Captain Larson and thirty-seven other survivors were picked up by the corvette *Hibiscus*.

For some days there had been unease in the British ranks about the conduct of those ships in the convoy sailing under a foreign flag. Captain

William Park of the Glasgow steamer *Loch Lomond* expressed his concern in writing:

> I would say that one of the ships in the convoy had been very bad at showing lights. The *Thyra*, a Norwegian ship, sailing astern of us, had been warned about showing lights in convoy, and as we had personally signalled to her about this on the night of the 17th October. There was a light showing from the after end of the bridge deck, and was seen frequently between 7 p.m. and 9 p.m.; another light was showing amidships in the vicinity of the engine-room. One night this ship dropped astern of the convoy, completely out of sight, but the next morning he caught up with us again. When we received orders to turn 90° the *Thyra* and another ship (I think it was the *Tiba*, a Danish ship) remained where they were. The *Tiba* had always been astern of her position and when the Commodore of the convoy signalled and asked why he was astern he received no reply.

There is no more heinous crime in the watch keeper's book than showing a light when in convoy at night. With U-boats about it was an invitation to sudden death. Not surprisingly, it was so often that the foreign-flag ships were accused of this wanton act, and the suspicion in the British ships was that these ships were signalling to the enemy. This would have been a very foolish act indeed, for the U-boat commander crouched at his attack sights in the conning tower had no means of discerning the nationality of the ship he was lining up on. The more plausible explanation lay in poor blackout arrangements on the foreign-flag ships. On the other hand, the British ships were not allowed to leave port without a tried and tested system in place. All doors opening out onto the deck were fitted with heavy blackout curtains and cut-out switches, while all ports had drop-down deadlights. Furthermore, British merchant seamen were frequently caught in air raids while ashore on leave, and they appreciated the consequences of showing lights when enemy bombers were overhead. It was extremely rare for a British merchantman to betray a convoy by showing lights.

Shortly after dawn on the 19th, and coincident with the arrival of Lieutenant Commander Russell's escort group, word was received from the Admiralty that U-boats had been sighted ahead of the convoy. Later in the day, the *Loch Lomond*, then sailing as the third ship of Column Three, received orders from the Commodore to drop back and take up position as No. Ninety-four, the rear ship of the starboard outer column. She had been designated as rescue ship for Columns Five to Nine. Her work would soon begin. Captain Park later reported:

> At about 9.20 on 19th October the convoy was attacked by submarines. We received a signal to turn 40 degrees to port. We heard several explosions. We saw that the *Uganda*, which had been the next ship ahead of us and was now on our starboard bow, had been torpedoed, and we also saw another ship, which later turned out to be the *Matheran*, in difficulties.
>
> While we were steaming to the *Uganda*, we noticed other boats nearer to us and also some men in the water, so we altered course and went to them first and picked them up. These were survivors from the *Matheran* and were chiefly Lascars. When we got alongside the boats they were afraid to jump to the ladders, so we had to lash them with rope and haul them on board. While we were doing this a destroyer came along and asked what the position was. I told the commanding officer about the *Uganda* and he went towards it. It was about 11.30 p.m. before we got all the survivors on board.

By the time the last of the *Matheran's* survivors had been hauled over the rails of the *Loch Lomond*, the convoy had pulled ahead out of sight, and Captain Park found himself faced with a challenging decision he could well have done without. His ship was alone on a dark and squally sea full of predatory U-boats, and he now had on board, in addition to his crew, seventy-two wet, exhausted and frightened survivors, some of whom were in need of medical attention. The safety of the North Channel lay only 250 miles away, and the temptation to make a full speed dash alone was very great.

While Park was weighing up the options yet another squall came racing down on the *Loch Lomond*, sweeping her decks with icy rain and reducing visibility to a few hundred miserable yards. Enough was enough. Park called his chief engineer to the bridge and explained the situation. There was no argument, and before the squall had passed, the *Loch Lomond*, with her boiler safety valves tightly screwed down, was burying her bows in the seas and for the first time since her trials on the Clyde six years earlier was striving to break the 15-knot barrier. The *Loch Lomond* was going home.

The *Loch Lomond's* bid for independence was short-lived. No sooner had she worked up to full speed than the corvette *Arabis* appeared out of the rain, swept alongside, and offered to escort her back to the convoy. Park had little choice but to follow meekly in the wake of the Navy ship, coming up with the rear ships of HX 79 at around 0100 on the 20th.

Two hours later, the *Loch Lomond* had resumed her position as rearguard of the starboard column and was adjusting her speed to stay on station, when it was reported to the bridge that a U-boat had been sighted on the port quarter. Captain Park immediately altered to put the submarine astern, at the same time instructing the radio room to send out an SSS alert. Meanwhile, the 4-inch gun's crew ran aft to man their gun. HMS *Arabis,* which was still nearby, closed the reported position of the U-Boat and dropped two depth charges, but saw nothing and had no Asdic contact. The submarine, it is presumed to have been U-38, had dived deep.

Over the next two hours, U-38 and the *Loch Lomond* played cat and mouse, the U-boat being sighted several times on the surface, and apparently following the British ship. Each time the enemy was sighted, Park put her right astern, but for some unexplained reason hesitated to order his gunners to open fire. He later reported:

> About 4 o'clock we saw either the same submarine or another one on our quarter about ¾ mile away and we kept him astern and then we lost sight of him. This continued for some time; we would see the submarine for about 10 minutes and then it would disappear. Every time we saw the submarine we put it astern and then when it disappeared we resumed our normal course of 115 degrees. In all we saw him about four times.
>
> During all this time we had our guns loaded and the crews standing by, but I did not want to fire until we had a reasonable chance of hitting the target.
>
> After 2 hours the submarine was still there and the last time we saw him he was a little nearer than before. Eventually the man at the gun said he thought he could see a vessel in the water astern. I said, 'Does it look like destroyer?' and he replied that he was not sure. I replied 'Do not fire unless you are sure, but wait until it gets lighter.

Subsequent research shows that the *Loch Lomond* was being stalked by two U-boats, firstly by Heinrich Liebe's U-38, and then Joachim Schepke's U-100. It seems highly likely that had the *Loch Lomond's* gunners been allowed to lob a few shells in the direction of their pursuers both Liebe and Schepke might well have beaten a hasty retreat. As it was, William Park's reluctance to shoot eventually cost him his ship.

At about 0630, while Captain Park was still debating whether to use his stern gun or not, U-100 fired a torpedo which struck the *Loch Lomond* on her starboard side about 100 feet from the stern. The explosion was like a clap of thunder, and was followed by a column of dirty water and debris soaring high in the sky from the after hold. Those on the bridge narrowly escaped injury when the slabs protecting the Hotchkiss gun shattered and showered them with broken lumps of concrete. Captain Park wrote in his report to the Admiralty:

> The ship took a 6° list to starboard and the Lascars we had taken on board all started clambering for the boats. We had two boats and neither of them had been damaged by the explosion. I gave no orders to lower the boats, but the Lascars climbed in and my own crew, not wishing to be left, got into the boat after them. The port boat got away very quickly before I had time to stop it being lowered. At the same time another crowd ran to the starboard boat, but fortunately before they lowered it we noticed that some timber from the after deck which had been dislodged by the explosion was dropping over the side and was floating to where we would have to launch the next boat. I gave the order to lower the boat quickly, and put the 3rd Officer in charge. This was about ½ hour after the explosion. I told the 3rd Officer to lie off and await orders. The Chief Officer who would normally have been in the port boat was still on board. There were altogether 3 of us remaining on board.. the Chief Officer, 2nd Officer and Wireless Operator of the *Matheran* and 2 Engineers, the 2nd Officer and myself from the *Loch Lomond*.

The situation of those remaining on board the *Loch Lomond* was precarious, as her list was increasing and she was slowly sinking by the stern. Much to their relief, when it was fully light, the minesweeper HMS *Jason* came in sight. Rockets were fired and flares burned, which the Navy ship answered by signal lamp. She made no move to take off Park and his officers, but nevertheless remained in the vicinity, a reassuring sight as she circled the area, probing with her Asdics for signs of the U-boat that had crippled the *Loch Lomond*.

Meanwhile, Captain Park ordered one of his lifeboats back alongside, and all those remaining on board the *Loch Lomond* abandoned ship. The occupants of the two lifeboats were picked up an hour later by HMS *Jason*. The minesweeper already had survivors from three other ships, the *Matheran, Bilderdijk* and *Uganda,* on board. These were joined by the *Loch Lomond's* crew of thirty-nine, plus the seventy-two men the rescue ship had saved from the *Matheran*, making a total 190 in all. The small sweeper bore a close resemblance to a River Clyde pleasure steamer on a busy bank holiday as she set off after the convoy.

The *Loch Lomond*, once a proud member of the fleet of Maclay & McIntyre, now abandoned, lay drifting forlornly astern of the convoy, her valuable cargo of steel and timber lost forever and soon to be haggled over by the underwriters at Lloyds. In the early afternoon, when HX 79 and its escorts had long disappeared over the horizon, U-100 came back to administer the coup de grâce. Schepke, unwilling to expend another of his dwindling stock of torpedoes, opted to use the derelict for gunnery practice. This proved to be a false economy, for the *Loch Lomond*, built to survive a lifetime of tramping in all weathers and conditions, absorbed seventy-nine 88mm shells before she finally rolled over and sank.

The shattered remnants of Convoy HX 79 found refuge in the North Channel next morning. The surviving ships were a forlorn sight; their funnels blackened by smoke, their salt-caked hulls running red with the rust generated by the Atlantic storms. Their arrival, ironically coinciding with the 135th anniversary of Nelson's great victory at Trafalgar, signified the end of one of the blackest periods in British maritime history. In the space of just fifty-six days, Dönitz's new U-boat packs had wreaked havoc amongst the transatlantic convoys, sending forty-six Allied merchant ships totalling 253,049 tons gross to the bottom. With them went 316,721 tons of cargo, cargo that would be sorely missed by Britain, now fighting alone against the awesome might of Hitler's war machine. But perhaps the most grievous loss was that of the 462 men who died with their ships. Sailors, firemen, stewards, engineers, navigators, captains, they were all irreplaceable.

In these early days of the Battle of the Atlantic, it had been demonstrated that Admiral Dönitz's *Rudeltaktik* could be the answer to Britain's overwhelming dominance of the ocean trade routes. Starting with the first tentative moves against Convoy SC 2, four U-boats, working together, and coordinated by radio from Lorient, had sunk 21,000 tons of shipping in forty-eight hours. Taking into consideration the fact that SC 2 was made up of fifty-three slow-steaming merchantmen with a weak escort screen, this first wolf pack attack could hardly be deemed an unqualified success. It was, however, an indicator of things to come.

The lessons had been well learnt when, in mid October, SC 7 came steaming over the horizon. Eight U-boats lay in wait in what had become their hunting ground 250 miles west of Bloody Foreland, and what followed was an unprecedented massacre that became known by the U-boat men as 'The Night of The Long Knives'. Of the thirty-five merchantmen making up the convoy, no fewer than twenty fell to Dönitz's torpedoes. SC 7's escort force, two sloops and a corvette, were hopelessly outclassed and could do little to prevent the slaughter. Otto Kretchsmer, in U-99, who alone sank seven ships, wrote in his War Diary:

Starshell was still being fired on either beam of the convoy in spasmodic bursts, having a curious ineffective result in the pale light of the moon. The nearest flares were falling 10 miles away and looked to the U-boat crew to be about as effective as a small child playing with matches in the middle of the Sahara Desert.

Commander Arthur Knapp, who in the Grimsby class sloop *Lowestoft* had led the defence of SC 2 and HX 72, summed up the situation succinctly:

Submarines are now operating amongst the convoys at night as surface vessels with the advantage of a minute silhouette and therefore extremely difficult to see in the dark, and the advantage of being able to dive quickly to avoid collision or make their getaway when sighted by merchant ships. Against this type of attack our Asdic is of little use, whether transmissions are used or not, and the only effective counter measures would appear to turn night into day and to use starshell, searchlights and flares from aircraft to carry out a high speed search in and around the convoy. Sloops, corvettes and trawlers are severely handicapped and of little use in any night action.

At this early stage of the war roughly half of British ocean-going merchant ships were defensively armed and, as might be expected, these ostensibly non-combatant ships had to be content with the Royal Navy's 'left-overs'. This usually amounted to a handful of machine-guns around the bridge to ward off attacking aircraft, and a 4-inch anti-submarine gun mounted on the stern. This complied with the terms of the Geneva Convention, which the Admiralty was then following to the letter. In consequence, any merchantman faced with a hostile submarine on the surface had only one option, and that was to put the enemy stern on and hope to run away, at the same time attempting to score a hit with the 4-inch. The last was a forlorn hope, for the majority of guns fitted to the merchant ships were more suited to be gathering dust in a war museum than being fired in anger. Furthermore, although some lucky ships carried small numbers of trained naval gunners, the majority of guns were manned by crew members who, by virtue of a three-day gunnery course reluctantly attended in a naval dockyard, were deemed to be proficient in the maintenance and firing of every conceivable weapon. The U-boats, equipped with the best guns Krupp Armaments could produce, manned by gunners trained to perfection, rarely lost the argument.

A sad footnote which illustrates the awesome power of the other enemy the convoys faced, and the pressure of work imposed on the small number of escorts available was written while the survivors of HX 79 were safe in dock discharging their cargoes.

On the night of 30 October, one of HX 79's escorts, the destroyer HMS *Sturdy*, having spent just long enough in port to refuel and reprovision, was back at sea, and on her way to escort the incoming slow convoy SC 8. She had rounded the Outer Hebrides and was on her way out into the Atlantic when she ran into a fierce westerly gale.

Conscious of the need to meet SC 8 before the U-boats gathered, *Sturdy's* commander, Lieutenant Commander George Cooper RN, decided to carry on into the teeth of the gale. A destroyer, by virtue of its calling, is built for speed rather than riding out an Atlantic storm, and as the night went on *Sturdy* buried her slim bows deeper and longer into the advancing waves so that at times she was almost completely submerged in the angry green water, burrowing through the depths like the enemy she was matched against. Inevitably, her twenty-two-year-old engines began to flag, and Cooper found it increasingly difficult to hold her up into the wind. Eventually, he found his ship being blown onto a lee shore on the west coast of the island of Tiree, and he was powerless to save her.

Carried bodily by the huge Atlantic rollers, the 1,000-ton destroyer was tossed ashore on the rocks like so much flotsam coming in on the tide. Lieutenant Commander M.J. Gibson, son of the *Sturdy*'s chief engineer, who was injured in the grounding, wrote many years later:

> The ship was driven onto the rocks and broke in two. I believe that
> an attempt to launch the sea boat was made. This resulted in its
> immediate destruction, sadly with the loss of its crew who were
> drowned. I am told that on shore the event was noted and a
> Merchant Navy captain, on leave and living nearby, managed to
> communicate with the ship by morse light advising the crew not to
> attempt to leave the ship until daylight. His advice was followed.
> Alas there was another later tragedy, the MN captain was lost on
> his next convoy.
>
> I understand that the crew of the *Sturdy* were picked up by
> another destroyer, leaving behind a destoring party. Meanwhile
> my father was taken to Oban cottage hospital from where my
> mother received word of what had happened.
>
> The outcome was that my mother and I set off for Oban. We
> arrived there on the day that another inbound convoy was
> attacked, with I believe casualties . . . Apart from a fractured
> kneecap, my father was in good order. As a relatively long stay was
> indicated I was dispatched to Tiree to see if I could recover any of
> my father's belongings . . .
>
> It is a long time ago now and memory dims. I do remember the
> hospitality and consideration that I received. I was treated as a
> guest, put up at the local hotel and transported out to the wreck
> site. An indication of the force of the gale was that the bows of the
> front section of the ship were actually in the grass on the shore.
> The stern section was about 40 yards off shore and only accessible
> by breeches buoy.

Chapter 13

The Lone Wolf

On the evidence of the four convoy actions already described, it would seem that in Dönitz's *Rudeltaktik* lay the answer to the severing of Britain's Atlantic supply lines. However, there were still powerful voices in Germany arguing in favour of the old tried and tested method of individual U-boats hunting alone, attacking any targets that came their way. In 1940, after a busy September and October, in which the U-boats attacked four major convoys, there was suddenly a scarcity of boats in the North Atlantic, mainly because those involved with the convoys were in port rearming, refuelling and repairing. The next big eastbound convoy, SC 11, provided the ideal opportunity for the single U-boat attack to be reassessed.

For reasons unknown, the usually efficient B-Dienst failed to warn Lorient of the approach of SC 11. The fact that the convoy was three days late in leaving Cape Breton may have been a factor. Thirty-eight ships strong, this slow convoy sailed from Sydney on 9 November, and for the first time it seemed that some effort had been made to provide a credible escort. HMS *Enchantress*, sleek and warlike in a fresh coat of Admiralty grey, cut an impressive figure as she criss-crossed ahead of the convoy, pennants flying and Asdics pinging. Unfortunately, as with so much of Britain's fighting power in these dark days, she was not all she appeared to be.

Enchantress, built by John Brown on the Clyde, had originally been fitted out as a sloop, but on completion in the spring of 1935 she had been commissioned as the Admiralty Yacht, her main mission in life being to accommodate the Board of the Admiralty whenever they chose to inspect the fleet. Her two 4.7-inch guns mounted aft were removed and replaced by extensive additional accommodation fit to house the Admirals in comfort. When she returned to normal service at the outbreak of war, this accommodation was removed, but her after guns were not replaced. This left *Enchantress* with just one 4.7 forward, which in early 1940 was supplemented by a 12-pounder and two quadruple 0.5-inch machine guns. Then, under the command of Commander Alan Scott-Moncrieff, RN, she had been assigned to convoy escort work.

Shortly before joining SC 11, *Enchantress* had been fitted with a Type 286 aircraft radar modified for shipboard use, a crude instrument capable of giving some warning of the approach of ships or aircraft, but little else. The resurrected sloop, with her 12-pounder HA/LA and machine-gun batteries was thus able to fight off an attack from the air, but she had little to offer against the U-boats.

The defence of SC 11 was considerably stiffened when, three days out of Sydney, *Enchantress* was joined by the 34,000-ton battleship HMS *Rodney*. To the uninitiated, at a stroke, the security of the convoy was ensured. Surely no U-boat would think seriously of attacking when this 24-knot monster, armed with nine 16-inch guns, an array of smaller armament and racks of depth charges, was in the vicinity? As it transpired, the battleship was never called upon to pit her strength against the U-boats. On 15 November *Rodney* was ordered to detach from SC 11 and seek out the German pocket battleship *Admiral Scheer* which, having sunk the *Jervis Bay* and savaged the convoy she was escorting, was at large in the North Atlantic posing an enormous threat to Allied shipping.

Although it had not started off well, 1940 was certainly proving to be a very good year for *Kapitänleutnant* Joachim Schepke.

Schepke had taken command of U-19 at the turn of the year. She was a Type IIB, 279 tons displacement with three bow torpedo tubes and two 20mm AA guns on deck, and by nature of her size was assigned to coastal work mainly in the North Sea. On her first war patrol, Schepke took her out of Kiel on 8 January 1940. His orders were to harass shipping sailing between British East Coast ports and Norway, which at the time was still neutral.

Lying off the Humber estuary just after midnight on 9 January, Schepke sighted a small deeply loaded vessel on a north-easterly course. She was the 1,345-ton Norwegian steamer *Manx*, bound from West Hartlepool with a cargo of coal for Drammen, in southern Norway. Completely alone, crawling along at a snail's pace, and unarmed, the *Manx* was a gift to Schepke. One torpedo was sufficient to send her and her cargo of coal to the bottom. Of her crew of nineteen, ten men survived the sinking, eight clinging to a capsized lifeboat, and two on a small raft. When rescue came, only six were still alive.

Before she went down, the Norwegian ship's wireless operator was able to send an SOS, which brought a British destroyer, on patrol nearby, racing to the scene, catching U-19 still on the surface. Schepke crash dived, but the destroyer's depth charges followed him down, and over the next two hours the U-boat was subjected to an unrelenting hammering as charge after charge exploded around her. Eventually, with her rudders damaged and her electric motors exhausted, she hit bottom and lay there unable to move.

It seemed that the crew of U-19 were doomed to die on the bottom of the North Sea, but fortunately for them Joachim Schepke was as resourceful as he was brave. As soon as the avenging destroyer had moved away, sufficient compressed air was released into the boat for the port diesel to be started, which in turn recharged the electric motors. Ballast was blown, and U-19 was manoeuvred to the surface using her motors as rudders. This was a relatively simple solution to an extremely dangerous and life-threatening situation, but in bringing it off Schepke showed something of his true potential.

Schepke and U-19 were back at sea again after only six days in port, and over the following eight months sank another eight ships of 14,372 tons. In May 1940 Schepke took command of the new Type VIIB U-100, and so began his amazing run of successes against the Atlantic convoys.

When Joachim Schepke returned from his third cruise in U-100, in which he had sunk three ships in HX 79, his accumulated sinkings stood at thirty-one ships totalling 135,970 tons gross. This charismatic 28-year-old, who was said to be 'confident, daring to the point of casual recklessness in his command', was also an ardent Nazi, a committed anti-Semite, and favourably regarded by Berlin. Along with Otto Kretchsmer and Günther Prien, he was now one of the top 'aces' of Germany's U-boat Arm.

Very unusually for the time of the year, Convoy SC 11 enjoyed fair weather for much of the Atlantic crossing. It was not until 22 November, when the ships were within 200 miles of the Irish coast that the cloud began to thicken and lower and a falling barometer signalled the approach of a depression. Twenty-four hours earlier, the lone escort

Enchantress had been joined by the three Canadian destroyers *Saguenay*, *Skeena* and *St Laurent*, and the Halifax-class frigate *Ottawa*, which were to guard the convoy on the final, and most dangerous leg of the crossing. Commander Scott-Moncrieff assumed command of the escort force, positioning the Canadian ships around the convoy, with *Skeena* acting as rearguard and rescue ship. At last, with five substantial warships protecting them, the merchantmen of SC 11 felt they could look forward to a successful conclusion to the voyage. However, their optimism proved to be premature.

When, on 7 November, 1940 U-100 set out from Lorient on her fourth cruise, the existence and sailing time of SC 11 was still unknown. Schepke's orders were to patrol 150 miles to the west of Bloody Foreland, ready to pounce on any Allied ship foolish enough to be sailing alone. From the outset, the cruise proved uneventful, and as day after day went by with not a ship, enemy or otherwise, darkening the horizon, Schepke and his men, who had for so long lived on the knife-edge of convoy warfare, found themselves facing the evils of boredom. The day to day routine went on; watches were changed, batteries charged, meals served, but tempers began to fray and small incidents that would have normally been ignored became major crises.

When, on U-100's fifteenth day out from Lorient, a howling gale came barnstorming in from the west, it was greeted with some relief. Boring watches spent in the conning tower searching in vain for the enemy suddenly became hours of exhilaration spent locked in combat with a sea gone wild. The wind rose to a screaming crescendo, the rain lashed down, and the steepening waves burst over the submarine's sharp bows, flooding her casings with a welter of green-tinged foam, and filling the air with icy spray. Riding the roller coaster of the heaving Atlantic swell, crackling oilskins streaming rain and spray, was enough to set the adrenaline running high even in the most stoic of old U-boat hands.

There were few in the ranks of SC 11 who greeted the sudden deterioration in the weather as a welcome diversion. With the wind whistling in the rigging and the spume blowing off the crests of the waves, it was plain to all that the Western Ocean was about to live up to its dreaded reputation. By nightfall it was blowing a full gale from the west and the once orderly columns of SC 11 were becoming more and more ragged. The ships, now embarked on the final leg of the voyage before entering the North Channel, were running before a following wind and sea that made precise steering essential. The slightest deviation from course allowed a quarterly sea to crash against the stern sending the ship slewing wildly, with the helmsman fighting to bring her back under control. Some of the older merchantmen had rod and chain steering gear and aboard them there was a constant worry that one of the chains might snap, a common occurrence when labouring in a heavy sea. SC 11 was rapidly becoming a mêlée of ships out of control.

In the wildly rocking conning tower of U-100 Joachim Schepke, one arm wrapped around the compass binnacle, the other raised to ward off the stinging spray, peered out into the blackness of the night. Despairing of finding the enemy in such dreadful weather, he was on the point of taking the boat down to find more comfortable conditions in the depths, when he caught the glimmer of a light ahead. The light was white, and from the way it was describing a slow arc against the sky it appeared to be a masthead light. Then, below the white light a faint green glow came into view. Against all the odds, Schepke had stumbled upon what seemed to be a lone ship, and the green light, her starboard side light, showing beneath the white indicated that she was eastbound. Unbeknown to Schepke, in the darkness ahead of him lay not one ship, but a whole convoy, and a convoy which was in disarray.

Station-keeping in a large convoy of ships sailing at night without lights has always been a hair-raising exercise, but on a night like this, with nil visibility due to rain and spray and ships sheering wildly from side to side in a quarterly sea, it was nigh impossible. Inevitably, two ships narrowly avoided a collision, prompting them to turn on their navigation lights. This was the signal for all the nervous bridge watch keepers of SC 11 to follow suit, and suddenly the darkness ahead of U-100 became a flickering kaleidoscope of white, red and green lights. Joachim Schepke, hunting alone, had struck gold.

On the bridge of the *Justitia*, owned by the Chellew Navigation Company of Cardiff, Captain David Davies was one of those forced to resort to showing navigation lights to avoid being run down by one of his neighbours. The 4,562-ton *Justitia*, carrying the usual cargo of steel billets and timber loaded in Savannah, Georgia, had originally been number 43 in SC 11, that is third ship in Column Four, but when the full force of the gale struck Davies had found it impossible to hold his ship on station. There were times when the huge following seas, their tops curling and foaming, slammed against her quarter with sufficient force to sweep her beam-on to the general course of the convoy. Whistles screeched, Aldis lamps flashed urgently, but it was only the exhibition of navigation lights that saved her from disaster.

What seemed at the time the only possible way of saving the *Justitia* from a messy collision turned out to be her death warrant. Joachim Schepke, having penetrated SC 11 on the surface from astern, lined up on the British ship's green starboard light, and fired a single torpedo at close range.

Schepke's torpedo found the *Justitia's* most vulnerable spot, blasting a hole in her engine room through which the sea poured unchecked. Given reasonable weather, the 5,000 tons of timber she carried in her 'tween decks and on deck would have kept the ship afloat long enough for her crew to abandon ship in safety, but drifting beam-on to the mountainous waves and listing drunkenly, she was quickly overwhelmed. She went down, taking Captain Davies and twelve of his crew with her. The remaining twenty-six men who survived were saved from the sea by HMS *Enchantress.*

Unseen and unheard in the confusion of the storm, and able to see only fleeting shadows through the fog of rain and spray, Schepke fired blindly at the next ship to lurch into his sights. She was the small Dutch steamer *Ootmarsum,* in exile from her home port of Amsterdam, and carrying a full cargo of iron ore for the steel mills of South Wales. Launched from a distance of no more than 600 yards, Schepke's torpedo broke the Dutchman's back, and she sank so fast that no one realized she had gone until heads were counted next morning. Her entire crew of twenty-five perished with her.

The convoy had by now lost all pretence of order, and was just a milling mass of frightened ships looking to escape this additional horror, death by explosion, that had been visited upon them. Some were showing lights, some were not, and many were on the verge of breaking away to seek more sea room in which to manoeuvre. One such was Reardon Smith's 4,740-ton *Bradfyne.* Under the command of Captain Rupert Vanner, the *Bradfyne* was full to her hatch coamings with 7,900 tons of grain, loaded in Montreal and consigned to Belfast. She had originally kept station as No. Ninety-three, third ship of the starboard outside column, but now the confusion was so great that Vanner had no idea of the position of his ship relative to the others.

All but hove to and at the mercy of wind and waves, the *Bradfyne* was the easiest of targets for U-100's torpedoes, one of which slammed into her at seventeen minutes past midnight. She was hit on the port side in her No. Two hold, immediately forward of the bridge. The explosion was muffled by the grain in the hold, but the upward blast was sufficient to reduce the bridge and accommodation below it to a smoking ruin.

As the sea invaded the *Bradfyne's* breached hull she slumped heavily to port, and seemed to be on the point of capsize. Then, with a groan that was almost human, she steadied up, finally assuming a crazy list of 20 degrees to port. How much longer she would last was a matter for conjecture. It was a terrible night on which to attempt to lower lifeboats, but Captain Vanner had no other option available. He gave the order to abandon ship.

The *Bradfyne* carried four boats, two 30-man lifeboats amidships, and two small jolly boats below the bridge. The jolly boats had been reduced to matchwood by Schepke's torpedo, and it was impossible to lower the starboard lifeboat, which was held fast in its davits by the list of the ship. Apprentice Paul Buchholtz takes up the story:

> . . . 22nd November, at 21.30 GMT, we were struck by a torpedo on the port side, forward of the bridge by No.2 hold about 100 feet from the bow, I do not know our exact position when we were torpedoed but our position at 2000 had been 55° 14' N. Our speed at the time was 6½ knots and the wind force 6 or 7 with a very choppy sea with huge waves. There was no flame or smoke, but all the superstructure and the bridge alleyway was broken and buckled. The ship listed immediately to port and we were unable to lower the starboard lifeboat. The Chief Officer ordered us to stand by the port lifeboat, and I got into this with a sailor as this was my boat station. The Captain gave the order to lower the boat, and just as this was being done the other apprentice jumped into the boat. By this time the *Bradfyne* was listing 15-20 degrees to port. Just as the boat was about halfway down a huge wave struck the boat, unlocking the falls and carrying away the painter. The boat remained against the ship's side with three of us in it. Another AB jumped into the boat when she was on top of a wave and about level with the railings on deck. We drifted rapidly astern and never had a chance to do anything and we never saw the ship again.

About an hour later we saw the light of flares from the directions in which the convoy had gone – we thought they might have been fired by destroyers around the *Bradfyne*. Before we lost sight of the *Bradfyne* we saw the Third Mate on the bridge letting off rockets and the Captain was signalling to some ship as we saw him with the lamp. The weather was very rough and the wind at gale force, so we were unable to do anything except lie to the sea anchor, even though we were continually shipping water. I tried hauling in the sea anchor and lying beam on to the sea, as being light (only four in a lifeboat for 30). I thought we might be more comfortable, but the reverse was the case as we shipped several heavy seas. After this we streamed the sea anchor together with two buckets which we found much more satisfactory.

On Sunday morning, 23 November, we sighted a ship but she did not see us: later in the day we sighted a flying boat coming directly towards us, but when it was about two miles off it turned and went away, although we lighted flares, fastening them to a boat hook and holding them in the air. Just before dark we saw another flying boat, but it never saw us.

After we had been afloat for three days and three nights a Norwegian ship, the *Norse King*, picked us up and landed us at Belfast.

It is not known what happened to the *Bradfyne* and those left on board on that storm-filled Atlantic night. One of the four survivors, Apprentice Terence O'Neill, testified:

We saw Captain Vanner and, I think, all the crew, judging by the size of the crowd, on deck after the explosion. Being as the torpedo hit in No.2 hold, it was possible that all the engine-room staff managed to survive and make it up to the deck, but it was too dark to identify anyone.

There was no panic, everyone was cool and calm, just waiting there quietly. There were two rafts left on the ship. We were quite helpless to manoeuvre the lifeboat and were soon swept away. We never saw the ship again.

The *Bradfyne* was fully radio equipped, and carried two radio officers, yet she does not appear to have broadcast an SOS. No trace was ever found of the ship and the thirty-nine men still on board, and it must be assumed that at sometime before dawn on 23 November the *Bradfyne's* cargo of bulk grain shifted, and she rolled over and sank.

With the whole of Scott-Moncrieff's escort force hunting him in earnest, the Canadians being particularly eager to get to grips with the enemy, Joachim Schepke beat a hasty retreat. When first sighting SC 11 he had reported the convoy to Lorient, anticipating that other U-boats in the area would join him. It now seems that, possibly due to the adverse weather, only U-93 was able to respond.

U-93, a Type VII C commissioned only four months earlier, was under the command of *Kapitänleutnant* Claus Korth. She had sailed from St Nazaire on 7 November, and in sixteen days at sea, constantly patrolling the convoy routes, had not fired a shell or torpedo in anger. This continued her run of bad luck experienced on her previous patrol. In an attack on the westbound convoy OB 228 Korth had sunk two small ships, but had immediately come under heavy depth charge attack by three escorts, narrowly escaping being blown to the surface. Having survived this first attack without damage, an hour or so later U-93 was again showered with depth charges by another avenging escort. The day finished with the U-boat being caught on the surface and bombed by a Sunderland of RAF Coastal Command. Once again U-93 escaped without damage, but this last incident had been quite enough for Claus Korth. He set course for home.

An unnatural peace had descended on SC 11 after Schepke had sent the *Bradfyne* down, and for three hours the only sounds to be heard were the howl of the wind and the crash of the waves. The convoy commodore, Vice Admiral Sir F.M. Austin, sailing in the 4,966-ton *Llandilo* leading Column Five, took advantage of the lull to attempt to restore order to the convoy, but he had little success. When Schepke came back just after 0300 on 23 November, ships were still milling around and navigation lights were flashing on and off. Schepke had no difficulty in picking out his next victim. She was the 2,205-ton Norwegian-flag steamer *Bruse,* one of Fred Olsen's out of Oslo, loaded with 1,550 tons of timber for the East Coast port of Ipswich.

Schepke's torpedo hit the *Bruse* amidships with catastrophic effect. The funnel toppled and went overboard, and the mainmast came crashing down on the boat deck, smashing two of the lifeboats and killing five men. Seconds later, with a horrendous screeching of metal on metal, the *Bruse* broke in two, the after part with the remainder of the lifeboats being swept away into the night. On board were the bulk of the little ship's crew, seventeen men.

When the German torpedo ripped their ship apart, Captain Ole Brekke, Second Mate Hans Jansen, and three seamen were on the bridge, stunned but still alive. As the seconds ticked by, they fully expected to meet their end in the icy waters of the Atlantic, but much to their surprise and great relief, the forward section of the ship, from the bridge to the bows, remained afloat. Engineless, rudderless, the derelict rolled crazily in the grip of the waves, but it showed no sign of sinking.

Gathering his wits, Captain Brekke ran to the wireless room, which was immediately abaft the wheelhouse, with the intention of sending off an SOS, only to find that the delicate transmitters had been destroyed by the blast. There now remained only the bridge distress rockets, which Brekke ordered to be fired.

The rockets soaring up into the cacophony of the storm seemed a forlorn hope, but once again the five survivors were in luck. *Skeena* was nearby and seeing the distress signals, she closed in on the broken ship. The Canadian destroyer made several attempts to come alongside, but this proved impossible in the violent weather prevailing. Lieutenant Commander James Hibbard decided to stand off until dawn.

Back on board the *Bruse,* the survivors were struggling to free a small liferaft which was lashed to the deck cargo. Two hours later, with still no sign of the dawn and no let-up in the weather, they heaved the raft over the side, and jumped after it. Seizing the opportunity, *Skeena* moved in and whisked them aboard.

Already on board *Skeena* was Able Seaman Johan Løkvik, the only man to escape from the after section of the *Bruse.* He had been sucked down with sinking wreck, but had fought his way to the surface, eventually finding and clambering on board a waterlogged lifeboat. *Skeena* searched for other survivors, but none were found.

It was thought that that was the end of the *Bruse,* but a few days later a patrolling aircraft sighted her fore part still afloat. The half ship, with its cargo still intact, was towed into the Firth of Clyde, where it was beached. Her deck cargo, and that remaining in the forward holds was then discharged. A survey revealed that the wreck was beyond repair, and what was left of the gallant little ship ended up in the breaker's yard.

Hidden in the depths of the storm. Schepke remained on the surface watching the *Bruse* break up. He then looked around for his next target, settling on a larger vessel. She was heavy with cargo and all but hove to as she breasted the advancing waves. She was the 2,694-ton, Norwegian-flag, *Salonica,* carrying 3,400 tons of pit props consigned to Newcastle, and commanded by Captain Ole Økland. Launched in 1912 from a Newcastle shipyard while the *Titanic* was setting out on her first and last voyage, the *Salonica* had spent twenty-eight hard years tramping the cross trades. Escaping from Norway in June 1940, she had already completed four Atlantic crossings under British control, but on this occasion age and the weather were getting the better of her.

A witness to the sudden destruction of the *Bruse* as she floundered in the heavy seas close on the *Salonica's* port side, Captain Økland decided that the time for being bunched up in a convoy was past. Ordering all crew to muster on deck wearing lifejackets, except the three men on watch in the engine room, he rang for full speed with the intention of making a lone dash for the North Channel.

Økland had made his move too late. Just as the *Salonica* began to show a brave turn of speed, Schepke's torpedo crashed into her boiler room and exploded with a thunderous roar. Third Engineer Andor Breivik and Stoker Jakob Tobler died in the great gush of scalding high-pressure steam that swept through the engine spaces.

With the way off her, the *Salonica* slewed beam-on to the heavy seas and took on a crazy roll. Her port lifeboats had been smashed by the blast, and when the starboard boat was swung out and lowered it capsized when it hit the water, hurling fourteen of the sixteen men on board into the sea. The other two managed to regain the ship by shinning up the boat falls.

Once again, it was *Skeena* that came to the rescue. Manoeuvring the destroyer skilfully, *Hibbard* came close alongside the sinking ship, providing sufficient lee for the nine men still on board to launch the jolly boat and row across to the *Skeena.* Of the fourteen men catapulted into the sea from the starboard lifeboat, seven were later pulled from the water by HMS *Enchantress.*

There was a lull in the attack while Schepke withdrew to reload, using the two spare torpedoes stowed on the submarine's deck, a herculean task in the weather conditions prevailing. Four hours elapsed and a grey dawn had broken before U-100 returned to the convoy.

Like so many others as daylight returned, Captain Peter Mortensen, master of the the Danish motor vessel *Leise Mærsk,* took the long lull to mean that the enemy had gone away. Sailing under the British flag for the Ministry of War Transport, the 3,136-ton *Leise Mærsk*, loaded with 4,500 tons of grain and general cargo from Three Rivers to Sharpness, was attempting to regain her station as third ship of Column Two when Schepke's torpedo blew her apart. Of her crew of twenty-four, only seven survived to be picked up by a Dutch salvage tug.

Unwilling to risk a brush with SC 11's escorting destroyers in daylight, Schepke held onto his last torpedo until darkness came again. At about 2000, U-100 was back mingling with the merchantmen, sailing unseen in amongst the columns.

Doggedly attempting to regain her position in the starboard outer column was another grain carrier, the 3,636-ton *Bussum*, owned by Vinke & Co. of Amsterdam. A veteran of the 1914-1918 war, when she had rescued survivors from the mined cruiser USS *San Diego*, the *Bussum* had already suffered major damage in this new war when she was bombed by German aircraft in the North Sea in May 1940. At about 2105 Schepke's final torpedo sent her spiralling to the bottom with her precious cargo. Fortunately, her entire crew of twenty-nine were rescued by HMCS *Ottawa*.

SC 11 was to suffer one more casualty, ironically at the hands of her own people. The 3,985-ton *Alma Dawson*, carrying a cargo of 5,900 tons of grain from Montreal to Ipswich, struck a British mine as she entered the Firth of Clyde. Her crew of thirty-five were picked up by the small Norwegian vessel *Spurt*, but the ship and cargo were lost.

In his lone and highly successful attack on Convoy SC 11 Joachim Schepke had sunk seven ships, ensuring that some 35,000 tons of desperately needed food and raw materials failed to reach British waters. This brought his confirmed total of ships sunk since setting out on his first war patrol in U-3 in September, 1939 to thirty-eight ships of 166,571 tons gross. U-100 was received with due ceremony on arrival in Lorient. Schepke, who had ably demonstrated what a single U-boat in the right hands might achieve, was awarded the Oak Leaves to his Knight's Cross a few days later.

On subsequent patrols Schepke and U-100 accounted for only three more Allied ships of 17,166 tons. At the end of December U-100 was taken into Kiel, where she spent two months undergoing a refit. During this time Schepke and his crew were used extensively for propaganda purposes, appearing in films, broadcasting and talking to potential recruits for the U-boat Arm.

It was with some relief to her crew that U-100 finally sailed from Kiel on 9 March 1941 to resume her role in the war. However, there was to be a reckoning a week later, when Joachim Schepke's luck ran out while he was involved in an attack of Convoy HX 112, which was heavily escorted by destroyers. U-100 was forced to dive and came under sustained depth charging. A report of the interrogation of prisoners stated:

> . . . Prisoners said that the first pattern of four or five depth charges exploded close to the U-boat. The depth gauge was said to have been damaged, and a number of light bulbs were smashed.
>
> It was stated that they had suffered further depth charging, and that extensive damage was caused in the U-boat; all pumps were put out of action, the instruments were all smashed, and the supply of compressed air gave out. The captain thought that the British would hear the air escaping. The floor plates were wrenched loose, water entered the bilges, and it was feared that the hydroplanes were no longer functioning properly.
>
> The U-boat sank deeper and deeper, as low as 230 metres (750 ft), according to prisoners; the crew felt very cold, and expected the hull to crash in at any moment.

Schepke was finally forced to surface, only to find the destroyers *Vanoc* and *Walker* waiting for him. A survivor from U-100 stated the following when under interrogation:

> The Diesels of "U 100" would not start, and it was found that they were not getting any fuel; then trouble was experienced with the electric motors. The captain became flurried and gave a wrong order; he ordered astern on the starboard motor, whereas he should have ordered ahead on the starboard motor. He quickly realized his mistake, but there was no longer time to correct it, and to turn the U-boat and fire a torpedo as the destroyer was approaching too fast, and by that time was too close. According to the German statements, torpedoes must run 150 metres (160 yards) before exploding. For a moment Schepke thought that the destroyer would pass astern of "U 100" but quickly saw that this was not likely.
>
> He shouted down to the crew to abandon ship, the men put on their life-belts and hurried up onto the bridge. Realising that it would not be possible to get their 8.8-cm gun into action, some

men made as though to man the 20-mm gun, but were at once dissuaded by their companions, who felt they would have no chance against the destroyer, which might then have left them to drown. The time was approximately 0318.

Five seconds before the collision, "Vanoc's" engines were stopped. The destroyer struck "U 100" almost at right angles just forward of the conning tower. "Vanoc" was brought up all standing.

The side of the U-Boat's hull and conning tower were smashed in, and the captain was caught and crushed between the stove-in side of the bridge and the periscope . . .

So died Joachim Schepke, horribly injured and dragged down into the depths by his sinking boat. It was an ignominious end to a brilliant career.

Chapter 14

The Year Ends

December 1940 opened with a return to the norm. When the next big eastbound convoy reached the Western Approaches Admiral Dönitz had re-mustered his forces and waiting in the wings were U-43 (Wolfgang Lüth), U-47 (Günther Prien), U-52 (Otto Salman), U-94 (Herbert Kuppisch), U-95 (Gerd Schreiber), U-99 (Otto Kretschmer) and U-101 (Ernst Mengersen). In support were the three Italian submarines *Argo, Giuliani* and *Tarantini,* making in all a formidable wolf pack.

HX 90, a fast convoy of thirty-five ships, with a quarter of a million tons of cargo on board, left Halifax for the United Kingdom on 21 November. This was no run of the mill convoy, for these ships, mostly British flag, were carrying desperately needed supplies, including sugar, grain, timber, steel, dairy produce, fuel oil, aviation spirit and phosphates. This, of all convoys, was a worthy target for every torpedo Dönitz was able to bring to bear.

After leaving Canadian waters, HX 90's sole escort was the armed merchant cruiser HMS *Laconia,* an ex-Cunard White Star liner of 19,695 tons. Armed with eight 6-inch and two 3-inch guns, the *Laconia* was typical of her class, too big and too slow to afford any effective protection to a convoy under attack. She was purely window dressing, but she was all the Admiralty had to offer.

The Convoy Commodore, 53-year-old Commander Victor Alleyne, RNR, sailing in the 5,848-ton *Botavon* at the head of Column Five, having served in the battleship *Renown* in the First World War, was only too well aware of the *Laconia's* shortcomings. But he had been assured that the destroyers of Western Approaches Command would join on or about 2 December, and until such time the convoy was safe in the *Laconia's* hands. Such promises are easy to make from behind a desk.

However, long before the U-boats arrived Commander Alleyne was to find his ships assailed by another enemy, the forces of nature at their most violent.

The North Atlantic in winter is no place for the faint of heart. The wide ocean is plagued by a wearying succession of low pressure systems sweeping across from west to east, each depression following so close on the heels of the other that they appear to merge into one continuous storm. Meteorological Office statistics record that the winter of 1940 in the North Atlantic was one of the worst in living memory, a record that holds good until this day.

The skies were already lowering when HX 90 left Halifax, and within forty-eight hours the clouds were trailing tendrils of icy rain across the rising seas. By the morning of 24 November, the long swells were assuming mountainous proportions and the breaking seas filled the air with salt-laden spray. As the day wore on, what had once been an orderly armada of ships was becoming a confused rabble as the heavily loaded merchantmen, the seas breaking clean over the decks of the smaller ones, struggled to maintain course and position in the convoy. By nightfall eleven ships had given up; the fight and were missing somewhere in the darkness astern, each fighting its own lonely battle with the rampaging elements.

When a feeble dawn finally broke on 26 November, the wind was howling like a banshee, and the rain was horizontal. Wedged in on the wildly gyrating bridge of the *Botavon*, Commander Alleyne shaded his eyes against the stinging rain and made a determined effort to make a headcount of the ships still holding together. Only thirteen were in sight, and they were only just holding their own.

For three more punishing days and nights the ships of HX 90 did battle with the North Atlantic at its worst. Miraculously, some semblance of order was preserved in the convoy, but ships still straggled and romped, drifting in and out of view, as did Wagner's *Flying Dutchman* of old. Rarely was Commander Alleyne able to count more than twenty in sight at once.

Finally, on the afternoon of 30 November, the storm gods relented. The wind dropped away, the clouds lifted and the angry seas gradually subsided, leaving only the long westerly swell to tell of the horrors of days past. One by one, missing ships began to reappear, and by nightfall HX 90 was twenty-nine ships strong and still reforming.

Sunday, the first day of December 1940, dawned fine and crisp, and with only just over two days steaming left to the North Channel there was a growing consensus in the battered, salt-stained ships that they were home and dry. Little did they know that just 100 miles ahead the outriders of Dönitz's wolf pack were casting about for signs of their prey. However, the U-boats were well to the north of HX 90's track, and if it had not been for the misfortunes of one ship, the convoy might well have slipped past them.

At 0700 that morning, the leading ship of Column Seven, the Belgian-flag *Ville d'Arlon* signalled the Commodore, saying that she was experiencing trouble with her steering gear, and would have to leave the convoy. The 7,555-ton cargo/passenger steamer *Ville d'Arlon*, under the command of Captain Albert Wilding, was bound for Liverpool with a general cargo. Commander Alleyne could do no more than wish her good luck, and by noon the Belgian ship was only a wisp of smoke showing on the horizon astern.

Surprisingly, the *Ville d'Arlon* rejoined at 1700 and at about this time HX 90's sole escort, the AMC *Laconia*, broke away to return to Halifax. The plan had been that the departure of the *Laconia* would coincide with the arrival of destroyers of Western Approaches Command. As always, the best laid plans have a habit of going wrong, and so it was with this one. When *Laconia* showed her stern, and made off at full speed for Halifax, the local escort was nowhere to be seen. HX 90 was rapidly nearing the U-boat danger zone, and other than a few ancient 4-inch guns manned by scratch crews, the convoy was unprotected.

Largely unknown to anyone except the plotters at Western Approaches Command in Plymouth, the waters in the approaches to the North Channel were becoming uncomfortably crowded. In close proximity to each other were three convoys, HX 90 inward bound, OB 251 westbound, and HG 47 homeward from Gibraltar. In all, ninety-eight extremely vulnerable merchantmen were within, or approaching the U-boat killing ground off Bloody Foreland, and their protection was shared between a pitifully small band of escorts. HX 90 was now completely alone, and would be so until OB 251 was out of the danger zone and her escorts could be spared for the incoming convoy. Meanwhile, northbound HG 47 had just two destroyers to patrol its large perimeter.

Twelve hours earlier, on the night of 30 November, U-101,

commanded by Ernst Mengersen, had reported to Lorient that she was cruising in position 55° N 23° W and had seen no sign of HX 90. Lorient advised her to search to the south-east. Mengersen, who had sunk only two ships since first taking command at the beginning of the year, complied willingly. And so it was that in the afternoon of 1 December, he sighted the *Ville d'Arlon*, then hurrying as fast as her 20-year-old engines would allow to rejoin HX 90. Suspecting, rightly it transpired, that he had sighted a straggler from an east bound convoy, Mengersen followed the Belgian ship at a discreet distance, at the same time informing Lorient of his discovery.

By the time the *Ville d'Arlon* was back on station with HX 90 Mengersen had been joined by Günther Prien in U-47 and Otto Salman in U-52. The three boats remained on the surface but out of sight, awaiting the arrival of darkness. When this came, it was not complete, for the Northern Lights were active and putting on a brilliant display. They gave sufficient light for the U-boats to close in on the convoy, while the rough seas masked their movements. Fortunately for HX 90, the enemy was not aware that the convoy was without escorts, otherwise the slaughter that occurred that night might have come sooner and been far greater.

The convoy had by this time succeeded in reforming its ranks. Thirty ships were present, steaming in nine columns each five cables apart, and maintaining a steady course of 060° at 8 knots. Mengersen came in from the starboard side and moved up to the head of the convoy. Once there, he trained his sights on the lead ship of the outside column, the 8,826-ton Anglo American Oil Company's motor tanker *Appalachee*, carrying 11,076 tons of aviation spirit and fuel oil for Avonmouth. He had chosen his target well.

Mengersen's torpedo crashed into the *Appalachee's* engine room, bringing her to a sudden halt. Fortunately, the highly volatile aviation spirit was in the forward tanks, so there was no catastrophic explosion and fire. Listing heavily as the sea rushed into her engine room, the tanker slewed to starboard and began to drift astern.

Instinctively, the ship immediately astern of the torpedoed tanker, went to her aid. She was the 4,958-ton British steamer *Loch Ranza*, loaded with timber and lead for Swansea. The *Loch Ranza's* bid to save life brought her into line for Mengersen's second torpedo, which went home forward of her bridge. By virtue of her timber cargo, the steamer remained afloat and upright, and was still able rescue thirty-two survivors from the *Appalachee's* crew of thirty-nine. Three hours later, the *Loch Ranza* was under way again and following the convoy at 5 knots. She was eventually taken in tow by a salvage tug and beached in Rothesay Bay. After extensive repairs, she returned to service with her owners, Maclay & McIntyre of Glasgow, in May 1941.

Curiously, Commander Alleyne was not yet aware that he had lost two ships. He later reported:

> At 20:15 two explosions were reported on the starboard wing of the convoy and gunfire. On making the bridge (less than 1 minute) I saw confused lights to starboard but certainly no gunfire. I did not see either a rocket of flare. There was a heavy rain squall and the starboard wing was 2.5–3 miles away. When visibility improved slightly I could see the rear ship of that column apparently coming on quite happily and no signals were made, so I concluded, and the captain agreed, that some ship had got tangled up with our right column, hence the commotion and lights. The explosions I could not account for and I did not myself hear any. Nothing was done and nothing further happened.

At first sight it may seem that Commander Alleyne's reaction to the unexplained explosions was bordering on the complacent. On the other hand, it must be remembered that the convoy was without escorts at the time, and even if ships had been torpedoed there was very little he could have done about it.

After torpedoing the *Loch Ranza*, Mengersen withdrew to reload and peace settled over HX 90 again. U–47 and U–52 were yet to make their presence known, and it seems they may have lost contact.

At 0100 on 2 December, the convoy altered course to 073° to approach the rendezvous with the local escort at dawn, an event eagerly awaited by the men who had endured the ocean crossing with only the minimal protection.

Half an hour later, the false euphoria of the convoy was shattered, when the *Ville d'Arlon*, back in position at the head of Column 7, hoisted two red lights, indicating that she was 'Not Under Command'. The Belgian ship's steering gear had failed again, and she was about to drop astern.

Nerves were already on edge and, not surprisingly, suspicions were aroused about the conduct of the *Ville d'Arlon*. She had made no effort to dim her red lights. In fact they were so bright that they must have been visible for many miles around, providing a perfect beacon for the U-boats to home in on.

U-101, her tubes reloaded, was by then attempting to regain contact with HX 90, and Ernst Mengersen was delighted when he sighted the *Ville d'Arlon*'s lights, a sure signal that he was on the right track. At about 0200 on 2 December, Mengersen was about to put a torpedo into the drifting *Ville d'Arlon*, when he sighted another U-boat on the surface close by. Having identified the stranger as Günther Prien's U-47, Mengersen chivalrously left the Belgian ship to him and moved on after the convoy. Prien quickly disposed of the *Ville d'Arlon*, sending her to the bottom with all her crew. He then followed in Mengersen's wake.

As the night of 1 December moved into the small hours of the next day, Commander Alleyne found himself faced with the ultimate nightmare that haunts every convoy commodore's waking hours. In what should have been its last night in open waters his convoy was still without its promised escorts, and now it was at the mercy of a pack of U-boats he could not see, and was unable to defend himself against.

Alleyne's fears were fully justified, for Mengersen and Prien had by then been joined by Otto Salman in U-52, Herbert Kuppisch in U-94, Gerd Schreiber in U-95, Otto Kretschmer in U-99 and Hans-Peter Hinsch in U-140. What followed over the next twenty-four hours can only be described as a complete and utter rout. The U-boats, completely unopposed, moved brazenly in and out of the columns of slow-moving ships, targeting and sinking ships at will. Torpedoes thundered, guns barked, distress rockets soared skywards, the sirens of the doomed ships wailed plaintively, men died. And in the face of all this mayhem Commander Alleyne fought to keep control. He later wrote in his report:

> I could not keep track of all the emergency turns as sometimes we had barely finished one when we had to go off again. We were like a helpless flock of sheep in a narrow lane with a dog each side. . .

The U-boats did not have it all their own way. Wherever possible, ships fought back, as did the North East Coast tramp *Dunsley*. Her master, Captain J. Braithwaite reported to the Admiralty:

> . . . I saw white lights and flares in the direction of the explosion and at 0328 we received an SSS from the LADY GLANELY. Presuming that the submarine would have left the vicinity we

steered towards the lights, in the hope of picking up survivors. At 0350 we saw the boats of the LADY GLANELY in the water and slowed down in order to go and help them. At 0410, when in position 54 41 N 18 41 W we sighted the submarine on the surface on our port beam about ½ mile away. The submarine opened fire and we replied at once. The submarine fired 3 shells and we fired 2 or 3. One of the shells from the submarine came in on our port beam and set the deck cargo on fire and then a shrapnel shell burst by the foremast on the port side. Another shell hit us on the poop; I do not know whether it burst inside or not but this made a big hole in the ship's side.

During this time we had opened fire and one of our shells appeared to hit the submarine; she did not fire at us any more but immediately disappeared. After some time another shell was fired at us, hitting us on our starboard beam. We were swinging at the time. This shell may have been fired by the submarine we first sighted, but I am of the opinion that there were two submarines in the vicinity and that this shot was fired by the second submarine. During the engagement we were machine gunned, but this did not do us any damage.

We then turned stern on to where we had seen the submarine and went off at full speed. We put out the fire which was close to the bulkhead, and the cargo was very little damaged. We then proceeded independently to Oban . . .

Captain Braithwaite's bald, almost self-effacing, statement of fact covering the action does little justice to the courage of the man and those under his command. This was a fight to the death – a sophisticated German fighting machine pitted against an ageing British tramp, her superannuated 4-inch manned by men who would not normally know a gun's breech from its barrel. But fight they did, and so lived to sail another day. Their one great regret was that they were prevented from going to the aid of the *Lady Glanely's* lifeboats, which disappeared into the night with their occupants, never to be seen again.

The *Dunsley* had one last errand of mercy to carry out before she reached the safety of Scottish waters. While HX 90 was under attack, her promised local escorts, the sloop *Folkestone*, the destroyer *Viscount* and the corvette *Gentian* were still shepherding Convoy OB 251. In desperation, Western Approaches Command had called in the armed merchant cruiser *Forfar*, then on the Northern Patrol, and directed her to go to HX 90's aid. Sending the 16,000 ton ex-Canadian Pacific liner into an area where the U-boats were swarming proved to be her death warrant. As soon as she approached the convoy she was spotted by Otto Kretchsmer in U-99, who immediately put a torpedo into her engine room slowing her down. Three more torpedoes followed over the next hour, the last of which hit the *Forfar*'s forward magazine and blew her bows off. One hundred and four men died with her, the remaining eighty-nine escaping in the boats, which were later sighted by the *Dunsley* as she left the convoy. Indirectly, it might be said that these men owed their lives to Ernst Mengersen, who in his attack on the *Dunsley* had caused Captain Braithwaite to go it alone.

The ships of Western Approaches Command that should have been protecting HX 90 during those crucial hours of the night, namely the destroyers *Viscount* and *Vanquisher*, supported by the Flower-class corvette *Gentian*, left the westbound convoy OB 251 at 1900 on 1 December. The plan was for them to rendezvous with HX 90 before midnight, but when they were on passage they heard the *Forfar*'s cries for help, and immediately altered course for the sinking AMC. They were too late to help the *Forfar*, and when they finally reached HX 90, they learned that the convoy, under continuous attack for twenty-six hours by an estimated pack of seven U-boats, had suffered grievously. At the same time, the ships of OB 251, which had dispersed after the escorts left, had come under attack, losing three of their number to U-43 and U-99.

As for HX 90, Commander Allyene's 'helpless flock of sheep', eleven ships and their cargoes had been lost, with three others damaged, while the armed merchant cruiser sent to defend them had also paid the supreme price. With these ships had gone a total of 345 irreplaceable men. And for those who had survived the U-boats the battle was still not finished. Commander Alleyne's log for the closing stages of the voyage reads:

Tuesday, Dec. 3

11:00 – Attacked from the air by large 4-engined bomber. He came down Column 4 & 5, dropped a bomb missing 43, S.S. *Hannington Court*, and then went off to attack S.S. *W. Hendrik* who was coming up astern about 4 miles. S.S. *Quebec City*, 42, had two wounded from gunning.

Plane dive bombed S.S. *W. Hendrik* and scored direct hit first time with aerial torpedo. Terrific explosion and the ship wreathed in flames for a few seconds, ship stopped blowing off steam. I believe she was hit twice more with smaller bombs.

Viscount and sloop standing by.

Several submarine alarms during the afternoon which sadly hampered making arrangements to split the convoy and organize for going through North Channel.

Wednesday, Dec. 4

Lot of rain coming down North Channel.

18:00 – Detached myself and *Ruahine* and proceeded for Bristol Channel at 10.5 knots.

Thursday, Dec. 5

Arrival Barry Roads, *Ruahine* in company 18:00, and very glad to get there. Since junction with Bermuda, I never had the convoy together as a whole, bad weather, the gales one after the other scattered them besides the ordinary machinery troubles. The only calm night we had Hitler scattered them again.

The year 1940 had proved to be the year of the U-boat in the North Atlantic. Hunting in packs, Dönitz's grey wolves reaped an unprecedented harvest of more than two million tons of Allied shipping, most of it in the autumn and winter months of the year. Storm force winds, blinding rain, fog and, ironically, periods of flat calms with bright moonlight, all worked in favour of the U-boats. In the six convoys covered by this book, involving 256 merchant ships, the U-boats sank sixty-five and damaged four. Thus, in the space of less than four months, 355,500 tons of shipping had been summarily sent to the bottom, taking with it a king's ransom of 310,000 tons of cargo and nearly 1,000 brave men whose experience and skills would not be easily replaced.

In all, the year saw the loss of 440 British, Allied and neutral ships totalling more than 2,000,000 tons gross. The majority were sunk by the U-boats in the Atlantic, and in return Dönitz lost only thirteen boats, eleven German and two Italian. As the German shipyards were turning out between eight and ten U-boats a month, the contest seemed destined to have only one end.

The Royal Navy did its best to stem the haemorrage of precious ships and men, but the escorts were too few, and often so old that the task they were set was completely beyond them. Commander Arthur Knapp, who was heavily involved in the defence of the convoys, had no hesitation in making his views known. He reported to the Admiralty:

Submarines are now operating amongst the convoys at night as surface vessels with the advantage of a minute silhouette and therefore extremely difficult to see in the dark, and the advantage of being able to dive quickly to avoid collision or make their getaway when sighted by merchant ships. Against this type of attack our Asdic is of little use, whether transmissions are used or not, and the only effective counter measures would appear to turn night into day and to use starshell, searchlights and flares from aircraft to carry out a high speed search in and around the convoy. Sloops, corvettes and trawlers are severely handicapped and of little use in any night action.

Appendix

Seventy years on, Frank Hyland, a seventeen-year-old apprentice in the *La Estancia* at the time, remembers the loss of his ship:

My ship, *La Estancia*, was almost new. She was on her second voyage when, loaded with nearly 9000 tons of brown sugar, we reached Halifax to join the convoy. We had left the UK and sailed 'light ship' (with no cargo) all the way to the Queensland Australian ports of Bowen and Mackay, before coming north again up the Pacific and through the Panama. Spirits on board were high as, not only would we now soon be home for a few days of leave, but every crew member had been given a seven pound gunny bag of sugar.

Having assembled, the fifty-odd ships started off, only to pause in our crossing at Bermuda to collect a few more ships. I believe the convoy then consisted of 59 merchant ships. Quite soon after this, the convoy was immersed in dense fog. And it was then that something quite remarkable happened. It appeared that orders had been given that in this eventuality every ship would make a sound signal on their whistle or siren. This was to be a number of short blasts to indicate the column she was in, followed by another series of blasts for their numerical position in that column.

The resultant cacophony would perhaps in other circumstances have been quite laughable! Here were nearly fifty ships, the crews of which were getting used to sailing completely blacked out at night, taking care not to jettison any rubbish, and not to make any more smoke than could be helped which might betray our position, now manufacturing so much noise that any surfaced U-boat for miles around would be in no doubt that something worthwhile was nearby!

During the rest of the war, I was in many convoys in fog, but this strange procedure was never repeated.

With the fog cleared, we continued on our way. My memories of the first part of that trip may well be merged with those of other Atlantic convoys, but I expect that many times we were summoned to our action stations and watched the thrilling sight of one or more of our escorts, flying their large black pennants dashing off to do their best to protect their charges. But the evening of 19th October was a deal different. Soon after it became dark, although there was some moonlight, we came under attack again, and about 2200 the first ship was torpedoed. Again, of course, we were at action stations. My position was as sight-setter on our four inch naval gun. All the (I think) six other members of the crew had been trained in their positions and with the third mate as gunnery officer, we felt ready to do whatever was needed. However, soon another ship was struck, then another, and our captain called down to the gun platform and told us to leave the gun and assemble with the rest of all hands on number three hatch. It turned out that this order probably saved many lives, including those of the gun's crew. Just before midnight a tanker which was abeam of us on the starboard side in the next column erupted into an inferno. It was an horrendous sight with gigantic gouts of flame billowing upwards. Most of us were engaged in watching this dreadful sight, when one of the crew called our attention to the port side of the ship. There, at a distance of just over half a cable, was a U-boat on the surface! Our ship must have made a perfect target silhouetted against the burning tanker as she drifted astern. The next instant I heard a rush of compressed air, which I now realize was the sound of a torpedo being fired. Then the whole ship shuddered so violently that several chaps fell over. A shower of sparks shot out of the funnel and the engine began to race out of control. Above all this noise the captain shouted to us from the bridge to abandon ship. It seemed obvious that the torpedo had hit us somewhere along the after deck and the explosion had shattered the propeller shaft.

The ship had two lifeboats, one on each side. These were already swung out in the ready to lower position and the process of abandoning was carried out (with one exception) by everyone in a calm and orderly fashion. The exception was an engineer whom I will identify no more clearly. Perhaps he had been close to the engine when it had gone berserk, whatever the reason, this poor chap was making a most terrible row.

Our captain had been right to give the order so quickly, because *La Estancia* was settling fast. The last few men to enter the boat hardly needed to use the Jacob's ladder, being able to almost step on board.

With our boat loaded we attempted to push clear of the ship, but as we were using our oars to do this, there was what I can only describe as a machine-gun sound as the hull rivets just forward of the bridge structure ripped apart. Then the whole foredeck of the ship rose slowly to a perpendicular position with the foremast extended along and above the rest of the now almost invisible ship! I think until then I had been numbed by what was taking place, but to look up and see this just above one's head. Yes – that was one of the few times in my life that I felt really afraid.

Our boat was only a few yards clear of the ship when suddenly, without seemingly any fuss, she was gone, the foc'sle being of course the last part of her we saw.

Now we were alone in our boat. Only later did I learn that the port boat, which we never saw, fared worse than us. The third mate losing his life in a way I never quite understood.

Then, floating as we were amongst the flotsam in the heaving, but not rough, ocean, a very strange thing happened . . . someone started to sing, others joined in, and them it seemed as though the whole of the lifeboat's crew were singing 'Roll out the Barrel' ! Astonishing? Yes. Unbelievable, No! My memory of some parts of that night may be a little hazy, but that singing during the night during a pack attack by (I have now learned) at least five submarines I shall never forget.

During the first half hour or so we didn't actually row anywhere – reasonable, I suppose – where would we row to?. Then we spied a floating body, and reaching this person, found it was our captain, spluttering and gasping, but still alive. I well remember one of the ABs leaning over the side and reaching under the water saying, 'You'll have to forgive me for where I'm grabbing you like this, Captain.' as he hauled our Master over the side by the seat of his pants!

About half an hour later we spied some red life-jacket lights in the water and found seven men floating together. Having got them on board, wet but uninjured, we learned they were from a ship called the *Ruppera*. She had been loaded with steel rods or some such cargo, and having been torpedoed she just plunged straight under. Later I received a letter of thanks from the owners to say that the men we picked up were the sole survivors from that ship.

It was about an hour after that when we saw a naval corvette closing us, and we made our way over and on to their remarkably low deck to be given a most warm welcome by the crew.

I cannot end this account without a few words of praise for the men on the corvette HMS *Coreopsis*. Even before the addition of us as survivors, their foc'sle must have been very overcrowded. Yet these men gave up their bunks for us and slept themselves just anywhere they could find – on tables or lockers – anywhere. And certainly not on the foc'sle deck, this was frequently awash with sea water, such was the incredible motion of these gallant little ships. Three days later we reached Greenock, where we were accommodated on the floor of some hall for a night or two, fitted out with a change of clothing, a railway warrant, and sent on our various ways.

Bibliography

Admiralty, *Weekly Intelligence Report*, Naval Intelligence Division

BdU KTB (War Diaries), www.uboatarchives.net

Beaver, Paul, *U-boats in the Atlantic*, Patrick Stephens, 1979

Beckman, Morris, *Atlantic Roulette*, Tom Donovan, 1996

Bennet, G.H. & R., *Survivors*, Hambledon Press, 1999

Brown, Anthony Cave, *Bodyguard of Lies*, W.H. Allen, 1976

Bucheim, Lothar-Gùnther, U-boat War, Collins,1978

Churchill, Winston, *The Second World War Vols I & II*, Cassell, 1950

Costello, John & Hughes, Terry, *The Battle of the Atlantic*, Collins, 1977

Course, Captain A.G., *The Deep Sea Tramp*, Hollis & Carter, 1960

Dönitz, Grand Admiral Karl, *Memoirs – Ten Years and Twenty Days*,
   Greenhill Books, 1990

Falls, Cyril, *The Second World War*, Methuen & Co., 1948

HMSO, *British Vessels Lost at Sea*, Patrick Stephens, 1984

Holm, John, *No Place to Linger*, Holmwork Publishers, 1985

Hoyt, Edwin P., *U-boats*, McGraw-Hill Book Co., 1987

Jones, Geoffrey, *Defeat of the Wolf Packs*, William Kimber, 1986

Lamb, James B., *The Corvette Navy*, Macmillan of Canada

Lewis, William J., *Under the Red Duster, Stackpole Books, 2003*

Lund, Paul & Ludlam, Harry, *Night of the U-boats*, W. Foulsham & Co.,
   1973

Ministry of Defence (Navy), *The U-boat War in the Atlantic*, HMSO

Padfield, Peter, *Dönitz-The Last Fùhrer*, Cassell & Co., 1993

Parker, Mike, *Running the Gauntlet*, Nimbus Publishing, 1994

Robertson, Terence, *The Golden Horseshoe*, Evans Bros. Ltd., 1955

Rohwer, Jùrgen, *Axis Submarine Successes 1939-1945*, Patrick
   Stephens, 1983

Roskill S.W., *The War at Sea*, HMSO, 1954-61

Showell, J.P. Mallmann, *U-boats Under the Swastika*, Ian Allen, 1987

Slader, John, *The Fourth Service*, Robert Hale, 1994

Stern, Robert C., *Type VII U-boats*, Arms & Armour Press, 1991

Terraine, John, *Business in Great Waters*, Leo Cooper, 1989

Thomas, David A., *The Atlantic Star 1939-1945*, W.H. Allan, 1990
Williams, Andrew, *The Battle of the Atlantic*, BBC Worldwide Ltd., 2002

Other Sources
www.uboatarchive.net
www.uboat.net
The National Archives, Kew

Index